Visio® 2003
FOR
DUMMIES®

D1515242

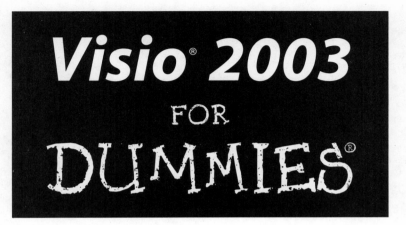

Visio® 2003 FOR DUMMIES®

by Debbie Walkowski

WILEY

Wiley Publishing, Inc.

Visio® 2003 For Dummies®

Published by
Wiley Publishing, Inc.
111 River Street
Hoboken, NJ 07030-5774

Copyright © 2004 by Wiley Publishing, Inc., Indianapolis, Indiana

Published by Wiley Publishing, Inc., Indianapolis, Indiana

Published simultaneously in Canada

For general information on our other products and services or to obtain technical support, please contact our Customer Care Department within the U.S. at 800-762-2974, outside the U.S. at 317-572-3993, or fax 317-572-4002.

Wiley also publishes its books in a variety of electronic formats. Some content that appears in print may not be available in electronic books.

Library of Congress Catalog Control Number: 2003116758

ISBN: 0-7645-5923-0

Manufactured in the United States of America

10 9 8 7 6 5 4 3 2 1

1O/RT/QR/QU/IN

About the Author

Debbie Walkowski has worked in the computer industry for more than 20 years in a variety of positions from sales and marketing to teaching and training. For the last 14 years, she has made writing her primary focus. Her company, the Writing Works, specializes in writing computer self-help books and providing writing services to companies such as Microsoft Corporation, Hewlett-Packard (formerly Digital Equipment Corporation), and AT&T Wireless Communications. She has authored 18 books on popular computer software including Microsoft Office, Microsoft Works, Microsoft PowerPoint, Microsoft Excel, Microsoft Project, Microsoft Windows, Visio, Quicken, Word Perfect, and Lotus 1-2-3.

Dedication

For Frank, the brightest and most enduring star in my life.

Author's Acknowledgments

When I was introduced to Visio nearly ten years ago, I was instantly impressed with the product. Visio was a fresh and creative answer to the drawing and diagramming challenges many business professionals faced. It was unique; nothing like it existed in the marketplace. The fact that Visio has survived the demands of a frenzied, fickle, and often unforgiving high-tech software industry is a testament to its quality, innovation, and usefulness.

Not only was I impressed with the product, I was bowled over by the quality and dedication of the people at Visio Corporation (then the owner of Visio). Throughout the process of writing three books on Visio, I found the people at Visio Corporation an invaluable resource — some of the finest, dedicated, top-notch professionals I have ever had the pleasure of working with. Stacy Dellas, Charlie Zaragoza, and Lorrin Smith-Bates, all top Visio corporate trainers, were always available to teach, demonstrate, and answer questions. Their contributions to my earlier Visio books still carry through to this edition of *Visio 2003 For Dummies*, my fourth book on this product.

Today Visio is owned by Microsoft Corporation. I would first like to thank Carla Hartwig, a Microsoft Product Manager for Visio, who provided much-needed details about Visio 2003 before its release and who continues to keep me updated on the product. At Wiley, I'd like to thank Terri Varveris, acquisitions editor, for giving me the opportunity to update my earlier book, *Visio 2000 For Dummies*. I credit Terri for recognizing the need in the marketplace for this update. My sincerest thanks go to Susan Pink, project and copy editor extraordinaire! Not only does she have excellent editing skills, she has the calm, in-control, unflappable personality that makes the editing process for the author so much easier. Susan often went above and beyond the call of duty; she is a real pro. Thanks, also, to Allen Wyatt, technical editor, whose dedication to accuracy helped make this book technically reliable. And finally, I offer my heartfelt thanks to my husband, Frank, who was not only endlessly supportive throughout this process but spent countless hours creating Visio drawings, testing Visio functions, and capturing figures for this edition of the book. I couldn't have completed this book on time without his help. My deepest thanks to *all* of you for your dedication to excellence!

Publisher's Acknowledgments

We're proud of this book; please send us your comments through our online registration form located at www.dummies.com/register/.

Some of the people who helped bring this book to market include the following:

Acquisitions, Editorial, and Media Development

Project Editor: Susan Pink

Acquisitions Editor: Terri Varveris

Technical Editor: Allen Wyatt, Discovery Computing Inc.

Editorial Manager: Carol Sheehan

Media Development Supervisor: Richard Graves

Editorial Assistant: Amanda Foxworth

Cartoons: Rich Tennant (www.the5thwave.com)

Production

Project Coordinator: Courtney MacIntyre

Layout and Graphics: Andrea Dahl, Lauren Goddard, Joyce Haughey, Stephanie D. Jumper, Michael Kruzil, Lynsey Osborn, Heather Ryan, Jacque Schneider, Melanee Wolven

Proofreaders: Laura Albert, TECHBOOKS Production Services

Indexer: TECHBOOKS Production Services

Publishing and Editorial for Technology Dummies

    Richard Swadley, Vice President and Executive Group Publisher

    Andy Cummings, Vice President and Publisher

    Mary C. Corder, Editorial Director

Publishing for Consumer Dummies

    Diane Graves Steele, Vice President and Publisher

    Joyce Pepple, Acquisitions Director

Composition Services

    Gerry Fahey, Vice President of Production Services

    Debbie Stailey, Director of Composition Services

Contents at a Glance

Table of Contents

Introduction

*O*kay, relax! I know as well as you do that you're not a dummy. But you may feel like one when it comes to using Visio — or any other software program you're not familiar with. Let's face it: No one is an expert with *every* computer program. And no one wants to feel like a dummy. That's what's so great about *For Dummies* books. They show you just what you need to know so you don't feel like a dummy anymore.

Visio can be a fun program to use, but it can also be intimidating at first. Why? Because there are so darn many types of diagrams, and we don't have a clue what some of them mean! (We'd all like to think we know, but the truth is, we don't.) The good news is, you don't *need* to. All you need to know is how to create diagrams that make sense for *you*, for your specialty, for your industry.

I am thrilled to be updating *Visio 2000 For Dummies*, published in July of 2000. Since then, Visio has been through big changes, not the least of which was the purchase of Visio by Microsoft Corporation. With the release of Visio 2003, Visio officially becomes part of the Microsoft Office suite of products, and future releases will be launched in sync with other Office products. Visio 2003 has undergone some exciting changes and incorporated great new features. This book brings you up-to-date on the latest advances for Visio and gives you tips on using Visio with other programs.

About This Book

Pay attention to the title of this book: If you are a programmer, this book is probably not for you! If you're "one of the rest of us" (and we're definitely in the majority!), this book is just what you need. You probably have a job to do — and I'm betting it's *not* to pore over the minute details of Visio's inner workings so you can impress your friends with your vast knowledge. You probably just want to find out enough about Visio so you can make drawings that *enhance* the job you do, not *become* it.

With this in mind, *Visio 2003 For Dummies* is designed to make you productive as quickly as possible. You find basic, useful information that helps you accomplish your goals. You find real-world examples and figures that *show* you how to do something rather than just *tell* you. You find concise step-by-step instructions for accomplishing specific tasks rather than a lot of rambling text that fills space and means nothing to you.

Conventions Used in This Book

Here's a summary of the conventions used in this book:

- ✔ When directions indicate that you type something, for example, "Enter **13** in the size box," the characters you type appear in bold.

- ✔ When I write *click*, I mean to click your left mouse button. If you need to right-click, I specify *right-click*.

- ✔ When I write *drag*, I mean to click and hold the left mouse button as you move the mouse. Release the mouse button when you're finished dragging.

- ✔ The term *shortcut menu* refers to the pop-up menu that appears when you right-click something on the screen. (Shortcut menus are not available for all elements in a drawing.)

- ✔ You can select commands using toolbar buttons, menu commands, or the Alt key. Because toolbar buttons are by far the fastest method, I always list them along with the menu command. (When toolbar buttons aren't available, I list only the menu command.) I specify a menu command by writing, for example, *Choose File⇨Save*, which means click the File menu to open it and then choose the Save option.

What You're Not to Read

If you're new to Visio and just want to know enough to create simple drawings or diagrams, you can safely skip Part IV. That section takes you deeper into customizing Visio and using some of its advanced features. Clearly, not every reader will become devoted to discovering advanced features. Browse through Part III for any features that you might find useful and have the time to work through. Also glance through Part V, which contains many interesting tips, tricks, and trivia that you might find very useful.

On the other hand, if you've used Visio before, you can safely skip Parts I and II, which offer basic getting-up-and-running information.

Foolish Assumptions

I assume that you have a reasonable working knowledge of Microsoft Windows. For this reason, I don't spend any of your valuable time in Chapter 1 describing how to find your way around Windows or how to work with dialog boxes. If you need to review these concepts, see *Windows XP For Dummies,* by Andy Rathbone (published by Wiley Publishing, Inc.).

How This Book Is Organized

Visio 2003 For Dummies is organized into five distinct parts. Use the parts to guide you to where you want to go on your Visio journey. The book is designed so that you can skip around to suit your needs.

Part I: Starting with Visio 2003 Basics

Part I lays the groundwork for your success with Visio. Every software program has its unique personality; Visio is no exception. Here you find conceptual information about Visio, get the Visio terminology down, discover how to recognize and work with what's on the screen, start Visio, save and open files, and print drawings.

Part II: Creating Visio Drawings

Part II is for those in a hurry because it teaches you the basics of creating a *simple* drawing. You find out about the basic elements of a Visio drawing and how to implement those elements in your drawing. I show you how to add and manipulate text, as well as how to work with margins and tabs, indentation, alignment, spacing, and more. You also see how to use and manipulate a drawing's connectors, the lines that connect one shape to another. (They're more than just simple lines, as you'll soon discover.)

Part III: Taking Your Drawings to the Next Level

In Part III you move into the intermediate features of Visio. Find out how to place shapes precisely on a drawing, create your own shapes, enhance and manipulate shapes, do more sophisticated stuff with connectors, and work with pages and layers.

Part IV: Advancing Your Knowledge of Visio

Certainly not every user needs to pursue Part IV! Here I show you how to create custom templates and styles, how to store data in shapes and report on that data, and how to protect your shapes and drawings from inadvertent changes. You also see how to use Visio drawings with other programs and save files for publishing on the Web.

Part V: The Part of Tens

One of the most useful sections of every *For Dummies* book, "The Part of Tens," is a collection of a variety of information. In *Visio 2003 For Dummies,* you find answers to ten frequently asked questions, ten "can I?" questions, ten "How to" pointers for useful tasks, ten tips for working successfully with Visio, and ten pointers to online resources for Visio.

Icons Used in This Book

The following icons are used in this text to call attention to specific types of information.

The Tip icon indicates information that's likely to save you time or information that will make you say to yourself, "Wow, I never knew that!" Be sure to read this stuff.

Wherever a Technical Stuff icon occurs, I explain in lay terms something that's bogged down in technical jargon. (Then again, sometimes the icon just points out technical trivia.) You won't find too many of these icons but when you do, the text is usually worth reading.

Definitely pay attention to the Warning icons. They're designed to warn you of impending doom or, at the very least, a possible problem you'd just as soon avoid.

Remember icons are designed as a gentle nudge rather than a blatant slam to the head. In other words, "Remember this — it may be important to you someday."

I use this funky little icon to point out weird stuff that Visio does every now and then.

This icon draws attention to the slick new improvements in Visio 2003.

Where to Go from Here

If you've never used Visio before, definitely start with Part I! Work your way through Part II as well, but don't feel that you must go beyond this point. If you've used Visio before, you might get crazy and start with Part V, skim Parts I and II and go directly to Parts III and IV to look for any features you might not be familiar with. Whether you are a beginner or experienced Visio user, be sure to look through Part V for answers, tips, and pointers to Visio-related Web sites.

Part I
Starting with Visio 2003 Basics

The 5th Wave · By Rich Tennant

"NIFTY CHART, FRANK, BUT NOT ENTIRELY NECESSARY."

In this part . . .

So your boss says you have to make a Visio drawing and you barely even know what Visio is? Well, this is the place to start.

Maybe you've seen other drawing programs. Visio, however, is a different animal. It's not really a drawing program, and it's certainly not a CAD program (thank goodness!). In this part, you understand what Visio is and what it does, you discover how to "speak" and "think" Visio, you negotiate your way around the screen, and you find out how to get help when you need it. You also print a drawing, something you'll no doubt find useful if you want to be productive!

Chapter 1

Visio 101

Close your eyes for a minute and picture the amount of visual information that comes to you on any given day. Magazines, newspapers, reports, television programs, and presentations illustrate a great deal of information in the form of charts, tables, graphs, diagrams, and technical drawings. These graphical elements often convey ideas far more quickly and clearly than long, boring paragraphs. You don't typically think of charts, diagrams, and graphs as *art*, but they are graphical, and this is where Visio comes in.

Although Visio is easy to use, you can benefit from a bit of explanation before you jump right in creating drawings. In this chapter, you become familiar with what you see on the Visio screen and find out how Visio works conceptually.

Getting the Scoop on Visio

In simple terms, Visio is a diagramming tool for business professionals, many of whom are self-confirmed non-artists. Although Visio is often referred to as a *drawing* tool, it isn't one, because it requires no artistic ability. It's more accurate to say that Visio is a *diagramming* tool. That's reassuring because even in highly analytical, non-art-related careers, you may be called upon to create a chart, diagram, or — perish the thought — a *drawing!* If the suggestion of drawing *anything* strikes terror in your heart, Visio can help.

Visio's grab bag of icons — or *shapes*, as Visio calls them — represents all sorts of things from computer network components, to office furniture, to boxes on an organization chart or a flow chart, to electrical switches and relays. You simply drag the shapes that you want into the drawing window and arrange and connect them the way that you want. You can add text and other graphical elements wherever you like.

For those of you with a computer-aided design background, *don't think CAD* with Visio! Although the finished product — a drawing — may look similar, Visio and CAD-based systems are different animals. If you're a self-confirmed CAD snob, that's okay, but don't underestimate or misunderstand Visio. Visio and CAD-based systems have different purposes and work entirely differently.

Comparing Visio products

Over the years, Visio has been available in several different flavors — Standard, Professional, Technical, and Enterprise — plus you could find advanced developer's tools in Visual Studio .NET and advanced network diagramming tools in Visio Enterprise Network Tools. Whew! All these versions became confusing and overwhelming to the average user, so Microsoft decided to simplify things and produce just two editions of Visio: Standard and Professional. The same "engine" drives both, but the audience for each is slightly different and the types of charts and diagrams you can create address different needs:

- ✔ **Visio Standard:** Designed for business professionals, this edition gives all kinds of business people — from product managers to financial analysts to sales and marketing professionals — the ability to create business-related charts and diagrams that illustrate business processes, marketing trends, organizations, project schedules, and so on.

- ✔ **Visio Professional:** Designed for technical users, this edition includes everything that Visio Standard includes and more. Network managers and designers, electrical engineers, IT managers, facilities planners, Internet specialists, Web designers and administrators, and software developers can use Visio Professional to create charts and diagrams that illustrate a wide variety of technical concepts and processes.

So how do you know which Visio is right for you? If you're involved in networks, IT, Internet or Web design, electrical engineering, architecture facilities planning and management, or software development, Visio Professional is the edition to use because it provides all the shapes and symbols you need to create simple or complex diagrams. If you're not involved in any of these fields but are a business professional involved in company sales, profits, marketing, or managing projects, Visio Standard is right for you. It includes all the shapes you need to create business-related charts, diagrams, and drawings, without cluttering your screen with shapes you'll never use (such as a proximity limit switch or a guided light transmitter).

A quick peek at some Visio features

Visio is often a misunderstood product, especially by those who've never used it. It's amusing to hear people say "Oh, Visio. That's that org chart software, isn't it?" That's like saying, "Oh, a Ferrari. That's a little Italian car, right?" Well, *that's* definitely an understatement!

Although Visio is a whiz at creating organization charts, that facility only scratches the surface of its capabilities and sophistication. The following list describes some of the things you can do with Visio:

- ✔ **Report on data:** Wouldn't it be great if you could store data in a drawing and then report on that data? With Visio, you can. Suppose you draw an office layout plan that includes cubicle walls, fixtures, office furniture, and telephone and computer equipment. You can store each piece of furniture and office equipment with data such as its inventory number, owner, and current location. Each computer equipment shape can include data about the manufacturer, hardware configuration, and Internet address assigned to it. From this drawing, you can generate property, inventory, and location reports. (See Chapter 13 for more information on storing and reporting on data in shapes.)

- ✔ **Generate drawings from data:** In contrast to the previous point, wouldn't it be great to be able to generate drawings from existing data? Again, with Visio, you can. Suppose you have employee data (name, title, department, reporting manager, and so on) stored in a text or spreadsheet file. You can generate an organization chart automatically from this data using Visio. Or suppose you manage projects and you have project tasks and durations stored in a spreadsheet or Microsoft Project file. You can automatically generate a Gantt chart from this data using Visio. If you use Microsoft Outlook, you can also bring data stored in Outlook into Visio and generate a calendar. (See Chapter 14 for more information on using external data in Visio.)

- ✔ **Use hyperlinks:** Often, you can't convey in a single drawing all the information necessary to make your point. You might want to refer the reader to a separate drawing, a Web site, or another document with related information. With Visio, you can add hyperlinks to a drawing or shape. This is an invaluable feature for pulling pieces of information together to present a comprehensive picture. (I discuss this feature in more detail in Chapter 14.)

- ✔ **Use the drill-down feature:** Jump quickly from an overview drawing to a detailed drawing and back again. For example, you can draw an overview map of a worldwide computer network and double-click the name of a city to see a drawing of that city's computer network. This drill-down feature is possible because Visio lets you define a shape's behavior when you double-click it. (See Chapter 13 for more information.)

Visio also provides impressive interoperability with other applications. You can

- Include clip art, figures, photos, sound, video, or objects from other programs in a Visio drawing.

- Create drawings, diagrams, and charts in Visio that you can later export to programs such as Microsoft PowerPoint, Microsoft Excel, Microsoft Word, and Microsoft Access.

- Save Visio drawings as HTML files and upload them to the Internet, or incorporate Visio drawings into Web pages.

What's new in Visio 2003?

Visio began as a straightforward business diagramming tool and steadily grew into a more sophisticated tool for creating highly technical and complex diagrams. While retaining all this sophistication, Visio 2003 gets back to basics by focusing on improving the fundamental capabilities of the product, expanding the business diagramming features, and making the program as easy to use as possible for new users.

Here are some of the new features in Visio 2003 Standard:

- A new brainstorming template that allows you to quickly and easily capture and organize random ideas

- A new drawing category for business process management, the emerging discipline that helps managers reduce costs by increasing efficiency in business processes

- The capability to add employee pictures to organization charts, as well as show dotted-line relationships between employees

- The capability to bring schedule information from Microsoft Outlook into Visio and create a customized calendar — and add calendar art

In addition to the preceding features, Visio 2003 Professional includes

- New network templates (for detailed networks and rack diagrams) to illustrate complex telecommunication and computer networks

- Updated and improved network shapes that reflect current market trends

- Updated and improved electrical engineering and building plan shapes

- A Microsoft Windows XP user interface template that lets developers prototype new user interfaces

✔ Enhancements to the Web site template that let you create more compact diagrams, edit shape text, and add new shapes, all much more quickly than in Visio 2002

✔ A new startup wizard for creating space plans

It's beyond the scope of this book to discuss all of Visio 2003's new features. Refer to *Visio 2003 Bible* (published by Wiley Publishing, Inc.)

Familiarizing Yourself with Visio Lingo

Like all software programs, Visio uses a particular terminology. You need to be familiar with the following terms before you begin creating diagrams and drawings:

✔ **Drag and drop:** The method Visio uses to create drawings. What are you dragging and where are you dropping it, you ask? You drag shapes and you drop them onto a drawing page.

✔ **Shape:** Probably the most important element in Visio. A *shape* represents an object of nearly any conceivable kind, such as a piece of office furniture in an office-layout diagram, a road sign in a directional map, a server in a network diagram, a box on an organization chart, or a bar on a comparison chart. Visio contains literally thousands of shapes. You can draw and save your own shapes, too, as I show you in Chapter 8.

✔ **Master shape:** A shape that you see on a stencil. When you drag a shape onto the drawing page, you're copying a *master shape* onto your drawing page, making it just one *instance* of that shape. Visio makes the distinction between *master shapes* and *instances* of shapes. But my advice is, don't clutter your mind with a trivial detail like this.

✔ **Stencil:** A tool Visio uses to organize shapes so that you can find the one you're looking for. A *stencil* is nothing more than a collection of related shapes. If you want to create a cubicle-layout diagram for your office, for example, you use the cubicles stencil, which includes shapes such as workstations, posts, panels, work surfaces, storage units, and file cabinets. Stencils are displayed in the Shapes pane on the left side of the screen so that the shapes are always available while you're working.

✔ **Template:** A collection of stencils in addition to predefined document settings. A *template* is essentially a model for creating a particular type of drawing. A template defines certain characteristics of the drawing so that the drawing is consistent. For example, when you use a Visio template for a specific type of drawing, Visio automatically opens one or more appropriate stencils, defines the page size and scale of your drawing, and defines appropriate styles for things such as text, fills, and lines. You can change any of these elements, but the point of using a template is to maintain consistency throughout the drawing. After all, your drawing may include several pages, and you want them to look as if they go together.

✔ **Connector:** A line that connects one shape to another. Perhaps the most common example of a connector is in an organization chart. The lines that connect the president to various groups in an organization and the lines that run through an organization are connectors. I tell you more about connectors in Chapter 6, but for now this definition is all you need to remember.

Jumping Head First into Visio

The best way to get started with Visio is to open a new drawing page, so you can cruise around the screen and get a feel for what's there. Then in Chapter 2, you create a drawing.

To start Visio, follow these steps:

1. **From your Windows desktop, choose Start⇨All Programs.**

2. **Choose Microsoft Office⇨Microsoft Office Visio 2003.**

   Visio displays the screen shown in Figure 1-1.

Take a look at what's shown on this screen:

✔ **Category:** The Category list shows sixteen items. These items represent the broad areas of drawing types, such as block diagrams, flowcharts, charts and graphs, and Web diagrams. When you select a category, the list of templates changes.

✔ **Template:** Within each category are a variety of templates (anywhere from two to two dozen) to choose from. Each one represents a different type of drawing in the broader category. For instance, in the broad category of Block Diagram, you can choose a template for creating a Basic Diagram, a Block Diagram, or a Block Diagram with Perspective. Most templates are available in metric or U.S. units of measure. When you click a category name, the list of available templates changes.

✔ **Getting Started:** The pane on the right side of the screen is labeled Getting Started, but the label changes depending on where you're working in Visio. For instance, when you select a template to create a drawing, the title changes to Template Help. If you choose Help⇨ Microsoft Office Visio Help after you're working on a drawing, the title changes to Visio Help. This can be confusing at first. I show you more about using the Help pane later in this chapter.

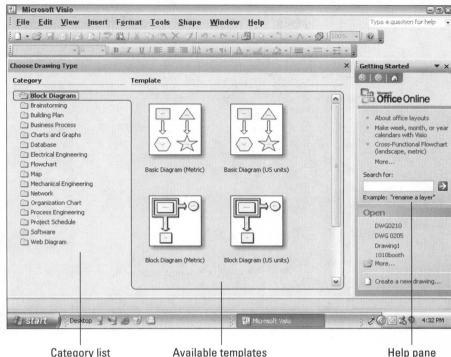

Figure 1-1:
A typical
Visio
opening
screen.

Category list   Available templates   Help pane

Getting familiar with the Visio screen

A typical Visio screen looks like the one shown in Figure 1-2. This screen is displayed when you select the Block Diagram category and the Basic Diagram (US units) template. In this section, you look at what's going on in this screen.

The screen is still divided into three primary areas:

- ✔ **Shapes pane:** On the left side of the screen, this pane contains three open stencils: Backgrounds, Borders and Titles, and Basic Shapes. Visio opens these automatically as part of the Block Diagram template.

- ✔ **Drawing window:** Resembling graph paper, this area is bounded by rulers on the top and the left, and by scroll bars on the bottom and the right. To the left of the bottom scroll bar is the navigation area, which displays tabs for each page in the drawing.

- ✔ **Template Help:** This is the infamous changing pane, labeled Getting Started in Figure 1-1. Now that a drawing category and template have been selected, this pane offers help on block diagram templates.

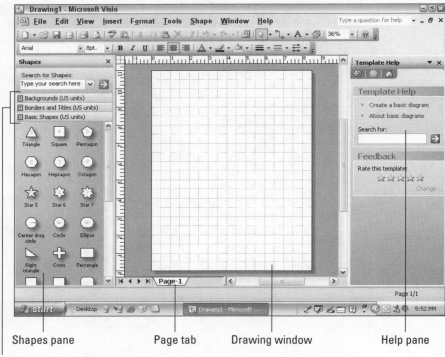

Figure 1-2:
A typical
drawing
screen in
Visio.

Shapes pane   Page tab   Drawing window   Help pane

Three open stencils

The Visio menu bar appears at the top of the window under the title bar. Below the menu bar are two open toolbars: the Standard and Formatting toolbars. The status bar, which provides information about your drawing, appears along the bottom of the drawing window. When a shape in a drawing is selected, the status bar displays the shape's width, height, and angle.

Checking out the menus

Visio's menu bar contains some typical menus found in almost every Windows application (such as File, Edit, Format, and Help). Even so, I suggest you review the contents of each menu for commands that you may not expect. The following list describes commands unique to Visio (even though some of the menus might look familiar):

✔ **Tools:** On this menu you find all kinds of tools for working with Visio shapes, the Visio drawing page, and the drawing itself. There are tools for setting Visio's color palette, rulers, grids, and so on. You find also the standard Microsoft options such as Spelling, Track Markup, Customize, and Options.

✔ **Shape:** The Shape menu contains commands for grouping, rotating, flipping, and aligning as well as commands for choosing a drawing's color scheme. You also find commands for changing the stacking order of shapes and doing some creative things such as fragmenting and intersecting shapes. (See Chapter 8 for details.)

The options on the Shape menu change depending on the type of drawing you're creating.

For certain types of drawings, Visio adds an additional menu to the menu bar. For example, when you create a Gantt chart using a Project Schedule template, Visio adds a Gantt Chart menu just after the Shape menu and before the Window menu (see Figure 1-3). On the Gantt Chart menu, you find commands specific to creating Gantt charts, such as adding and deleting tasks, linking tasks, and setting working hours. Other types of drawings that add a menu to the menu bar are Brainstorming, Database, Building Plan, Organization Chart, and Process Engineering. The options on these menus are specific to the type of drawing you create. As soon as you close the drawing, the menu option disappears.

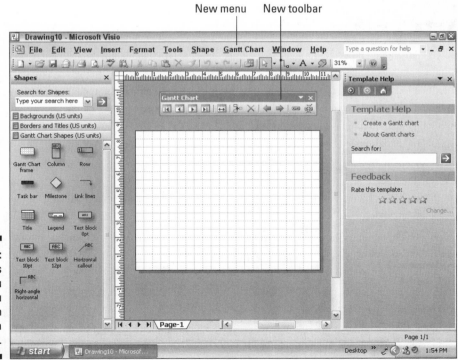

Figure 1-3:
Visio inserts a new menu in the menu bar when you create a Gantt chart.

Working with toolbars

Visio has a dozen or so toolbars, two of which are displayed automatically when you start the program. The two default toolbars are Standard and Formatting. You can hide either of these, and you can display additional toolbars as well.

After you begin to recognize the toolbar buttons, it's much faster to click a button than select a menu command. I list a lot of these buttons on the Cheat Sheet at the beginning of this book.

Throughout this book, I try to maximize the drawing window shown in each figure by displaying only the necessary toolbars.

To hide or display toolbars, right-click anywhere in the toolbar area. On the shortcut menu that appears, click a toolbar name. Toolbars that have a check mark next to them are displayed; all others are hidden (see Figure 1-4).

All Visio toolbars can be docked at different locations on the screen. Just grab the vertical bar at the left end of any toolbar and drag it to a new location on the screen. A moved toolbar automatically becomes its own window, and you can position it anywhere you like on the screen by dragging its title bar.

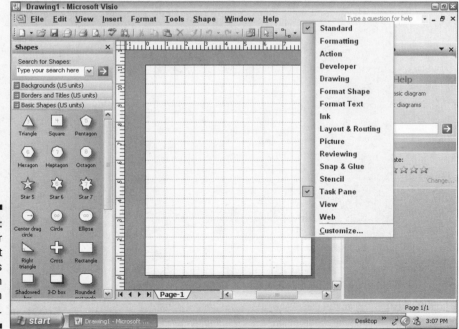

Figure 1-4:
The toolbar shortcut menu lets you turn toolbars on and off.

If you're a toolbar fanatic, you might want to customize the toolbars by adding buttons you use most often and deleting buttons you never use. You can also choose any buttons you want and create a new toolbar.

Creating a toolbar

To create a custom toolbar, follow these steps:

1. **Choose View➪Toolbars➪Customize.**

   Visio displays the Customize dialog box.

2. **On the Toolbars tab, click the New button.**

   Visio displays the New Toolbar dialog box.

3. **In the Toolbar Name field, type a name (see Figure 1-5), and then click the OK button.**

   Visio adds the new name to the list of toolbars and displays a new, blank toolbar on the screen. (It's small, but it's there!)

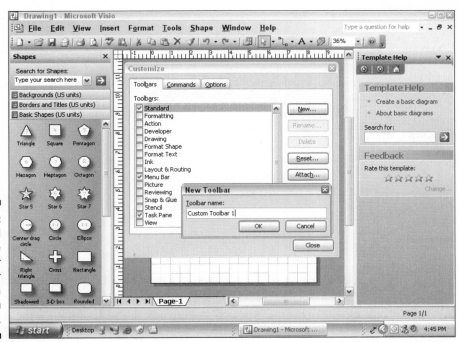

Figure 1-5: You can add and delete toolbar buttons or create a custom toolbar.

4. **If you want to add buttons to the new toolbar, drag and drop the new blank toolbar into the toolbar area, and then follow the steps in the next section "Modifying a toolbar."**

5. **Click Close to close the Customize dialog box.**

Modifying a toolbar

If you just want to add a button here or there, consider modifying an existing toolbar rather than creating a new one. Either way, follow these steps to add buttons to any toolbar:

1. **Display the toolbar that you want to change.**

   To do so, right-click the toolbar area and select the toolbar.

2. **Right-click the toolbar and choose Customize.**

   Visio displays the Customize dialog box.

3. **Click the Commands tab.**

   Categories are on the left and commands are on the right, as shown in Figure 1-6.

Figure 1-6:
Choose a toolbar on the left and buttons on the right.

4. **Click a category on the left, and then scroll through the list of commands (buttons) on the right.**

5. **Drag the button from the dialog box to the location on the toolbar where you want the button to be added.**

   Yes, that's right. Drag it right out of the Customize dialog box and onto the toolbar! When you release the mouse button, the new button becomes part of the existing toolbar at the point where you dropped it.

Deleting a button from a toolbar

To remove a button from a toolbar, follow these steps:

1. **Display the toolbar that you want to change.**
2. **Right-click the toolbar and choose Customize.**

   Visio displays the Customize dialog box.
3. **Drag the button that you want to delete off the toolbar.**

   If you want to delete additional buttons, repeat this step.
4. **Click the Close button to close the Customize dialog box.**

Getting Help When You Need It

Have you ever felt overwhelmed by too many people offering advice and assistance? Well, you might feel that way with Visio 2003: Help is so abundant, you might not be sure where to turn first.

In this section I cover a lot of options for getting help. Don't let all this information overwhelm you! The best way to work with Visio Help is by exploring it and trying new things. With practice, you'll become quite adept!

Using the Help pane

In this section, you start with the concept of a Help pane, which Visio displays automatically on the right side of the screen. In Figure 1-1, for example, the pane is labeled Getting Started. In Figure 1-7, the same pane is labeled Visio Help. To display this pane, choose Help⇨Microsoft Office Visio Help.

When you first start Visio, the Help pane progresses through these three steps:

- ✔ **Getting Started:** This is the help you get when you start Visio.
- ✔ **Template Help:** This help is available after you select a drawing template.
- ✔ **Visio Help:** This help pane appears when you click Help⇨ Microsoft Office Visio Help.

The Back, Forward and Home buttons help you navigate the Help screens you've visited. These screens are like a filmstrip. The Back button moves backward through the filmstrip, Forward moves forward, and Home button takes you to the beginning: Getting Started.

Forward   Type a question

Back   Home

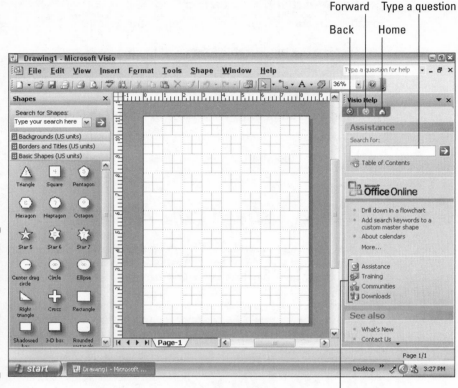

Connect to online help

Figure 1-7:
This pane
is Help
Central,
giving you
access to
local help
and online
help.

It's a bit of a misnomer to use the name Help pane because the pane is used also as a Reviewing pane, a Clip Art pane, and more. When used for something other than Help, the Forward and Back buttons take you to whatever information you displayed recently. To switch the pane from a Help pane to display something other than help, click the down arrow at the right end of the pane's title bar.

Let's focus on the Visio Help pane, as shown in Figure 1-6, because this is the one you will use most often. In the Assistance section, you can type any question and Visio will display a list of possible solutions from its local Visio help files. Click whatever interests you and the answer is displayed in a separate window, including step-by-step instructions if they apply.

To broaden your search for answers on the Internet, click any of the icons in the Microsoft Office Online section — Assistance, Training, Communities, or Downloads — and connect directly to the appropriate Microsoft Web page. (Of course, you must have live access to the Internet to use these Help options.) Each one opens in a separate window. Here's a brief description of what you'll find:

- ✔ **Assistance:** Takes you directly to Microsoft's assistance page for any Office product, including Visio. This page includes hints, tips, articles, templates, clip art, and more. Whatever you're looking for, you can probably find it here.

- ✔ **Training:** This is a slick new feature that actually talks to you for the first few pages and then launches you on your own to learn how to use various Visio functions.

- ✔ **Communities:** Click here to go to the Microsoft Office Newsgroups Web page, where you can share information with other users worldwide about Visio or any other Office product.

- ✔ **Downloads:** Click here to check for updates and other downloads for any Microsoft Office product, including Visio.

When you're finished with any of these Web pages, just click the X in the upper-right corner to close the window.

When you find some great help online that you'd like to refer to at another time, choose Favorites⇨Add to Favorites on your Web browser, and then select a folder where you want to save the Web page.

As if you don't have enough options in the Help pane, remember that you can always return to Visio's menu bar and click the Help menu there. (I warned you that Help was excessive!) The Help menu includes some options not found in the Help pane:

- ✔ **Getting Started Tutorial:** Click here if you want a step-by-step guide that walks you through Visio. (Technically, this is not truly a tutorial because you don't create a drawing. Instead, you find out about the *process* for creating a drawing.)

- ✔ **Diagram Gallery:** This is a great place to look if you don't know what type of drawing to select. It gives you examples of many different types of Visio diagrams so you can decide which one is best for conveying your information.

Want to make your voice heard without ever speaking a word?

If you want to help Microsoft continually improve Visio, consider participating in the Customer Experience Improvement Program. This program offers a way for you to give anonymous feedback to Microsoft about how well Visio is working for you and meeting your needs as an individual user. To participate or to find out more about this program, choose Help⇨ Customer Feedback Options. (If you want to speak your mind and prefer not to be anonymous, you can always drop Microsoft a line by choosing Help⇨Contact Us.)

Don't forget tool tips

Like most Windows programs, Visio also uses tool tips. When you point to a button on a toolbar and *hover* over it (pause without clicking), a tip pops up to tell you the name of the button. This is especially helpful when you're learning Visio.

Visio expanded the concept of tool tips to its stencils. When you hover over a stencil shape, a tip pops up and gives the name of the shape and a description, as shown in Figure 1-8.

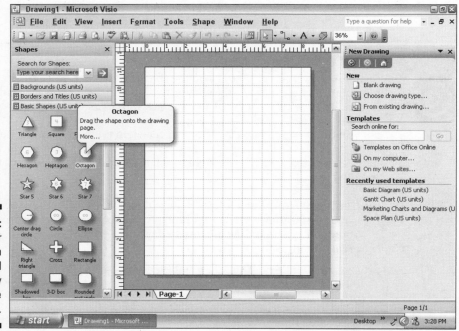

Figure 1-8:
Hover over a shape on the stencil to display Visio shape tips.

If you don't want to view tool tips or stencil tips, choose Tools⇨Options, and then click the View tab. Click to remove the check mark from Toolbar ScreenTips and Other ScreenTips, and then click OK.

Closing Visio

When you're ready to close Visio, choose File⇨Exit. If you haven't recently saved all open files, Visio prompts you to do so for each file. Choose Yes to save or Cancel to return to Visio without saving the drawing.

Chapter 2

Creating and Saving a Simple Visio Drawing

In This Chapter

▶ Creating a drawing

▶ Opening and arranging stencils

▶ Using the Pointer Tool button

▶ Adding shapes

▶ Navigating a drawing successfully

▶ Viewing drawings in different ways

▶ Saving your drawing

▶ Opening your drawings

---

*V*isio is a powerful program with many sophisticated features. It can be intimidating at first, but it doesn't have to be if you begin at the beginning — with a simple drawing.

In this chapter, you find out the standard way to create a simple drawing, bring shapes in, and move around on the screen. You also discover how to create drawings using different methods and how to save a drawing and reopen it later.

Creating a Drawing the Standard Way

Although you can create a drawing in several ways (which you learn about later in this chapter), Visio makes the standard way as easy as possible by guiding you through the choices.

To create a drawing, follow these steps:

1. **If Visio is not already running, choose Start⇨Programs⇨ Microsoft Office⇨Microsoft Office Visio 2003.**

   The opening screen appears, as shown in Figure 2-1.

2. **On the left side of the screen, click a category.**

   In the Template area, Visio displays a sample of the types of drawings, diagrams, or charts available in that category. Use the scroll bar, if necessary, to display all available templates.

3. **Click a template.**

   Visio creates a new drawing page. One or more stencils are automatically opened on the left side of the screen (see Figure 2-2, which displays an Audit diagram).

Now you're ready to create a drawing. Notice that the mouse pointer on the screen is an arrow. Visio automatically selects the Pointer Tool button on the Standard toolbar when you start a new drawing. You discover more about using this tool later in the chapter.

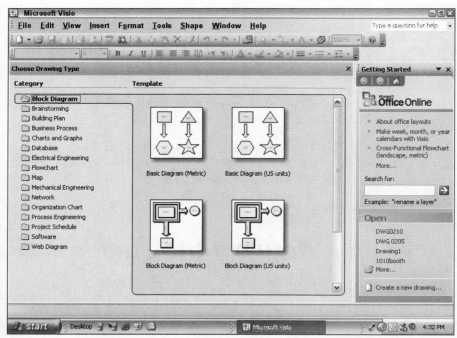

Figure 2-1:
The Visio opening screen displays 16 categories of diagram types.

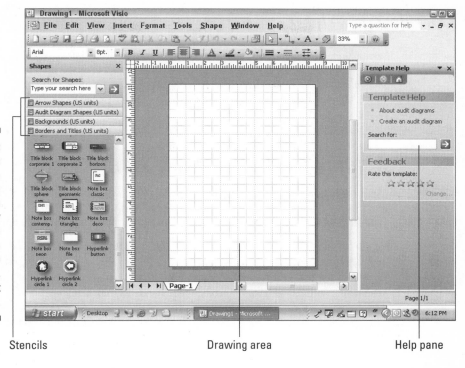

Figure 2-2:
Visio sets
up the
drawing
page
specifically
for the type
of drawing
you choose
(in this case,
the Audit
diagram).

Stencils   Drawing area   Help pane

Where's the template?

You might think of a template as a visible form with blanks or boxes to be filled in. In Visio, a *template* can be confusing to a new user because there isn't anything to see. Instead, the template sets up your drawing for the type of drawing you want to create. For example, if you choose Marketing Charts and Diagrams as your template (from the Charts and Graphs category), Visio automatically does the following:

✔ Opens five stencils (Marketing Diagrams, Marketing Shapes, Charting Shapes, Backgrounds, Borders & Titles) on the screen. These can appear in any order.

✔ Sets the drawing page size to 8 ½ x 11, the page orientation to Portrait, and the drawing scale to 1:1

✔ Chooses an appropriate font, point size, and color

✔ Chooses a variety of other settings such as line color and width, shadow position, text alignment, and bullet or numbering style

Working with Stencils

When you choose a drawing category and template, Visio automatically opens the stencils you need to create your drawing. But you're not limited to the stencils that open automatically. You can close some and open others, as I discuss later in this chapter. For now, you see how stencils work and what you can do with them.

Moving and arranging stencils

Most templates automatically open more than one stencil. Figure 2-3 illustrates the nine — yes, count them, *nine* — stencils that open automatically when you select the Part and Assembly Template for Mechanical Engineering.

The default docking location for stencils is the Shapes pane, on the left side of the screen. Stencils are stacked atop one another with just the title bar showing. As you open additional stencils, they're added to the stack. This stacking arrangement saves space for the drawing area.

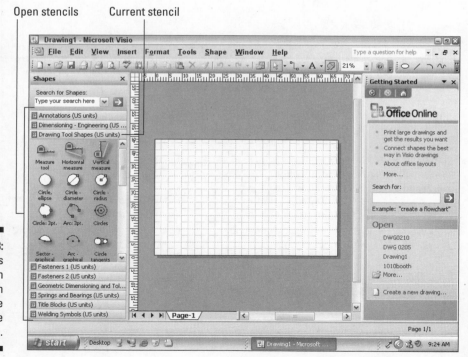

Figure 2-3:
Visio stacks open stencils on the left side of the screen.

You can change the docking location to the top, bottom, or right side of the screen. A fourth option is to float a stencil so that it appears in a separate window with its own Close and Minimize buttons. This option lets you place the stencil anywhere you want on the screen, move it, resize it, and minimize it.

To reposition a stencil, click the title bar and drag the stencil to another location on the screen. The stencil docks itself depending on where you release the mouse button. For example, if you drag the stencil to the bottom of the drawing area, the stencil docks itself there. If you drag it to the top of the drawing area, it docks there. If you want a stencil on the right side of your screen, first close the Help pane, and then drag the stencil there. If you drag a stencil anywhere else on the screen, it floats in its own separate window.

In Figure 2-4, stencils appear in every possible location; left, right, top, bottom, and floating. You can arrange stencils any way you like. Notice that the more stencils you display at once, the smaller your view of the drawing area.

Stencil docked on the top   Floating stencil

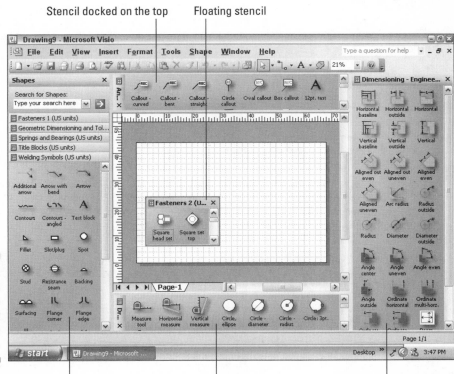

Figure 2-4:
Visio lets you arrange stencils any way you like.

Default docking location   Stencil docked on the bottom   Stencil docked on the right

A step-by-step method for creating drawings

You've seen it before. The okay-what-do-I-do-now stare that creeps across someone's face when he or she starts a new program. As they say, it always pays to have a plan. At least with a plan, you can *pretend* you know what you're doing!

Use this checklist whenever you create a drawing using a template:

- ✔ Know what kind of drawing you want to create so you can choose an appropriate drawing category.

- ✔ Start a new drawing by choosing a template in that category.

- ✔ Open any additional stencils that you may want to use (see the section "Opening additional stencils" in this chapter).

- ✔ If you want your drawing to have multiple pages, add them now (see Chapter 9).

- ✔ Drag and drop shapes from the stencil onto the drawing (see Chapter 4).

- ✔ Connect the shapes (see Chapter 6).

- ✔ Add text to the drawing (see Chapter 5).

- ✔ Apply a color scheme to the drawing (see Chapter 7).

- ✔ Save the drawing.

- ✔ Print your drawing (see Chapter 3).

The process can be far more involved than this. You can create background pages, add layers, incorporate hyperlinks, insert objects from other programs, and so on. But this is the basic process you follow each time you create a drawing. Refer to this list until you're more comfortable working with Visio.

Closing stencils

To close a stencil displayed in the stack in the Shapes pane, right-click its title bar and choose Close. The title bar of a floating stencil or a stencil docked somewhere other than in the Shapes pane contains an X. Click the X to close the stencil.

Opening additional stencils

If you want to use a shape that's not available in any of the open stencils, you can open additional stencils. In fact, you can open as many stencils as you have room for on your screen.

If you're not sure which stencil you need to open, check out the "Finding the Shapes You Want" section in Chapter 4, where you find out how to search for shapes.

To open a stencil, follow these steps:

1. **With your drawing displayed on the screen, choose File⇨Shapes.**

   A list of drawing categories appears. This list mirrors the category list that appears when you start Visio. Each category has a right-pointing arrow.

2. **Point to the category you want.**

   A list of all stencils in that category appears, as shown in Figure 2-5.

3. **Click a stencil name.**

   The stencil opens and is displayed on the left side of the screen. For information about arranging stencils, see the "Moving and arranging stencils" section earlier in this chapter.

Selecting a Pointer Tool Button

Before you can place or select shapes in a drawing, you need to use the Pointer Tool button. Fortunately, Visio selects the Pointer Tool button for you automatically when you start Visio. The button itself is located on the Standard toolbar (see Figure 2-6).

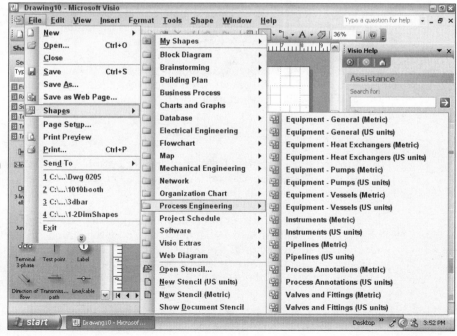

Figure 2-5: The submenu lists the same categories you see on Visio's startup screen.

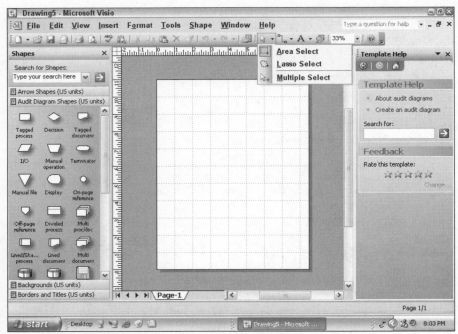

Figure 2-6:
The Pointer
Tool button
has three
variations.

In the drawing area, the pointer is a simple white arrow just like the one used in many other software programs. Visio calls this standard Pointer Tool *Area Select*. The Pointer Tool has two other variations:

- **Lasso Select:** This lets you select shapes by drawing a lasso around them. You use this setting most often when your drawing is dense with shapes and you want to select specific shapes in an area.

- **Multiple Select:** This setting causes the mouse to automatically add to your selection each time you click a shape.

To choose the Lasso Select or Multiple Select button, click the down arrow next to the Pointer Tool button on the Standard toolbar, and then click the variation of the tool that you want.

Unfortunately, the mouse pointer on your screen doesn't change to reflect the type of Pointer Tool you select. You can only tell which Pointer Tool is selected by the behavior of the pointer after you start using it. Later in this chapter, you use these pointers to select multiple shapes. For now, continue using the standard Area Select tool.

Working with Shapes

Shapes are the essence of all Visio drawings. The first thing you do to create a drawing is to add shapes. Later you can add connectors, text, and other elements to the drawing.

Adding a shape to a drawing

So, how do you get shapes into a drawing? You drag them in. It's almost too simple. In the same way that you drag a window's title bar or drag a stencil to a new location on the screen, you drag a shape into a drawing. Point to a shape in the stencil, click and hold down the left mouse button, and then drag the shape into the drawing area. Release the mouse button when the shape is where you want it. (As simple as it is, don't be surprised if you click a shape, click the drawing area, and then wonder why your shape isn't there. This may happen a few times before you remember to hold the mouse button and *drag!*)

You can drag a shape into a drawing as many times as you want — the master shape stays on the stencil. As you drag a shape into your drawing area, you see an outline of the shape on the screen. When you release the mouse button, the actual shape appears in your drawing and remains selected (green handles are displayed around the perimeter of the shape) until you click a blank area of the drawing page.

You can also drag a whole bunch of shapes into a drawing at once. Suppose you're creating a directional map and you know you want to use these shapes from the Landmark Shapes stencil: airport, townhouse, ferry, river, hospital, and sports stadium. Hold down the Shift key as you click each shape. In the stencil, each shape you click remains highlighted. When you select the last shape, release the Shift key and drag the shapes into the drawing. Visio stacks the shapes on top of each other (slightly staggered so that you can see each one). Now you can arrange them however you like.

If the shape is not exactly the size that you want and you just can't wait to adjust it, see the "Sizing up your shapes" section in Chapter 4.

Selecting a shape

Selecting a shape in a drawing is even easier than dragging it onto a drawing — just click the shape. When you select a shape, its green selection frame and handles become visible (see Figure 2-7). You need to select a shape before you can move it, copy it, delete it, or change it in any other way.

Selection handles

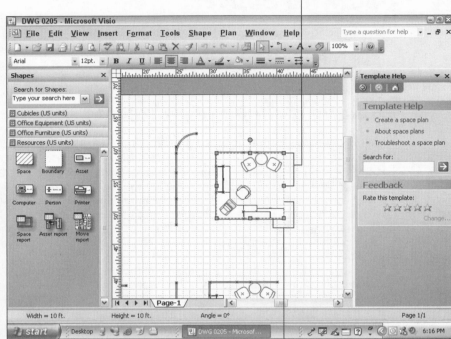

Selection frame

Figure 2-7:
The bright
green
handles and
dashed
frame tell
you the
shape is
selected.

A shape displays different types of selection handles depending on the tool you use to select the shape. You find out more about controlling, working with, and manipulating shapes in Chapter 4.

Selecting more than one shape at a time

Sometimes you may want to perform the same task (such as moving, copying, rotating, or flipping) on several shapes at a time. You can use one of three methods to select multiple shapes:

✔ **Use the Area Select Pointer Tool button and hold down the Shift key as you click each shape that you want to select.** As you select shapes, they're enclosed in a *selection box* (a green dotted rectangle). Green handles appear at the corners of the selection box (see Figure 2-8). All selected shapes are outlined in magenta (the first one in a bolder outline).

First shape selected

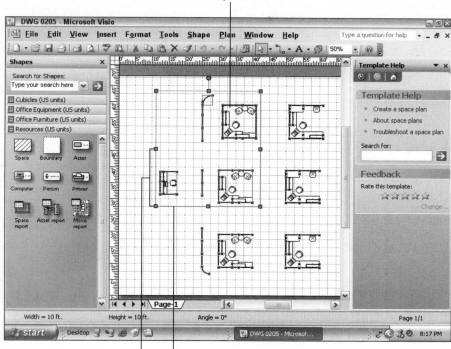

Figure 2-8:
The selection box encloses all selected shapes, which are individually outlined in magenta.

Selection handles   Selection box

✔ **Use the Area Select Pointer Tool button and drag a selection box around multiple shapes.** This method is shown in Figure 2-8. Just drag the mouse around the shapes that you want to select, and then release the mouse button. You must fully enclose all the shapes that you want to select; if you cut across a shape, it isn't selected.

✔ **Use the Lasso Select Pointer Tool button and click and drag the mouse pointer around the shapes you want to select.** This method is shown in Figure 2-9. As you drag, a lasso on the screen follows your path. As soon as you release the mouse button, the selected shapes are enclosed in a rectangle just like the one shown in Figure 2-8.

✔ **Use the Multiple Select Pointer Tool button and click each shape that you want to add to the current selection.** (You don't need to hold the Shift key or do any dragging with this option.) When you're finished, you need to remember to turn off this pointer by choosing a different one. Otherwise, Visio continues selecting shapes every time you click one!

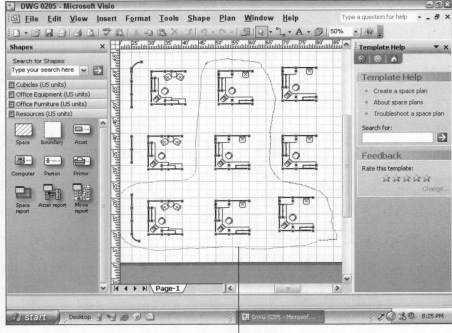

Figure 2-9:
Lasso
Select lets
you select
shapes the
way you
might
outline them
with pencil
and paper.

Figure 2-9:
Lasso
Select lets
you select
shapes the
way you
might
outline them
with pencil
and paper.

Selection lasso

If you select multiple shapes and then decide to exclude one of them, you can deselect it without deselecting all the shapes. Hold down the Shift key and click the shape you want to remove. You can tell that you successfully deselected the shape because the selection box shrinks to *exclude* the shape. To deselect all selected shapes, click any blank area of the drawing or press Esc.

To select all shapes in a drawing quickly, press Ctrl+A or choose Edit➪ Select All.

Navigating Through a Drawing

Often drawings contain multiple pages, and you need to be able to move from one page to another quickly. The drawing shown in Figure 2-10 contains four pages. The name of each page appears on a tab at the bottom of the drawing window on the navigation bar. To move from one page to another, just click the page tab. Visio highlights the tab for the page that's currently displayed.

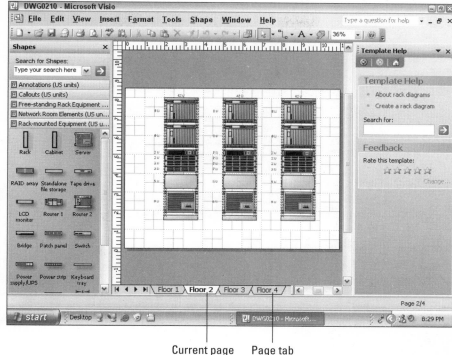

Figure 2-10:
Tabs appear
for every
page in the
drawing; the
current
page tab is
highlighted.

Current page   Page tab

If the navigation bar isn't wide enough to display all the page names, put
your mouse pointer over the right end of the navigation bar until the pointer
changes to a double-headed arrow. Now you can drag the navigation bar to
the right until it displays all the page tabs in your drawing. (This shortens
your scroll bar, but you can still scroll.)

Zeroing In on a Drawing

As you work on a drawing, it's nice to be able to zoom in on a particular area.
Visio gives you several options for zooming in and out.

Using the Zoom button

The typical way to adjust your view of a drawing is to use the Zoom button
on the Standard toolbar. Next to the Zoom button (the one that displays a
percentage) is a drop-down arrow. When you click this arrow, a list of percentages (50%, 75%, 100%, 150%, 200%, and 400%) is displayed, along with
three other options (see Figure 2-11).

Zoom options

Type a percentage here

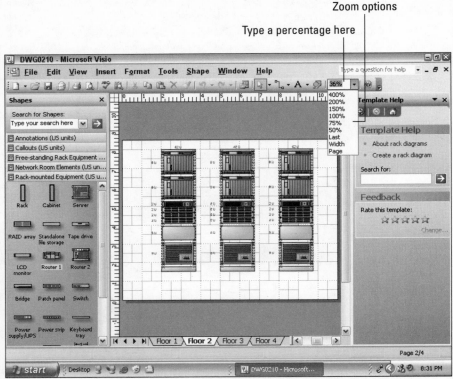

Figure 2-11:
The Zoom
button
offers
preset zoom
percentages
and other
options.

Just click the percentage you want, type a percentage, or click one of the following options:

- ✔ Last: Returns to the last percentage used
- ✔ Width: Displays the width of the page
- ✔ Page: Displays the entire page

These options appear also in the View menu under Zoom, but using the Zoom toolbar button is faster.

My favorite way to zoom — and by far, the fastest — is to hold down the Ctrl key and use the scroll wheel on the mouse. Scrolling forward (away from you) zooms in; scrolling backward (toward you) zooms out. Of course, this method requires a scroll wheel on your mouse. If your mouse doesn't have one, you can zoom using Ctrl+Shift. When you press and hold these keys, the mouse pointer changes to a magnifying glass with a plus sign. Click the left mouse button to zoom in; click the right mouse button to zoom out. To zoom back out again to display the entire drawing, press Ctrl+W.

When you're zoomed in close, you can *pan* (move right, left, up, or down) through a drawing by using the scroll bars.

Using the Pan and Zoom window

When you're working on an enormous drawing, it's easy to lose your bearings when you zoom in on a specific area. Using the scroll bars to pan through a drawing can get cumbersome. A great way to keep your perspective on a drawing and navigate at the same time is to use the Pan and Zoom window, shown in Figure 2-12. This tiny window gives you a full-page view of your drawing; a zoom box marks the area you're currently zoomed in on. You can use the zoom box simply to keep an eye on the area you're working in, or you can move it to a different location in the drawing.

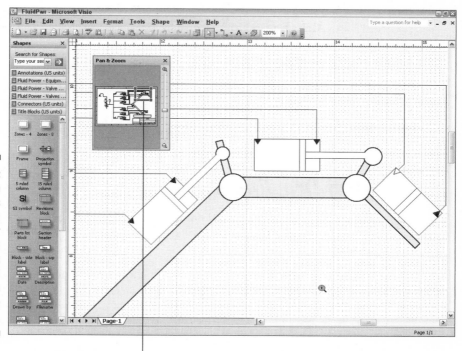

Figure 2-12: The zoom box marks the area of your drawing that's magnified on the drawing page.

Portion displayed in the drawing area

To experiment with the Pan and Zoom window, follow these steps:

1. **Choose View⇨ Pan & Zoom Window.**

   Visio displays the Pan and Zoom window. The red rectangle outlines the area of the drawing you're currently viewing.

2. **To zoom in on a different area of the drawing:**

   a. **Place the mouse pointer over the red rectangle until the pointer changes to a four-headed arrow.**

   b. **Drag the red rectangle to a new location in the drawing.**

3. **To move to a different location in the drawing, point anywhere outside the red rectangle and drag the mouse.**

   A new rectangle is drawn automatically and Visio shifts your view of the drawing.

4. **To resize the red rectangle (which changes the size of the area you view in the drawing):**

   a. **Move the mouse pointer over the red rectangle until the mouse pointer changes to a two-headed arrow.**

   b. **Click and drag the mouse in any direction to resize the rectangle.**

   Visio automatically shifts your view of the drawing to the boundaries defined by the red rectangle.

Like other windows, you can make the Pan and Zoom window a floating window by dragging it anywhere on the screen. Or you can dock it along any edge of the drawing area just by dragging it.

Using Drawing Explorer

Drawing Explorer is like central database administration for your drawing. It keeps track of a truckload of drawing data (some you might think trivial!), such as

- Number and name of the foreground and background pages
- Order of the pages
- Shapes used on a specific drawing page
- Layers used on a specific drawing page
- Styles used throughout the drawing
- Master shapes used throughout the drawing
- Fill pattern, line pattern, and line ends used in the drawing

Why would you possibly care about this kind of information? For some drawings, you may not care and won't even bother to open Drawing Explorer. But just knowing that the information is readily accessible can be helpful.

Drawing Explorer displays information about a drawing in a hierarchical format. It's modeled after Windows Explorer, which uses a tree structure, folder and document icons, and the – and + symbols to indicate whether or not a folder is empty. In Figure 2-13, the first line in the Drawing Explorer window displays the path name for the drawing. Below the path name are various folders, beginning with Foreground Pages. Page-1 contains the Shapes folder, which is open. The highlighted shape name (Display) is selected automatically in the drawing.

Notice the thumbtack icon in the title bar of the window in Figure 2-13. When the window is docked, the thumbtack looks like it's tacked to show that the window is thumb tacked in place. If you hover over the button, the tool tip says Turn On AutoHide. If you click the thumbtack and then move the mouse away from the window, the window closes but the title bar remains on the screen. When you want to use the window again, just move your mouse over the title bar and the window reappears.

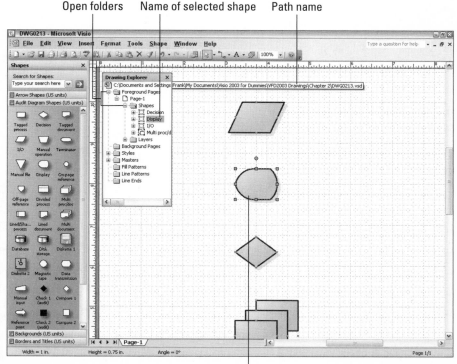

Figure 2-13:
Drawing
Explorer
displays a
wealth of
information
about your
drawing in a
hierarchical
format.

To open Drawing Explorer, choose View⇨Drawing Explorer. Use Drawing Explorer the same way you use Windows Explorer; click the + symbol to the left of a folder to see its contents. You can right-click any folder or folder entry to display a shortcut menu. The options available on the menu are unique to the item you click. For instance, if you right-click the Foreground Pages folder, the shortcut menu lets you insert or reorder pages.

The best way to find out about Drawing Explorer is to play with it: open and close folders and right-click everything. You'll soon become familiar with the type of information that's available and your options for using it.

If you open an existing drawing while the Drawing Explorer window is open, it remains open and reflects the data of the current drawing. To close Drawing Explorer, click the Close button (the X) in the upper-right corner of the window.

You can move, dock, or auto-hide the Drawing Explorer window by following the same methods used for the Pan and Zoom window. Refer to the "Using the Pan and Zoom window" section earlier in this chapter.

Saving Drawings

When you've spent a lot of time creating a drawing, the last thing you want to do is lose it! You should save a drawing as soon as you create it and continue saving it every few minutes (or at least every time you add anything significant to it). This is a habit I've developed after too many bad experiences losing work that I often slaved over for hours.

Saving a drawing the first time

The first time you save a drawing, Visio displays the Save As dialog box. Follow these steps to save your drawing:

1. **Choose File⇨Save.**

   Visio displays the Save As dialog box, as shown in Figure 2-14.

2. **Click the folder where you want to save your drawing.**

   If necessary, use the icons on the left or click the drop-down arrow on the Save In box to navigate to the folder where you want to save your drawing.

3. **In the File Name box, type a name for your drawing.**

4. **In the Save As Type box, click Drawing if it's not already selected.**

   For information on the different file types, see the "Saving a drawing in another file format" section, later in the chapter.

5. **Click the Save button.**

   Visio saves your file and keeps your drawing on the screen.

Current folder

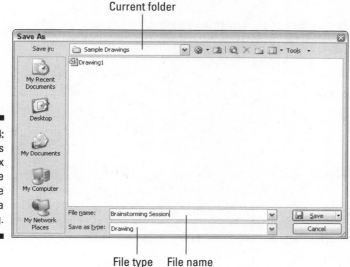

File type   File name

Figure 2-14:
The Save As
dialog box
appears the
first time
you save a
drawing.

Setting up AutoSave

To train your brain to remember to save, set up Visio to save files automatically for you. *This is not a substitute for saving files yourself!* However, in the event of a power failure (or a clumsy coworker kicking out your power cord), Autosave allows you to recover a file in the state in which it was last saved. Here's how to set up a time interval for saving files.

1. **Choose Tools⇨Options.**

2. **Click the Save tab.**

   The screen shown in Figure 2-15 appears.

Enter a time interval here

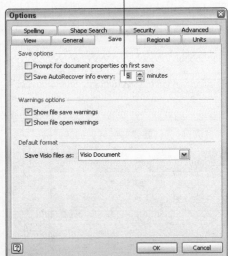

Figure 2-15:
You can
specify the
time interval
for auto-
saving.

3. **Click the Save AutoRecover Info Every option. Use the up or down arrow to select a time interval.**

   I suggest 5 or 10.

4. **Click OK.**

Saving a drawing as a template

It's also possible to save a Visio drawing as a template. Many corporations find it useful to create and save custom templates because they can incorporate their company logos and other company-specific information. See Chapter 12 for more information about creating and saving custom templates.

Saving a drawing in another file format

In Visio, you have many options for saving drawings in different file formats. Don't let the humongous list of file types intimidate you. Many of these you'll never use, but it's nice to know that they're available should you ever find the need.

Visio defaults to the Drawing file type; which is the type you'll use most often. You can also save a Visio drawing as a Visio 2002 file type, if necessary, but you can't save a drawing in an earlier version of Visio (such as Visio 5).

- ✔ Drawing
- ✔ Stencil
- ✔ Template
- ✔ XML Drawing
- ✔ XML Stencil
- ✔ XML Template
- ✔ Visio 2002 Drawing
- ✔ Visio 2002 Stencil
- ✔ Visio 2002 Template
- ✔ Scalable Vector Graphics
- ✔ Scalable Vector Graphics Compressed
- ✔ AutoCAD Drawing
- ✔ AutoCAD Interchange
- ✔ Web Page
- ✔ Compressed Enhanced Metafile
- ✔ Enhanced Metafile
- ✔ Graphic Interchange Format (GIF)
- ✔ JPEG File Interchange Format
- ✔ Portable Network Graphics
- ✔ Tagged Image File Format (TIFF)
- ✔ Windows Bitmap
- ✔ Windows Metafile

Using a Visio Wizard to Create a Drawing

Most programs use only one standard way to create a new document, but Visio gives you several options. I describe one method — using a wizard — in this section. You can also create a drawing at any time after Visio is running as follows:

1. **Choose File⇨New⇨Choose Drawing Type.**

   Visio displays the opening screen.

2. **Choose a category on the left.**

   Visio displays sample drawing types.

3. **Click a template.**

   Visio creates a new drawing page and opens the appropriate stencils.

If you've used other Microsoft programs, you're probably familiar with wizards. If not, a wizard is a tool that guides you through the steps you need to perform a task quickly and easily. Wizards can be used for almost any type of task. In Visio, they help you create specific kinds of drawings.

Visio 2003 isn't consistent in the location or availability of wizards. And there isn't any way to search for a wizard. Some appear on the Template list when you select a drawing category, such as the Organization Chart Wizard. Some, such as the Space Plan Wizard, pop up automatically when you choose the building plan drawing type and space plan template. Others are on special menus, such as the Calendar menu that appears when you select the Project Schedule drawing type and the Calendar template. Table 2-1 lists the known wizards in Visio 2003 and where to find them.

Table 2-1	Wizards in Visio 2003
Wizard	*How to Find the Wizard*
Database	Choose Tools⇨Add-Ons ⇨Run Add-On or Tools⇨Add-Ons⇨Visio Extras.
Database Export	Choose Tools⇨Add-Ons ⇨Run Add-On or Tools⇨Add-Ons⇨Visio Extras.
Organization Chart	Create a drawing using the Organization Chart category, and then choose Organization Chart Wizard. Or choose Tools⇨Add-Ons⇨ Organization Chart.
Import Outlook Data (to create a calendar)	Create a drawing using the calendar template (which displays the Calendar menu), and then choose Calendar⇨Import Outlook Data Wizard. Or choose Tools⇨Add-Ons ⇨Run Add-On.
Space Plan	Choose File⇨New⇨Building Plan⇨Space Plan.
Import Timeline	Create a drawing using the Project Schedule⇨ Timeline template (which displays the Timeline menu), and then choose Timeline⇨ Import Timeline Data.

Wizard	How to Find the Wizard
Export Timeline	Create a drawing using the Project Schedule⇨ Timeline template (which displays the Time-line menu), and then choose Timeline⇨ Import Timeline Data.
Import (Microsoft) Project Data (for Gantt chart)	Create a drawing using the Project Schedule⇨ Gantt Chart template (which displays the Gantt chart), and then choose Gantt Chart⇨ Import Project Data.
Export (Microsoft) Project Data (for Gantt chart)	Create a drawing using the Project Schedule⇨ Gantt Chart template (which displays the Gantt Chart), and then choose Gantt Chart⇨ Export Project Data.
Generate Site Map (Web site)	Create a drawing using the Web Diagram cate-gory, and then choose General Site Map.

Opening Drawings

After you've created and saved some Visio drawings, you need to know how to reopen them. You can open drawings saved in the current version of Visio or a previous version of Visio, and you can open and work on more than one drawing at a time.

Opening a saved drawing

After you've saved a drawing, you can open it again in a few different ways. If Visio isn't running and you need to start it, use these steps:

1. **Choose Start⇨Programs⇨Microsoft Office⇨Microsoft Office Visio 2003.**

   The opening screen appears (refer to Figure 2-1).

2. **In the Getting Started pane on the right side of the screen, see whether the file is listed in the Open section.**

   Recently opened files are listed in the Open section. You can also click the File menu and check to see whether the file you want is listed at the bottom of the menu.

3. **If you find the file you want, click it to open it.**

4. **If the file isn't listed, choose File➪Open.**

   The Open dialog box appears.

5. **Navigate to the folder where you stored the file, highlight the file name, and then click the Open button.**

   Your drawing is displayed and all appropriate stencils are opened.

Opening a drawing saved in a previous version of Visio

You can open a file saved in *any* previous version of Visio, including Visio Standard, Professional, Technical, or Enterprise. Open the file just as you would any file you saved in Visio 2003. If the file used stencils or templates that are no longer available in Visio 2003, the Shapes pane is empty. You can choose Files➪Shapes to open any stencil and apply it to the drawing. When you're finished working, you can resave the file in Visio 2000 format or in Visio 2003.

Previous versions of Visio allowed you to save a workspace (with the .vsw file extension). Visio 2003 doesn't provide this option, but you can still open a workspace file. If you want to save a workspace file in Visio 2003 (or Visio 2002), Visio saves it as a drawing file (with the .vsd file extension).

Opening more than one drawing at a time

In Visio, you can work with more than one drawing at a time. The file you open becomes the active drawing; any other drawings that are already open remain open. All open drawings are listed at the bottom of the Window menu.

To open a drawing while working in Visio, follow these steps:

1. **Choose File➪Open.**

   The Open dialog box appears.

2. **Navigate to the folder where your file is located.**

3. **In the document list, click the file that you want to open.**

4. **Click the Open button.**

If you want to view more than one drawing on the screen at the same time, choose Window⇨Tile or choose Window⇨Cascade. The Tile option arranges drawings side-by-side on the screen. The Cascade option stacks the windows on top of one another and slightly staggered so you can read the title bars.

After the drawing windows are open, you can rearrange them by dragging the title bars or resizing the windows. For more information on arranging windows on your screen, see *Windows XP For Dummies* by Andy Rathbone (published by Wiley & Sons Publishing, Inc.)

Chapter 3

Printing Visio Drawings

For the most part, printing in Visio is a breeze — not much different from printing from any other Windows application. If your drawing doesn't vary from the template, without any major changes to the page size or orientation, you can often just click Print and get exactly the results you expect. However, sometimes your drawings won't be this straightforward. What if your drawing is larger than the paper? What if it's small and you want it to fill the page? What if your drawing is wider than it is tall, and it won't fit on standard paper? In this chapter, you find the answers to these questions and discover what you need to know to print all kinds of drawings (or selected portions of drawings) successfully.

Understanding How Visio Prints

The most important concept to keep in mind when printing with Visio is that the printer paper size and the drawing page size are independent of one another. The *printer paper size* refers to the paper you use in your printer. The *drawing page size* refers to the paper you see represented in white (usually shown with grid lines) in the drawing window on the screen.

Most of us use printers that handle 8½-by-11-inch or 8½-by-14-inch paper. Sometimes the printer may handle tabloid size paper (11-by-17 inches). And if you work in an architectural firm, an engineering lab, a graphics design firm, or a large corporation with vast resources, you might have access to a plotter as well, which prints on large rolls of paper up to 60 inches wide. The truth is, it doesn't matter what your printing resources are. Visio can print your drawing no matter what size paper your printer handles.

When you use a Visio template to create a drawing, it sets up your drawing page size and printer paper size so that they match. Depending on the type of drawing you're creating, it might set up the page in *portrait* mode (taller than it is wide) or *landscape* mode (wider than it is tall). Visio matches the drawing page size to the printer paper size and keeps the drawing page size that way unless you do something to change it. It's okay to change it! (Visio wants to work the way you work, not force you to conform to inflexible rules.) You just need to know how it will affect your printing if you do.

Preparing to Print

Before you print any drawing, you should do the following:

- ✔ Check to see whether the printer paper size and the drawing page size are different
- ✔ Center your drawing
- ✔ Use Print Preview to get a look at how your drawing will print

In this section, you find out more about the importance of each of these steps and how to do each one. (You could try skipping these steps, but if you do you'll just be wasting paper!)

Checking the printer paper and drawing page sizes

To compare the printer paper size and the drawing page size, choose File➪Page Setup to display the Page Setup dialog box shown in Figure 3-1. This dialog box lets you make any necessary changes to the printer paper size and the drawing page size.

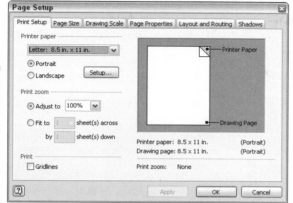

Figure 3-1:
Here, you
see the
drawing
paper size
and printer
page size
together.

The Print Setup tab is where you make changes to the printer paper size. To make changes to the drawing page size, you use the Page Size tab. (For now, you can ignore the rest of the tabs in this dialog box.)

The terrific feature of this dialog box is the illustration on the right, which appears in both the Print Setup tab and the Page Size tab. The illustration shows you a picture of both the printer paper size and the drawing page size on top of one another, so you can tell immediately how things are lining up.

Figure 3-1 shows a drawing in which the printer paper size and the drawing page size line up perfectly in portrait mode. (In this example, I used a template to create a drawing and didn't change the drawing page size or the orientation.) You don't need to do anything special to print successfully except preview your drawing, as you see later in this chapter.

But what if you go to print your drawing and the Page Setup illustration looks like the one in Figure 3-2? The printer paper size and drawing page size don't line up. You know you need to do some adjusting before you print, but what do you change?

The illustration shows you that your drawing paper is in landscape mode and your printer is set to print in portrait mode. This means that if you have any shapes in your drawing that fall *outside* the area shown by the printer paper, they won't print. (Even if you don't have shapes outside the printer paper area, your drawing won't be centered neatly on the page.)

In this example, the problem is one of orientation and is easy to solve: Change either the printer paper orientation to match your drawing (refer to Figure 3-2) or change the drawing page orientation to match the paper (refer to Figure 3-3). Your choice depends on the content of your drawing and how you want it displayed. Whichever you choose, the goal is to have the orientation and size of the paper match the orientation and size of the drawing page.

Page orientation options

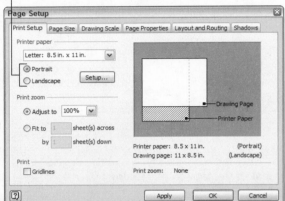

Figure 3-2:
A discrepancy between the printer paper size and drawing page size.

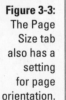

Figure 3-3:
The Page Size tab also has a setting for page orientation.

Page orientation options

Previewing your drawing

You should always preview your drawing after checking the page and paper setups. Why? Because the Print Setup and Page Size dialog boxes show you how the printer paper size and drawing page size compare to one another; they don't show you anything about the drawing itself and where the shapes are located. Print Preview gives you a preview of the actual drawing. You can display the print preview screen by clicking the Print Preview button on the Standard toolbar or by choosing File➪Print Preview.

Your goal in Print Preview is to see that all shapes fall inside the wide gray border around the edge of the paper, which indicate the drawing's margins. These page margins are visible only in Print Preview — another good reason to check here before printing! Any shape that falls across the margin lines won't print correctly. Everything is A-okay in the drawing shown in Figure 3-4. You can see that the page is set to print in portrait mode and that all the shapes fall within the page margins.

If your drawing's shapes fall across page margins, you can try several options. You can print on larger paper, adjust the placement of the shapes in the draw-ing, tile the drawing, or reduce the size of the drawing to fit the paper. Tiling and reducing the drawing are discussed later in this chapter in the "Printing oversized drawings" section. Refer to Chapter 4 for information about moving shapes in a drawing. To print on larger paper, refer to the preceding section.

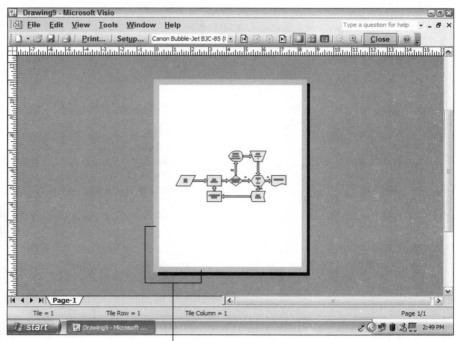

Figure 3-4:
In Print Preview the gray border indicates page margins.

Page margins

A clear view in Print Preview

If you've never used Print Preview before, here are a few tips. Notice in Figure 3-4 that Print Preview has its own toolbar. The first four buttons — New Drawing, Open, Save, and Print Page — also appear on the Standard toolbar. The remaining buttons are described in Table 3-1. You can use these buttons to change your view of Print Preview. Click the Close button when you want to return to your drawing in Visio.

Table 3-1		Print Preview Toolbar Buttons
Button	*Name*	*What It Does*
🖨	Print	Displays the Print dialog box
Setup...	Setup	Displays the Page Setup dialog box
Canon Bubble-Jet BJC-E5	Current Printer	Displays the current printer and lets you choose a different one
◀|	First Tile	Displays the first tile (if you selected the Single Tile option)
◀	Previous Tile	Displays the tile before the one currently displayed (if you selected the Single Tile option)
▶	Next Tile	Displays the tile after the one currently displayed (if you selected the Single Tile option)
▶|	Last Tile	Displays the last tile (if you selected the Single Tile option)
▤	Single Tile	Displays a single tile in a tiled drawing
⊞	Whole Page	Displays all the tiles in a tiled drawing
▤	Current View	Displays only the area of the drawing that was displayed before you chose Print Preview

Button	Name	What It Does
	Zoom Out	Reduces your view in the print preview window (you can see more of the drawing)
	Zoom In	Magnifies your view in the print preview window (you see less of the drawing)
Close	Close	Closes the print preview window and returns to the normal drawing view
	Help	Changes the mouse pointer to a question mark and displays help on the item you click

Printing Your Drawing

When you've checked the settings for the printer paper size and the drawing page size, and you've centered and previewed your drawing, you're ready to print. With your file open, follow these steps:

1. **Choose File⇨Print.**

   The Print dialog box appears, as shown in Figure 3-5.

2. **Choose the printer you want to use if more than one is available.**

Figure 3-5:
Specify the printer settings, pages to print, and number of copies.

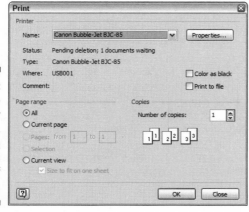

3. **If you want to check the settings for your printer:**

   a. **Click the Properties button.**

   b. **Adjust the printer settings as you normally do.**

   c. **Return to the Print dialog box.**

4. **In the Page Range section, choose All, Current Page, Selection, or specify a range of pages by typing page numbers.**

   You can specify a range of pages only if the drawing has more than one page. Similarly, you can specify to print the Selection only if you made a selection before displaying the Print dialog box.

5. **Specify the number of copies you want to print.**

6. **Click OK.**

Some Windows applications give you the option of printing a group of selected pages, such as 2, 4, and 7. Visio doesn't provide this option. To print a group of selected pages, you need to print each page individually in the Pages: from option. For example, to print pages 2 and 4, you would type 2 and 2 in the Pages: from option, click OK to print that page, type 4 and 4 in the Pages: from option, and click OK.

Now that you know the basics of printing, let's look at some special considerations for printing, such as centering a drawing, including headers or footers in a drawing, printing gridlines, and printing partial drawings. These are common tasks, but they require a little extra effort to set up.

Adding Headers and Footers to a Drawing

A *header* refers to text that appears at the top of each page of a drawing; a *footer* is text that appears at the bottom of each page. Headers and footers are optional. If you decide to add them to a drawing, you can include text such as a title, a file name, a date, or automatic page numbers. You decide where you want them to appear in the header or footer area: at the left margin, centered, or at the right margin.

Headers and footers apply to every page in a drawing.

Often you want headers or footers to include the time, date, file name, or page number. Visio adds these automatically when you select one of these items. You can insert the following items:

✔ Current date (short)

✔ Current date (long)

✔ Current time

✔ File extension

✔ File name

✔ File name and extension

✔ Page name

✔ Page number

✔ Total printed pages

When you choose one of these items, Visio enters a formatting code in the dialog box, such as &t for the current time. Don't let this throw you; the correct information is automatically inserted when you print the drawing. Note that you can use more than one of these items for each location in the header or footer. For example, if you want a centered header to include the page number, page name, and file name, click all three options in the Header Center box. Just be sure to add spaces between each entry.

To add a header or footer to a drawing, follow these steps:

1. **Choose File⇨Open to display your drawing.**

2. **Choose View⇨Header and Footer.**

   The Header and Footer dialog box appears.

3. **In the appropriate Header or Footer text box (Left, Center, Right), type the information that you want to appear, such as "Company Confidential."**

   If you want Visio to automatically insert the date, time, file name, or other information, click the right arrow at the end of the Left, Center, or Right text box (see Figure 3-6) and then click the option you want. If you're inserting more than one option, add appropriate punctuation and spacing.

   You can enter as many characters as will fill one line. (The exact number depends on the font size you choose in Step 5.) If you enter more characters than will fit across the page, the characters overtype at the right margin.

4. **In the Margin boxes, type a size for the header margin and footer margin, if you want.**

   You shouldn't need to adjust margins unless you want an extra-wide margin.

The margin setting for a header is the distance from the top of the header text to the top edge of the page. For a footer, it is the distance from the bottom of the footer text to the bottom edge of the page. Unlike in other programs, Visio headers and footers do not print inside the page margin area; they print inside the drawing area.

Figure 3-6:
The Header and Footer dialog box makes it easy to enter titles or special text such as the date or file name.

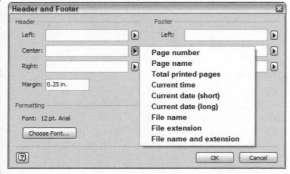

5. **To format the header and footer text:**

    a. **Click the Choose Font button.**

        The Choose Font dialog box appears, as shown in Figure 3-7.

    b. **Choose a font, size, style, special effects, and color for the header and footer text.**

Formatting applies to all header and footer text; you can't format each one individually.

    c. **Click OK to close the Font dialog box.**

Figure 3-7:
Choose a font, size, style, and color for header and footer text.

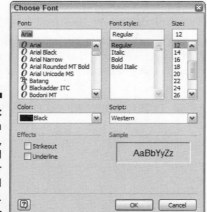

6. **Click OK to close the Page Setup dialog box.**

Click the Print Preview button on the Standard toolbar or choose File➪Print Preview to see how your header and footer text will look when you print your drawing. (Header and footer text is only visible in Print Preview or on the printed drawing.)

In a tiled drawing (one that's printed across several sheets of paper), Visio prints headers and footers on each sheet. You may want to put header and footer information on a background page (a separate page that works as an underlay) instead. For details about creating background pages, see Chapter 9. For information about tiling a drawing, see the "Printing oversized drawings" section later in this chapter.

Printing Gridlines

When measurements are important to your drawing, it's useful to print the gridlines that show up in the drawing page window. To print gridlines, follow these steps:

1. **Open your drawing file.**

2. **Choose File➪Page Setup.**

   The Page Setup dialog box appears.

3. **Click the Print Setup tab if it isn't already selected (see Figure 3-8).**

4. **In the Print area near the bottom of the dialog box, click the Gridlines option.**

5. **Click OK.**

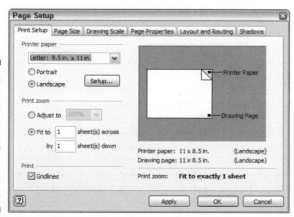

Figure 3-8: The Gridlines option toggles on and off each time you check the box.

Printing Part of a Drawing

It's nice to know that you can always print a portion of a drawing if you need to. Maybe you're drawing includes a lot of shapes and you want to print only a few of them. Or maybe a portion of your drawing is still in flux and you want to print everything except that portion. You can choose the shapes you want to print and prevent the others from printing by not selecting them. Use these steps:

1. **Open the drawing you want to print.**

2. **In the drawing, select only the shapes that you want to print.**

3. **Choose File⇨Page Setup to check your drawing's paper size and orientation, and then click OK.**

4. **Choose File ⇨Print Preview or click the Print Preview button on the Standard toolbar.**

5. **Choose File⇨Print.**

   The Print dialog box appears

6. **Choose the printer settings as you normally do.**

7. **In the Page range area, click Selection.**

8. **Click OK.**

   Visio prints only the shapes you select.

Reducing and Enlarging Printed Drawings

When you create an *oversized drawing* (one that's larger than the paper in your printer), you can see right away in Print Preview that the drawing won't print on a single sheet of paper. It might make sense to tile the drawing (that is, print it across several sheets of paper). But if you need the drawing to print on one page, another option is to change the print scale. Changing the *print scale* lets you print the drawing at a smaller percentage of its original size. It's like creating a reduced copy of a drawing on a copy machine.

Conversely, when a drawing is too small, you can enlarge the print scale and make the drawing easier to read when you print it.

Note that print scale is different than from the drawing scale. *Print scale* is simply a percentage of the original drawing size. *Drawing scale* expresses a relationship between the size of real-world objects and the size at which they're shown in a drawing. You find out how to change drawing scale in Chapter 7.

Altering the print scale of a drawing

To change the print scale of a drawing, use these steps:

1. **Open your drawing file in Visio.**

2. **Choose File⇨Page Setup.**

   The Print Setup tab of the Page Setup dialog box appears, as shown in Figure 3-9.

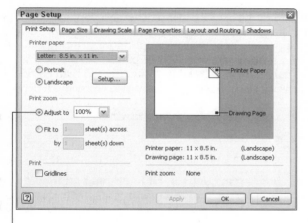

Figure 3-9:
You can print to scale or tile a drawing.

Adjust print scale

3. **In the Print zoom area, click the Adjust to option.**

   Enter a number smaller than 100 percent to reduce the printed size of the drawing. To instead enlarge the drawing, enter a number greater than 100 percent.

4. **Click OK to close the Page Setup dialog box.**

5. **Choose Print⇨Preview or click the Print Preview button on the Standard toolbar.**

   Make sure your drawing fits on the drawing page.

6. **Repeat Steps 2 to 5 if necessary to adjust the drawing.**

You may expect your drawing to change on the screen, but it doesn't. This is because you've altered the *print* scale, not the *drawing* scale. Again, like reducing or enlarging a page on a photocopier, the size of the original doesn't change. Only the copied result changes.

If you need to print the drawing at regular scale, follow the previous steps to change the percentage back to 100 before you print again.

Printing oversized drawings

Suppose you create a very large drawing, say 2½ feet wide by 3 feet high. If you have a plotter, printing the drawing is a breeze. Just enter the page size and drawing size in the Page Setup dialog box as described earlier in this chapter, preview the drawing, and then print.

But what if you don't have access to a plotter and you want to print the drawing at actual size (because, for example, you want to use the drawing in a presentation for a large audience). Another option for printing an oversized drawing is to print it on separate sheets of paper and tape or paste the sheets together. This is called *tiling* a drawing. Using the following steps, you specify exactly how many sheets of paper you want your drawing to fit on:

1. **Choose File⇨Open to display your drawing.**
2. **Choose File⇨Page Setup.**

   The Print Setup tab of the Page Setup dialog box appears.
3. **In the Print zoom area, click the Fit to option and then enter the number of sheets across and the number of sheets down.**
4. **Click OK.**

To view exactly how your drawing will be tiled when printed, click the Print Preview button on the Standard toolbar, or choose File⇨Preview. The gray lines in the print preview screen represent the borders between pages. Another way to view tiles while you're working is to choose View⇨Page Breaks. This option displays the same page borders right on the drawing page so you can make adjustments as you work without switching to Print Preview.

Fitting the drawing on the number of pages you specify affects the printed copy but not the scale of the drawing. To "untile" a large drawing, return to the Page Setup dialog box and reset the zoom percentage to 100%.

Setting Shapes Not to Print

Sometimes it's just as important *not* to print a shape or shapes as it is to print others. For example, if you're printing an office layout plan, your employees are interested in seeing the cubicle layout but don't need to see the wiring components. Or maybe you've named a new department head in your company but you don't want your employees to see the name of the new boss on the organization chart yet. Maybe you're planning office space but aren't sure some of the office furniture you've ordered will be available. These are all cases when you might want to set a specific shape or shapes to not print in your drawing.

To set a shape not to print, follow these steps:

1. **Open your drawing.**

2. **Right-click the shape you want to set for nonprinting and choose Format⇨Behavior.**

   The Behavior dialog box appears.

3. **If the Behavior tab is not already selected, click it (see Figure 3-10).**

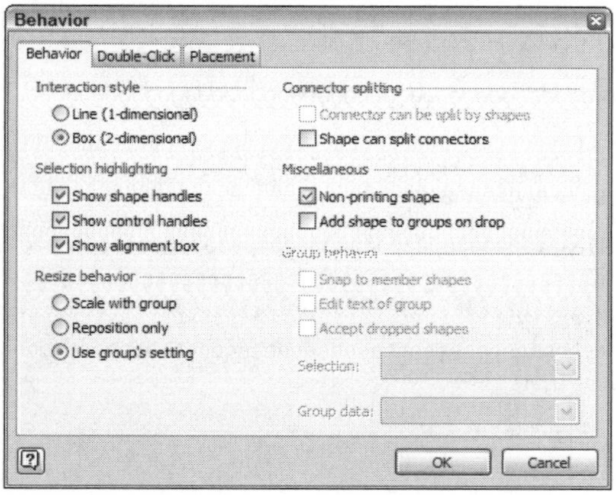

Figure 3-10: The Non-printing shape option toggles on and off each time you click it.

4. **In the Miscellaneous section, click the Non-Printing shape option.**

5. **Click OK.**

To make sure that the shape is set to not print, click the Print Preview button on the Standard toolbar or choose File⇨Print Preview. The shape should not appear on the print preview screen. When you print the drawing, the shape will not print.

To make the shape print again, follow the previous set of steps and click to unselect the Non-printing shape option in Step 4.

Printing Reviewers' Comments

Visio 2003 incorporates some advanced reviewing and markup features. (See Chapter 14 to find out about annotating and reviewing Visio drawings.) When you've had one or more people take the time to review a drawing for you, it's nice to be able to print the drawing showing their comments. To do this, follow these steps:

1. **Open the drawing you want to print.**

2. **Choose View➪Markup to display reviewer's marks on the drawing.**

3. **Choose View➪Reviewing Pane.**

   The pane to the right of the drawing window summarizes the reviewers' comments. Or if the Help pane is already displayed, click the down arrow in the title bar and choose Reviewing to switch to the Reviewing task pane.

4. **In the Show Markup Overlays section of the pane, click Show All.**

5. **Choose File ➪Print Preview to preview the drawing.**

6. **Choose File➪Print.**

   The Print dialog box appears.

7. **Choose print settings as you normally do, and then click Print.**

Visio prints your drawing showing all reviewers' comments. To return to printing the drawing without reviewers' comments, choose View➪Markup again to unselect this option.

Printing a Background Separately

Visio lets you create backgrounds for the pages in your drawings. A background is assigned to and appears behind a page in the drawing. To find out more about creating and using backgrounds, see Chapter 9.

If your drawing contains a background page, you might find it useful to print the background separately from the rest of the drawing. This is an easy task because the background is stored as a separate page in a drawing. Follow these steps:

1. **Open the drawing file that contains the background page.**

2. **Click the Background tab at the bottom of the drawing window to make it the current page.**

3. **Choose File ⇨Print Preview to preview the drawing.**

4. **Choose File⇨Print.**

   The Print dialog box appears.

5. **Click the Current page option, and then click OK.**

   Only the background page prints.

Printing Layers Separately

Visio lets you place shapes on separate layers in a drawing. There are many circumstances where it makes sense to print layers separately. For example, in a drawing that depicts a building or a home plan, only the plumber cares about seeing the pipe layout and only the electrical team cares about seeing the wiring and telecom layout. If you place these components on individual layers, you can print the layers separately. For details on creating layers and printing them separately, see Chapter 10.

Part II
Creating Visio Drawings

The 5th Wave   By Rich Tennant

After his flowchart deteriorated to stick figures, Donald the technophobe decided to give Visio a try.

In this part . . .

This is where you find all the basic stuff you need to know to create a drawing. You find out how to add shapes to a drawing and work with them, how to connect shapes, and how to add text so you can describe your drawings. You won't do any fancy stuff here, but you will understand enough features of Visio to be productive.

Chapter 4

Discovering What Visio Shapes Are All About

Shapes are the most important elements of Visio; they're the building blocks you use to create diagrams, drawings, charts, and graphs. Regardless of the type of drawing you create — a flowchart, a network diagram, an architectural drawing, a project timeline — you create each drawing by using shapes. Visio includes many types of shapes that not only *look* different but also *behave* differently. In this chapter, you discover many different types of shapes, what makes them different, and how to work with them in your drawings and diagrams.

I'm a firm believer in doing things as quickly and easily as possible. Often, using menu commands isn't the quickest way. I'm partial to keyboard short-cuts, so in this chapter you'll see me favoring them — though I do point out other methods available for accomplishing a particular task.

Discovering What's In a Shape

If you think you may not have enough shapes to choose from when you're building your drawings, think again. Visio includes thousands of shapes!

Shapes are stored in *stencils*, which are collections of related shapes displayed in their own window on your Visio screen. You'll create most drawings by using the shapes that Visio supplies, but you can create and store your own shapes as well. Chapter 8 covers creating and storing shapes.

A shape can be as simple as a single line or as complex as an industry-specific network component for a computer system. Unlike clip art, shapes have certain "smart" characteristics. For instance, if you add text to a shape and then resize the shape, the text reformats automatically to the new size. Shapes with glued connectors (like the lines that connect boxes on an organization chart or flowchart) stay connected when you move them. A pie chart isn't just a pie chart. You decide the number of slices it should have, and when you want to adjust percentages, the shape adjusts automatically. A bar chart shape adjusts the length of its bars automatically after you type a percentage for one of the bars (see Figure 4-1).

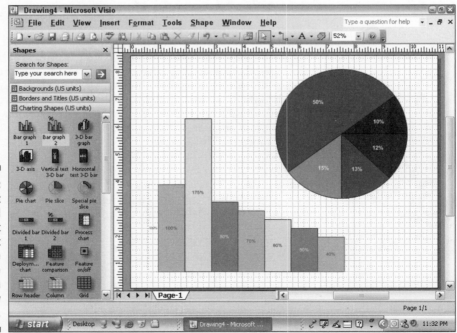

Figure 4-1: Pie chart slices and bar chart bars adjust to the proper size when you enter a new percentage.

You can control a particular aspect of a shape, such as the angle and direction of the vanishing point of a three-dimensional shape like a cube. (The *vanishing point* is the point at which parallel lines of a three-dimensional object appear to converge.) You can store data (for example, inventory numbers, service dates, or serial numbers), with a shape and generate reports from the stored data. (For more information about storing data in shapes, see Chapter 12.) If you're a software developer creating a custom Visio solution, you can program specific behavior into shapes. You can see why Visio shapes are called *SmartShapes*. Many have built-in brainy behavior.

Examining open and closed shapes

Shapes can be classified as either *open* or *closed*, as shown in Figure 4-2. An open shape is one in which the endpoints aren't connected, such as a line, an arc, or an abstract shape. A closed shape is a fully connected object such as a polygon.

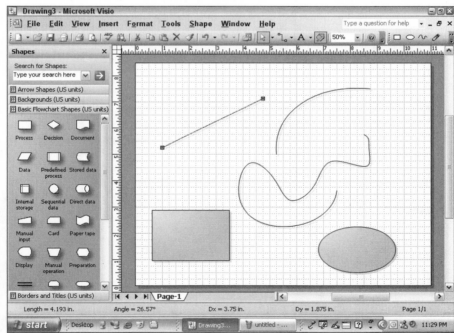

Figure 4-2: Check out these examples of open and closed shapes.

What difference does it make whether a shape is open or closed? You can fill a closed shape with a color or a pattern. You can't fill an open shape, but you can add endpoints such as arrowheads and other symbols.

Comparing one- and two-dimensional shapes

All Visio shapes are either one-dimensional or two-dimensional. Two-dimensional shapes have length and height. When you select a two-dimensional shape with the Pointer Tool button, you can see its selection frame and selection handles (see Figure 4-3).

The *selection frame* is a green dotted line that fully encloses a shape. *Selection handles* are green squares that appear at the corners and sides of a frame. (Later you see that handles can look different when you select a shape using a different tool.) The handles enable you to change the shape's length and height. Even a nonrectangular shape (such as a pie chart) displays a rectangular frame with side and corner handles when the shape is selected.

Selection frame   Selection handle

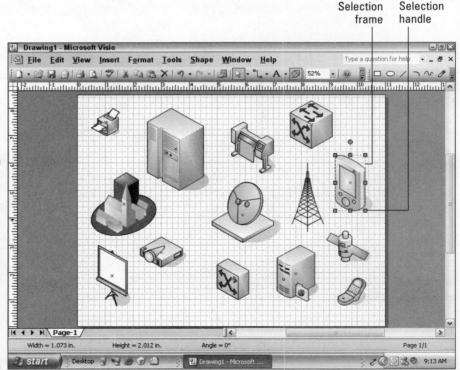

Figure 4-3: Two-dimensional shapes have length and height and display a selection frame with selection handles when selected.

A line is an example of a one-dimensional shape. It has only two *endpoints* — small green boxes — that are visible when you select the line (see Figure 4-4). The beginning point — that is, the point from which you begin drawing — contains an x; the endpoint contains a (+) symbol.

You can resize the length of a one-dimensional shape, but not its height; a one-dimensional shape has no height. (A line has *thickness*, which you can alter by using a formatting command. Thickness is not the same as height.)

An arc is considered a one-dimensional shape, although it may seem to be two-dimensional. Notice in Figure 4-4 that an arc has only two endpoints; it doesn't have a frame with handles at each corner and side. The handle at the top of the arc is called a *control handle*, which enables you to adjust the bend of the arc. See the "Controlling Shapes" section later in this chapter to find out more about working with control handles on other types of shapes.

You see a shape's handles only when the shape is selected. The type of handle you see depends on the tool that you use to select the shape. You see more examples of shape handles throughout this chapter.

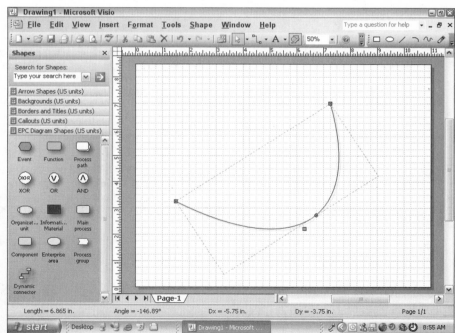

Figure 4-4: One-dimensional shapes display two endpoints when selected.

Working with Shapes

After you have shapes in your drawing, you'll want to do all kinds of things to them, such as moving, copying, pasting, deleting, and resizing. These are some of the most common tasks you do with shapes that don't involve altering the shape itself. Table 4-1 shows some toolbar buttons you use to work with shapes.

Table 4-1	Standard Toolbar Buttons for Working with Shapes	
Button	**Name**	**What It Does**
✂	Cut	Removes the selected shape from the drawing and makes it available for pasting
📑	Copy	Saves a copy of the selected shape and makes it available for pasting
📋	Paste	Places the selection that you cut or copied into the drawing
✕	Delete	Removes the selected shape without making it available for pasting
🖌	Format Painter	"Picks up" the formatting of a selected shape and makes it available to another shape
⬇	Stamp	Places the selected shape into the drawing whenever you click it (rather than dragging a shape repeatedly from the stencil)

To drag a shape, you have to click the shape with the left mouse button and hold the button down as you move the shape.

Moving shapes

After you have shapes in your drawing, you'll move them around a lot until you get them exactly where you want them. Moving a shape is simple; just drag the shape wherever you want it. As you drag a shape, watch the vertical and horizontal rulers. The shape's top, middle, and bottom points are indicated on the ruler by faint dotted lines. If you want to place a shape three inches from the top border of your drawing and two inches from the left border, for example, you can see exactly where the shape is aligned by watching the indicators on the ruler.

You can restrict the movement of a shape by holding down the Shift key as you drag the shape. If you drag the shape horizontally, it moves only to the right and left and keeps its vertical position. If you drag the shape vertically, it moves up and down and keeps its horizontal position.

See Chapter 7 for additional information on how to snap shapes into alignment by using rulers, a grid, and alignment commands that can make the placement of your shapes more exact.

Nudging shapes

Sometimes a mouse can be a clumsy instrument to use. What if you need to move a shape exactly 1/32 of an inch? It's just not going to happen with a mouse! Visio lets you nudge shapes. *Nudging* is essentially bumping a selected shape by using the arrow keys on the keyboard. When you nudge a shape, the shape moves in tiny increments, usually to the nearest ruler subdivision. Variables such as the ruler scale, grid, and zoom percentage can determine how much the shape moves.

Try this quick and easy way to reposition shapes:

1. **Click the shape that you want to nudge.**
2. **Position the shape by pressing the up, down, right, or left arrow key repeatedly.**
3. **When your shape is positioned where you want it, click anywhere on the drawing page to deselect the shape.**

If you want to nudge several shapes at the same time, hold down the Shift key as you select the shapes you want and then use the arrow keys to nudge the selected shapes as a unit.

Copying and pasting shapes

Copying and pasting shapes is something you do often when creating a drawing. If you know you want to use a shape more than once, you could drag the shape from the stencil into the drawing each time you want to use it. But wouldn't it be better to drag just one instance of the shape into your drawing, make any necessary changes to it (such as changing its size, color, fill, or text), and then copy it to other places in the drawing? Especially when you're modifying the shape, it's easier to copy the shape from one place in the drawing to another, rather than start all over again from the stencil.

As I've said before, I prefer to do things as quickly and easily as possible, so my favorite method for copying and pasting a shape is to do both tasks in one step. Hold down the Ctrl key, drag the shape you want to copy, and then release the mouse button in the new location. As soon as you press Ctrl, you see a (+) symbol attached to the mouse pointer. This tells you Visio will *add* (or copy) the shape rather than move it. Presto! You've copied and pasted all in one simple step.

If you're using a lot of the same shape in your drawing, another quick way to copy and paste all at once is to select the shape and then press Ctrl+D (short for Edit⇨Duplicate). The shape is pasted to the right and slightly below the copied shape. Now you can move it wherever you want.

If you prefer the two-step method for copying and pasting, here are the different ways to copy a shape after you select it:

- ✔ Press Ctrl+C
- ✔ Right-click the shape and choose Copy from the pop-up menu
- ✔ Click the Copy button on the Standard toolbar
- ✔ Choose Edit⇨Copy

All these methods place a copy of the shape (or shapes) on the Windows Clipboard.

To paste the shape in a new location, do one of the following:

- ✔ Press Ctrl+V
- ✔ Right-click a blank area of the drawing page and choose Paste from the pop-up menu (the shape or text most recently copied is pasted)
- ✔ Click the Paste button on the Standard toolbar
- ✔ Choose Edit⇨Paste

You can continue to paste multiple copies of the shape until you use a copy command again to copy a different shape.

Stamping shapes

Here's another nifty button if you need to use a shape over and over again in your drawing. It's the Stamp button, and it works just like a rubber stamp. Wherever you stamp the button, the shape is pasted into your drawing. This is the best method to use if you just want to use shapes as-is from the stencil because it saves you the trouble of repeatedly dragging the shape from the stencil.

Follow these steps to use the stamping button:

1. **Click the Stamp button (refer to Table 4-1) on the Standard toolbar.**

   If the button isn't on your toolbar, click the down arrow at the right end of the toolbar (Toolbar Options), choose Add or Remove Buttons⟳ Standard, and then click the Stamp button to add it to your toolbar.

2. **In the stencil, click the shape that you want to stamp.**

3. **Drag the mouse pointer into the drawing area.**

   Notice that your mouse pointer now looks like a stamp.

4. **Click where you want to stamp the shape.**

   Keep clicking until you've added all the stamped shapes that you want in your drawing.

5. **Click the Pointer Tool button (it looks like an arrow) to switch back to the regular mouse pointer.**

Sizing up your shapes

In many cases, you'll want to resize shapes for your drawings. Visio makes resizing simple. Use the following steps to adjust the size of shapes.

1. **Select the shape with the Pointer Tool button.**

2. **Do one of the following:**

   • Drag a side handle to change the shape's width.

   • Drag a top or bottom handle to change the shape's height.

   • Drag a corner handle to change the height and width at the same time. Visio maintains the shape's height-to-width proportions when you drag at the corner.

3. **Release the mouse button when the shape is the size that you want.**

If your shape contains text, the text reformats automatically as you resize the shape. (See Chapter 5 to find out how to enter text in shapes.)

These steps may seem to imply that all shapes are parallelograms. They're not; but remember that every two-dimensional shape has a rectangular frame, which *is* a parallelogram, so that the shape can be resized in width, height, or both proportionally.

If you want a shape to be a specific size, for example, 2-by-1½ inches, watch the status bar at the bottom of the screen as you resize the shape. The status bar displays the shape's height and width as you move the mouse.

You can also use Visio's Size and Position window to specify the size and location of a shape in a drawing. To display this window, choose View⇨Size and Position Window (see Figure 4-5). Type the height and width you want for your shape and then press Enter. To close the window, click the Close button in the window's title bar.

Like other windows, you can make the Size and Position window a floating window by dragging it anywhere on the screen. Or you can dock it along any edge of the drawing area just by dragging it.

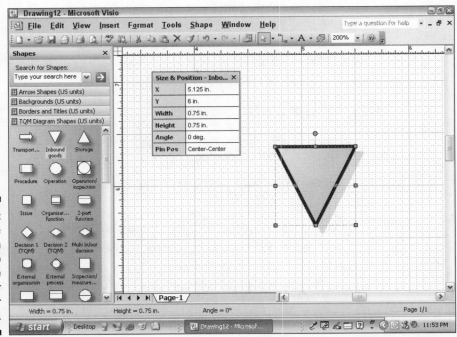

Figure 4-5:
Use the Size and Position window to enter the exact size or location for a shape.

Deleting shapes

You can delete a shape in one of four ways. First select the shape and then do one of the following:

- ✔ Press the Delete key on the keyboard
- ✔ Press Ctrl+X
- ✔ Click the Cut button on the Standard toolbar
- ✔ Choose Edit➪Cut

Pressing the Delete key is the easiest way to delete a shape. But if you think you may want to bring the shape back again, use Ctrl+X or Cut instead. That way, the shape is stored on the Clipboard so that you can paste it in the drawing again (as long as you paste it before you cut anything else).

You can use the same method to delete more than one shape at a time. Select all the shapes you want to delete (either click them or draw a selection box around them) and then choose one of the four delete options. (Refer to Chapter 2 to find out how to select multiple shapes at once.)

If you delete something by mistake, you can choose Edit➪Undo (or press Ctrl+Z) to bring it back. By default, Visio has 20 levels of Undo, so you can undo up to the last 20 commands that you performed. (If you think you want more, you can set up to 99 levels of Undo! Choose Tools➪Options, click the General tab, and type a number in the Undo Levels box.)

Controlling Shapes

You already know that when you select a shape using the Pointer Tool button, the shape displays selection handles, which are small green squares on the shape's rectangular frame. These usually appear at the four corners and the sides of a shape's frame.

Selection handles allow you to resize a shape, but you might want to make other changes. For example, you might want to change the width of bars in a bar chart or the magnitude or a curve. Or you might want to change the vanishing point for a three-dimensional cube. You can't use selection handles to accomplish any of these tasks, but Visio provides different types of handles, points, and vertices that allow you to make these kinds of changes to a shape, as shown in Table 4-2. In this section, you find out how to use these handles, points, and vertices to change different aspects of a shape.

Table 4-2	Handles, Points, and Vertices Used for Controlling a Shape		
Shape	*Color*	*Name*	*What It Does*
◈	Yellow	Control handle	Varies depending on the type of shape. It might adjust the direction an arrow points or the width of bars in a bar chart.
⬡	Green	Control point	Changes the curve or symmetry of a line segment
⬤	Green	Rotation handle	Rotates a shape to a different angle
◉	Green	Eccentricity handle	Adjusts the magnitude and angle of an arc
✦	Green	Vertex	Changes the point at which two line segments meet
✳	Blue	Connection point	Marks the location where you can glue a shape

Note: When a handle, point, or vertex appears in gray on the screen, it's locked and can't be changed.

Not all shapes contain all the handles and points shown in Table 4-2! For example, control handles appear on some shapes and often apply to an aspect of the entire shape, whereas control points appear only on part of a shape, such as lines, line segments, arcs, and freeform curves. Some shapes might not contain vertices and others won't include eccentricity handles. Don't panic if you can't find a handle or point when you're expecting one. If it's not there, it's probably not necessary.

When I start talking about the color of handles and points, you'll have to use your imagination or try to duplicate the examples on your own screen. The black-and-white figures in the book put you at a disadvantage, but being able to recognize the colors of these handles and points is important.

Adjusting shapes using control handles

When you select a shape, the control handles — if the shape has any — appear somewhere on or near the shape and enable you to control some aspect of the shape. Every shape's control handles have a purpose. The purpose varies depending on the shape to which the control handles are attached. To discover what a shape's control handles are used for, select the shape, and then hover the mouse over the control point to display the tip for the control handle.

An example of a bar chart is shown in Figure 4-6. The yellow diamonds are control handles. The control handle near the bottom allows you to adjust the width of the bars; the control handle near the top allows you to adjust the overall height of the bars.

The control handles for the shapes in Figure 4-7 have a different function. In this 3-D block diagram, the Vanishing Point shape is used to define the vanishing point for all shapes in the drawing. But each 3-D shape in the drawing has its own control handle that lets you change the shape's individual vanishing point.

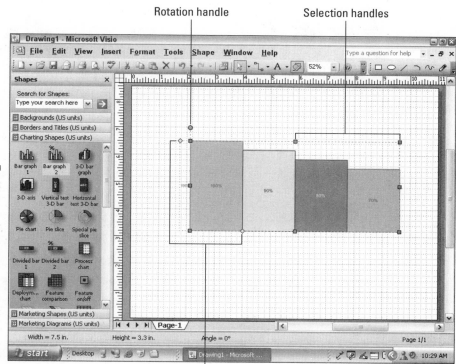

Figure 4-6: When selected, this bar chart shape displays control handles that let you alter the dimensions of the bars.

Rotation handle

Selection handles

Yellow control handles

Control handle for the cube's vanishing point

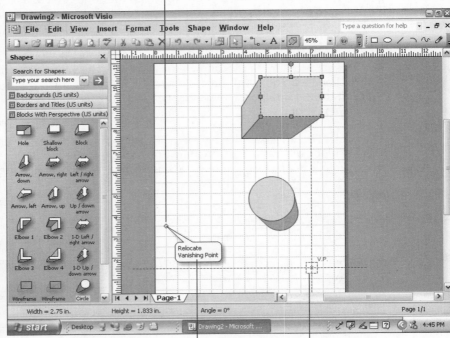

Figure 4-7:
The cube's
vanishing
point was
changed
using its
control
handle.

Control handle tip   Vanishing point for the drawing

Adjusting a shape's control handle is simple. Just select the shape using the Pointer Tool button, and then hover over the control handle until the tip appears. The tip might say something like "adjust corner rounding" or "adjust pie slice." Drag the control handle until you get the result you want — that's all there is to it!

Adjusting shapes using control points

Control *points* (as opposed to control *handles*) appear on lines, line segments, arcs, and freeform curves. (These elements might be freestanding or part of a more complex shape.) A control point lets you control the shape of a line, an arc, or a curve. (When you hover over a control point, the tip says "Bend Shape.") Another way to describe the function of control points is to say that they let you control the shape of a shape. So, if you want to make a straight-sided rectangle look like a bulging rectangle, for example, you drag a control point on the rectangle's line segments. Think of a control point as a rubber band point.

To work with a shape's control points, you must select the shape using the Line, Arc, Freeform, or Pencil Tool button on the Drawing toolbar. (If the Drawing toolbar isn't displayed, right-click in the toolbar area and select the Drawing toolbar from the pop-up menu.) These drawing tools are shown in Table 4-3. When you select a shape using one of these tools, Visio first displays the shape's control points and vertices. Then a split-second later, Visio displays the selection frame and handles.

Let Visio display all these handles and points before you move the mouse! If you move the mouse away too quickly, some handles and points might not be displayed.

Table 4-3	Drawing Toolbar Tools for Displaying a Shape's Vertices and Control Points	
Button	**Name**	**What It Does**
	Line Tool	Lets you draw a line
	Arc Tool	Lets you draw an arc
	Freeform Tool	Lets you draw "freeform" in any direction
	Pencil Tool	Lets you draw lines, arcs, or circles, depending on how you move the mouse

To adjust a control point, choose one of the drawing tools from Table 4-3, and then select the shape. Control points are displayed as green circles with an X inside. When you click a control point to select it, the point turns magenta until you release the mouse button in its new position. Figure 4-8 shows how a pentagon shape looks before and after its control points are moved.

Shaping corners

Just as control points enable you to bend line segments, *vertices* let you reshape the angle at which line segments meet. You can display a shape's vertices (green diamond-shaped points) by selecting a shape with any of the drawing tools shown in Table 4-3.

Rotation handle   Selection handles

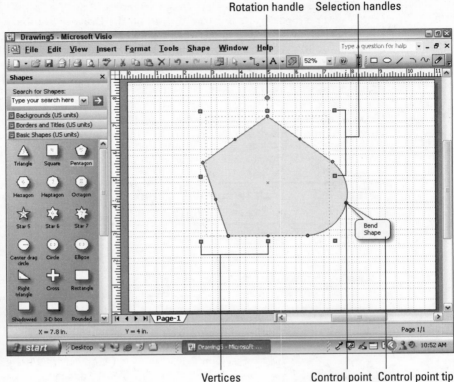

Figure 4-8:
You can
curve a line
segment by
dragging
its control
handle.

Vertices   Control point Control point tip

Hover over a vertex and the tip says "Adjust Corner." When you click on a vertex to select it, it turns magenta. Once selected, you can you can drag it in any direction, changing the length and angle of the lines that form the vertex. If you want to alter a leg of a star, for example, drag the vertex (see Figure 4-9). To find out how to add or delete vertices, see Chapter 8.

Visio seldom displays vertices on shapes that you drag into a drawing from a stencil. That's because many Visio shapes are complex enough that moving a vertex may destroy the shape. However, you can always display vertices on shapes that you draw. See Chapter 8 for information about drawing your own shapes.

Rotating shapes into place

Many Visio shapes can be rotated so that you can place them at the angle you prefer. To display a shape's rotation handle, you don't need to select the shape using a drawing tool; the Pointer Tool button works just fine. The round, green *rotation handle* usually appears outside the perimeter of the selection frame and selection handles. When you point to the rotation handle, the mouse pointer changes to a single curved arrow. When you hover over the rotation handle the handle tip says "Rotate Shape."

Every rotation handle has an accompanying *center of rotation* pin, marking the point around which the shape rotates. The center of rotation pin is a small green circle with a + symbol.

To rotate a shape, drag a rotation handle using a circular motion. The mouse pointer changes to a rotation pointer (four arrows in a circular shape), and you see an outline of the frame as you rotate it around the center of rotation. See Figure 4-10. A shape's rotation pin is usually located in the center of the shape, but you can move it. If you want to rotate a rectangle around its lower-right corner, for example, drag the center of rotation pin to the lower-right corner of the rectangle and then rotate the shape. (Check out Chapter 8 for more details on rotating shapes.)

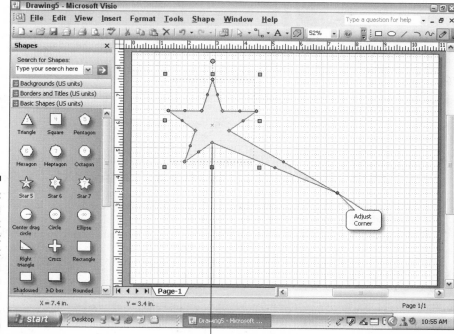

Figure 4-9:
Drag
a vertex
to adjust
the point
at which
two line
segments
meet.

Vertices are green diamond shapes

Rotation handle (the green circle)

Rotation mouse pointer (the four arrows)   Center-of-rotation pin

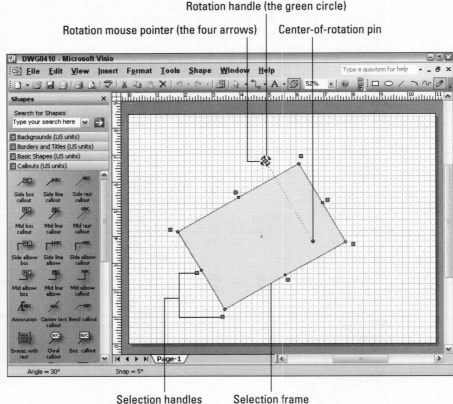

Figure 4-10:
Drag the
rotation
handle in a
circular
motion to
rotate a
shape.

Selection handles   Selection frame

Modifying arcs using eccentricity handles

In simple, non-techie terms, an elliptical shape is an oval. In Visio, an elliptical shape can also be *part* of an oval, as in an oval-shaped arc. All elliptical shapes in Visio have *eccentricity handles*, which are designed to let you adjust its *off-centeredness* or *eccentricity*. For example, if you draw an arc, you use the eccentricity handles to change the angle at which the arc sits relative to its endpoints.

Eccentricity handles are visible only when you select a shape using the Pencil Tool button. First you see the arc's control point, a small green circle with an x in it. As soon as you click the control point, it turns magenta and the shape's eccentricity handles are displayed on either side of it, joined by a green dotted line. The eccentricity handles are also green circles with an x inside. The dotted line represents the angle at which the curve sits relative to the curve's endpoints (see Figure 4-11).

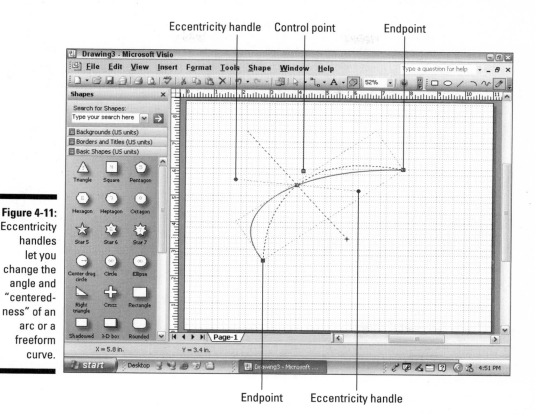

Figure 4-11: Eccentricity handles let you change the angle and "centered-ness" of an arc or a freeform curve.

To change the magnitude of an arc, click the control point at the top of the arc and drag it in any direction. If you want the arc to angle differently, drag either eccentricity handle up or down. To change an arc's eccentricity (in effect, its "bend" point), drag either eccentricity handle closer to or farther from the control point. (The closer the eccentricity handles are to the control point, the more circular the arc becomes.) The best way to figure out how to work with eccentricity handles is to play with them!

Using connection points

Connection points are the places on a shape where the endpoints of other one-dimensional shapes (such as lines) can connect to the shape. For example, the boxes in an organization chart have connection points where the lines connect to the boxes. (Note that not all shapes have connection points.)

You can display connection points by choosing View➪Connection Points. These small, blue Xs can appear almost anywhere on a shape — but usually appear at corners, midpoints of lines, or centers of shapes (see Figure 4-12). You can clutter your screen by displaying connection points all the time! I recommend that you display them only when you need them. To turn off connection points, choose View➪Connection Points.

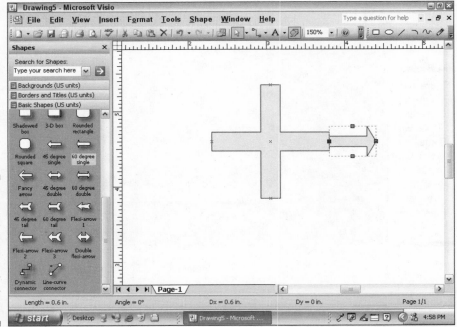

Figure 4-12: Connection points mark locations where you can glue other shapes or connectors.

Finding the Shapes You Want

Visio offers so many different shapes on so many different stencils, keeping them all straight is difficult. What if you recall seeing just the right shape for a drawing but don't remember which stencil it's on? Or what if you're looking for just the right shape — one you've never used before — and you don't want to search through dozens of stencils looking for it? Well, now you don't have to!

Visio 2003 makes it easy to find shapes by using the Search box right in the Shapes pane (see Figure 4-13). Just type a word such as *flag* or a combination of words such as *circuit breaker* and Visio searches for shapes matching your description.

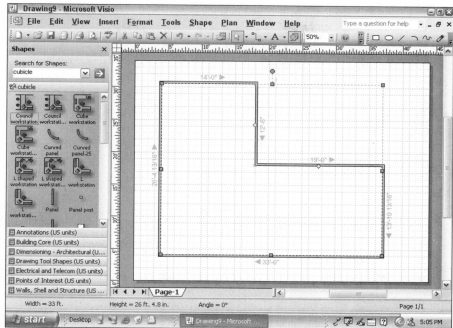

Figure 4-13:
Visio
displays the
shapes it
finds in a
new stencil
window.

To use the search feature, follow these steps:

1. **In the Search for Shapes box (in the Shapes pane on the left side of your screen), type a single word or a combination of words.**

2. **Click the green arrow next to the search box.**

   Visio searches for shapes that match your description. If shapes are found, they're displayed in a new window with the search word or phrase you used as the title bar. If shapes are not found, Visio displays "Could not find a match. Please search again."

3. **Use any found shapes the same way you use other shapes; just drag them into your drawing.**

If your search word or phrase is too broad, Visio finds too many shapes. If the results found total more than 100 shapes, Visio displays a message asking whether you want to review the results. Click Yes to view them all, or click No to end the search and then type a more specific search word or phrase.

When you use Search for Shapes, Visio searches for shapes stored on your computer as well as on the Internet. This is the default setting for searching. You can change this search setting, among others, using the following steps:

1. **Choose Tools⇔Options.**

   The Options dialog box appears.

2. **Choose the Shape Search tab (see Figure 4-14).**

   In the Search locations area, note that the Everywhere box is checked, as well as the My Computer and the Internet boxes. You can uncheck any of these boxes to limit your search.

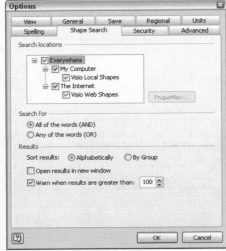

Figure 4-14:
You can
customize
the way
Visio
searches
for shapes.

3. **In the Search For area, choose All of the Words (AND) or Any of the Words (OR).**

4. **In the Results area, choose to sort results Alphabetically or By Group.**

5. **If you want results for each search to appear in a new window, choose Open Results in a New Window.**

   This is a good option to choose if you want to save the shapes in a custom stencil. When this option is not checked, results from a new search replace old search results.

6. **To change the Warn When Results Are Greater Than setting, use the up or down arrow or type a new number.**

7. **Click OK.**

Another way to find a shape is to search for a shape that's similar to one already in your drawing. For example, suppose your drawing contains a personal computer shape and you want to find a similar shape. Use the following steps to search for similar shapes:

1. **Right-click a shape in your drawing and choose Shape.**

   The menu shown in Figure 4-15 appears.

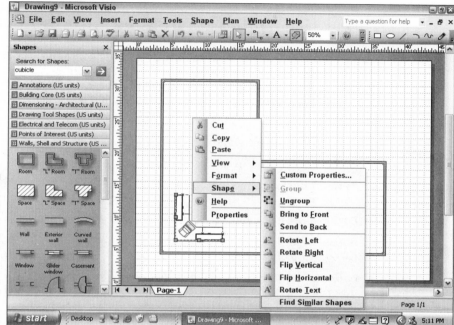

Figure 4-15:
You can find similar shapes quickly by right-clicking a shape in the drawing.

2. **Choose Find Similar Shapes.**

   Visio searches for similar shapes and displays the results in a stencil in the Shapes pane.

3. **Drag the shape into your drawing just like from any other stencil.**

To find out more about creating custom shapes and stencils and saving them, see Chapter 12.

Jazzing Up Your Drawings

Some drawings and charts are appropriate without any frills or fluff. But sometimes, black shapes and text on a white background can be *really* boring. This is especially true if you plan to use your drawings as part of a presentation or add them to a publication. If you have the flexibility to add interesting graphic elements and color, by all means, do so! Visio has some slick features for jazzing up your drawings.

Using the Visio Extras stencil shapes

There are times when you want to include in a drawing some graphical elements that don't qualify as clip art. They're more functional than clip art. Examples of this type of graphical element are borders, title blocks, legend blocks, and measurement scales. Visio includes a huge collection of stencils that contain these types of shapes.

To see a sample of these shapes, choose File➪Shapes➪Visio Extras. On the submenu, you find the following stencils:

- ✔ **Annotations:** A collection of shapes (callouts, text blocks, arrows, symbols) you can use to describe or call attention to parts of your drawing.

- ✔ **Backgrounds:** Designs you can add as a backdrop to your drawing.

- ✔ **Borders and Titles:** Predefined page border styles and title boxes from elegant to technical.

- ✔ **Callouts:** A varied set of callout shapes used to grab attention and describe areas of a drawing (more choices than those found in the Annotations stencil).

- ✔ **Connectors:** A huge collection of every type connector imaginable.

- ✔ **Custom Line Patterns:** Options for custom line patterns for one-dimensional shapes.

- ✔ **Custom Patterns (scaled and unscaled):** Options for custom fill patterns for two-dimensional shapes.

- ✔ **Dimensioning (architectural and engineering):** Measurement specifications for scale drawings.

- ✔ **Drawing Tool Shapes:** A collection of circles, arcs, lines, measuring tools, and polygon shapes.

- ✔ **Embellishments:** Cool and weird stuff like Egyptian corners, Greek borders, art deco frames, and wave sections.

- ✔ **Symbols:** Internationally-recognized signs and symbols.

- ✔ **Title Blocks:** A vast array of every conceivable title block, used in architectural drawings, maps, revisions, file names, drafts, and more.

Figure 4-16 illustrates some creative ways to use these stencil shapes.

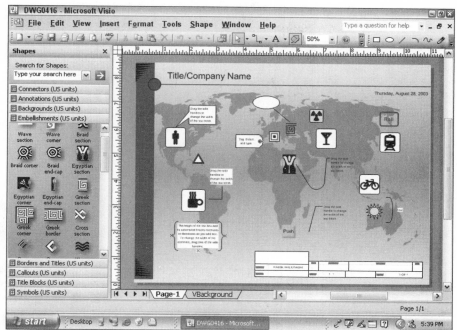

Figure 4-16:
All the shapes in this figure came from Visio Extras stencils.

Applying a color scheme

Another way to spice up your drawings is to apply a color scheme. A *color scheme* is a predefined set of colors assigned to the foreground, background, text, fills, and various shapes in a drawing. Figure 4-17 shows a plain black-and-white drawing; Figure 4-18 shows the same drawing with a color scheme applied. (Of course, you can't see the color in the figure, but you get the idea!)

To apply a color scheme to a drawing, follow these steps:

1. **Open the drawing and click a blank area to unselect all shapes.**

2. **Right-click anywhere in the drawing area and choose Color Schemes. Or Choose Tools➪Add-ons➪Visio Extras➪Color Schemes.**

   The Color Scheme dialog box appears, as shown in Figure 4-19.

3. **In the Choose a Color Scheme list, highlight a color scheme and then click Apply.**

   Grab the title bar of the Color Scheme dialog box to move the box out of the way. Then you can see how the color scheme looks in your drawing.

4. **To try other color schemes, repeat Step 3.**

5. **When you're satisfied with the color scheme, click OK.**

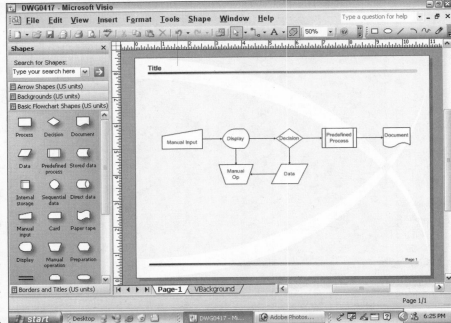

Figure 4-17:
A typical
drawing
with no
spectacular
elements,
color, or
formatting.

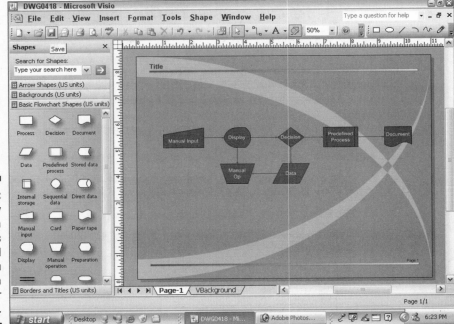

Figure 4-18:
Every
element of a
drawing is
colored
when you
apply a
color
scheme.

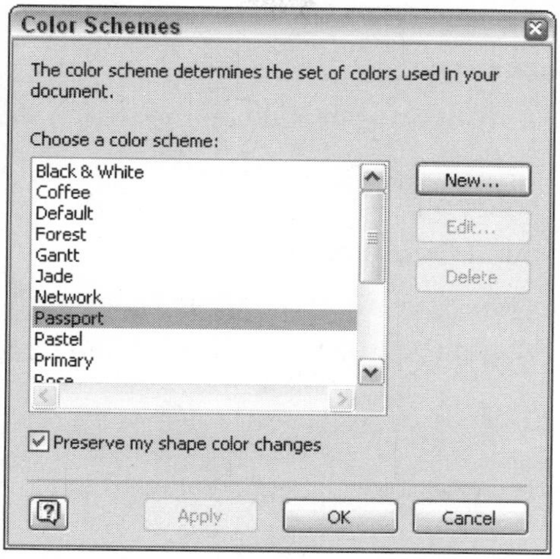

Figure 4-19:
Use the
Color
Schemes
dialog box
to choose
from more
than a
dozen color
schemes for
your
drawing.

If you prefer, you can create your own color scheme and choose your own colors for the foreground, the background, shadows, the line color, and the text. Use these steps to create a custom color scheme:

1. **Open an existing drawing or create a new one.**

2. **Right-click anywhere in the drawing area and choose Color Schemes. Or Choose Tools⇨Add-ons⇨Visio Extras⇨Color Schemes.**

3. **Click the New button.**

   The New Color Scheme dialog box appears, as shown in Figure 4-20.

Figure 4-20:
Choose
colors for a
custom
color
scheme.

4. **In the Name box, enter a name for your color scheme.**

5. **In the Style box, choose a style.**

   The changes you see in the drawing depend on the stencil shapes used in the drawing.

6. **Choose a foreground color:**

   a. **Click the Foreground Color button.**

      The Colors dialog box appears, as shown in Figure 4-21.

   b. **Choose a color from the Standard tab or click the Custom tab to blend a color.**

   c. **Click OK.**

      Visio returns to the New Color Scheme dialog box.

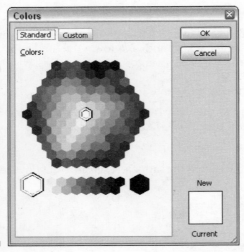

Figure 4-21:
Choose a color from the Standard tab, or click the Custom tab to create a custom color.

7. **Repeat the process for the background color, shadow color, line color, and text color as follows:**

   a. **Click the appropriate button in the New Color Scheme dialog box.**

   b. **Choose a color from the Standard tab or click the Custom tab to blend a color.**

   c. **Click OK.**

8. **In the New Color Scheme dialog box, click OK.**

   Visio returns to the Color Schemes dialog box. The name you gave your color scheme now appears in the list.

9. **Click your new color scheme name and then click Apply.**

   Visio applies the color scheme to your drawing.

10. **To adjust the chosen colors, repeat Steps 6 through 9.**

11. **Click OK to close the Color Schemes dialog box.**

Notice that the New Color Scheme dialog box has a button called Use Current Document Style Colors. If your drawing already uses a color scheme, you can click this button to base a new color scheme on the current colors used.

Chapter 5

Adding Text to Your Drawings

· ·

· ·

*E*ven though they say one picture is worth a thousand words, a little bit of explanation can often help! It's highly unlikely that you'll create all your drawings without any text, so read on to find out how to add freestanding text as well as text to shapes, and then format it the way you want.

Understanding Text Blocks

All text in a Visio drawing is contained in a text block. A *text block* is a special frame for holding text. Most Visio shapes have a text block attached to them. For example, every shape in a flowchart has an attached text box, where you enter data to describe the process or decision represented by the flowchart symbol.

A shape's attached text block goes wherever the shape goes. But you won't see a text block unless you enter text in it — and even then you see only the text itself. (Text blocks aren't outlined by a visible frame.)

In some cases, you may want to add text to a drawing that's *not* attached to a shape. This is called a *text shape* or *freestanding text*. A title for a drawing is a good example of freestanding text. It's obviously text, but it isn't attached to any of the shapes in the drawing; the text block itself is the shape.

Adding Text

In this section, you add text to a shape in a drawing and then add freestanding text. As you work with raw text (that is, the text itself before you format, color, or otherwise jazz it up), you use the buttons on the Standard toolbar shown in Table 5-1.

Button	Name	What It Does
Table 5-1	**Standard Toolbar Buttons for Working with Text**	
	Copy	Places a copy of the selected shape in the paste buffer
	Paste	Places the contents of the paste buffer in the drawing
	Pointer Tool	Lets you select a shape or shapes
	Text Tool	Lets you create a stand-alone text block (unattached to a shape)
	Text Block (drops down below the Text Tool button)	Lets you move, rotate, or resize a stand-alone text block or one attached to a shape
	Format Painter	"Picks up" the characteristics of the selected text so you can apply it to other text

To add text *to a shape* in your drawing, follow these steps:

1. **Double-click a shape to select it and display its text box.**

   The shape's text box is a green dotted outline on a white background. It isn't always inside the shape; sometimes it's outside but near the shape.

2. **Begin typing text in the shape's text block.**

   If your screen zoom is set to anything less than 100%, Visio immediately zooms in on the shape's text block when you begin typing.

   Continue typing. Visio keeps up with you even if you enter a 400-line caption. (Well, that may be a bit of an exaggeration.) If you enter more than one line of text, Visio automatically wraps the text to the next line. You can press Enter any time to begin a new line of text. If you enter more text than the text block can hold, Visio enlarges the text block as you continue to type.

3. When you've finished typing, click anywhere outside the text block.

Voilà! You see the original shape again, along with your text.

Figure 5-1 shows how extensively you can use text in a drawing. Sometimes a so-called drawing contains more text than graphics!

If you enter a lot of text, the text block may become larger than the shape itself. To make the text fit inside the shape, you have a few options. Enlarge the shape, and the text block (including the text in it) reformats automatically as you resize the shape. (Refer to Chapter 4 for more about resizing shapes.) If your drawing won't allow you to enlarge the shape, you can change the size of the text block or change the text's font size. See the "Working with Text and Text Blocks" section later in this chapter.

If a shape has an associated text block, you can't tell where the text block is going to show up until you type something in it. If you're curious about the text box's location before you enter text, you can display it quickly by clicking the shape and then pressing F2.

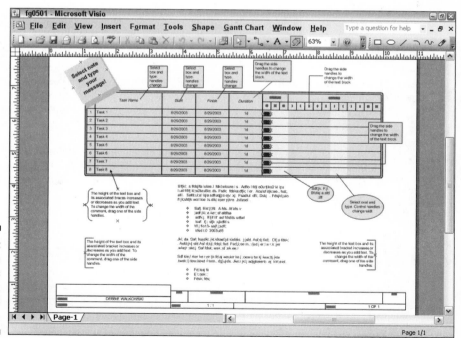

Figure 5-1: Some drawings contain a great deal of text.

The formatting of text in a text block is different depending on the shape you work with. Some shapes left-align text, others right-align text, and still others orient the text vertically. Templates control the way text is aligned and formatted. (This actually isn't weirdness. A logical reason exists for these differences, but they can catch your attention if you're not expecting them.) For more information on changing text characteristics, see the "Changing the Way Your Text Looks" section later in this chapter.

In many circumstances, you'll want to include text that's not part of a shape. Titles, callouts, and fine print such as copyright notices are three examples that come to mind. You can include *freestanding text* in a drawing easily by following these steps:

1. **Click the Text Tool button on the Standard toolbar.**

   Your mouse pointer changes to look like a sheet of paper with text.

2. **Drag the pointer to draw a text box as large (or as small) as you want. Or double-click to have Visio draw a text block for you.**

   Your text block is outlined by a green dotted line and an insertion point appears in the center.

3. **Type your text.**

4. **Click anywhere outside the text block or press Esc.**

Note that in Step 2, the insertion point appears in the center of the text block because the text is set to be center-aligned. For more information on changing this setting, see the "Changing alignment" section later in this chapter.

You can also type in a text block using the Pencil, Line, Freeform, Rectangle, or Ellipse Tool buttons to create your own shapes. Just double-click the shape and add text in the way just described. For more information about creating shapes, see Chapter 8.

Technically, freestanding text isn't really freestanding. It's a shape in and of itself. Visio calls it a text shape. Does that matter? Not really. You just need to know that text is always enclosed in a block; it never just floats around aimlessly!

Working with Text and Text Blocks

In any drawing, you invariably manipulate text in *some* way, whether you edit, copy, paste, move, resize, change the alignment, alter the margins, shift the tabs, and so on. This section helps you make these changes after you enter text.

If you're familiar with word-processing programs such as Microsoft Word, you find that Visio handles text in nearly the same way. If you're already a pro at performing editing tasks, you can whiz right past these sections that discuss copying, pasting, moving, and deleting.

Editing text

It's inevitable. The moment you click outside a shape to save your text that you thought was perfect, you realize you need to change it. Maybe you want to add text, delete text, reword what you wrote, or just start all over again. Changing text in Visio is easy. Follow these steps:

1. **Select the Text Tool button, and then click a shape to display its text (see Figure 5-2).**

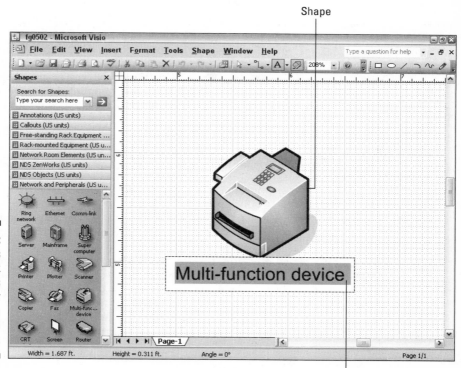

Figure 5-2: A shape's text block appears either in or somewhere near the shape.

2. **Click the mouse where you want to change the text.**

   You see the insertion point after you click.

3. **Begin typing, selecting, deleting, or backspacing to make your changes.**

   - **To delete characters to the right of the insertion point:** Press the Delete key.

   - **To delete characters to the left of the insertion point:** Press the Backspace key.

   - **To select the text and type over it:** Highlight the text you want to delete (use the mouse or hold down the Shift key and use the arrow keys). Then begin typing new text. Whatever you type replaces the text you selected.

4. **After you make changes to your text, click anywhere outside the text block.**

   Your original shape or text shape is visible again.

You can also open a text block by double-clicking the shape using the Pointer Tool (on the Standard toolbar), but watch out! If you use this method, Visio automatically selects all the text in the shape. If you don't want to replace all the text, be sure to click somewhere in the text block to position the insertion point before you begin typing. If you begin typing without positioning the insertion point, Visio replaces your text with whatever you type. If you replace text accidentally, use Edit⇨Undo or press Ctrl+Z to bring back your old text.

Copying and pasting text

Sometimes you may want to copy text from one place to another — anything to avoid retyping! Actually, copying text is a good idea for another reason: consistency. If you want a chunk of text to be exactly the same somewhere else in your drawing, the best way to ensure this is to copy the text.

It doesn't matter whether the text you're pasting is attached to a shape or is freestanding text. You follow the same basic steps for copying and pasting. First, select the text to copy. If you don't select a text block to paste to, but instead paste the text by clicking a blank area of the drawing, Visio pastes the text into a new text block somewhere near the middle of the drawing page. You can then move the text block where you want it.

You copy and paste text using the following steps:

1. **Click the Text Tool button on the Standard toolbar, and then click a shape.**

   The shape's text block appears.

2. **Select the portion of text that you want to copy.**

3. **Click the Copy button on the Standard toolbar, press Ctrl+C, or choose Edit⇨Copy.**

4. **Choose where you want to paste the text:**

   • To paste into a shape's text block, double-click the shape.

   • To paste a text-only shape, click any blank area of the drawing.

5. **Click the Paste button on the Standard toolbar, choose Edit⇨Paste, or press Ctrl+V.**

The text that you copy remains on the Windows Clipboard until you copy something else. If you need to paste again and again, feel free!

After you select text, the quickest way to choose the Copy and Paste commands is from the pop-up shortcut menu. Just right-click after selecting text to display the shortcut menu.

Moving a text block

It isn't always obvious where Visio places a shape's text block until you enter some text in it or select the shape and press F2. In either case, you might find that you don't like the position of a text block and want to move it. In Figure 5-3, the text block for the star on the left covers up part of the shape. You could reduce the font size, but then your text might not be readable. A better solution is to move the text out of the star, as I did with the star on the right.

To move a text block independently of its shape, you use the Text Block button. Follow these steps:

1. **Click the Text Block button on the Standard toolbar.**

   Your mouse pointer changes to look like a sheet of paper with lines of text.

   To access the Text Block button, you click the down arrow next to the Text Tool button on the Standard toolbar. Refer to Table 5-1 to see what both buttons look like.

2. **Click the shape that has the text you want to move.**

   The green text block frame and handles become visible.

3. **Move the mouse over the text block frame until the pointer changes to a double rectangle.**

   Notice when you hover the mouse pointer over the frame, the tool tip says "Move Text Block."

4. **Drag the text block to reposition it.**

   Visio repositions the shape's text block to the position you choose.

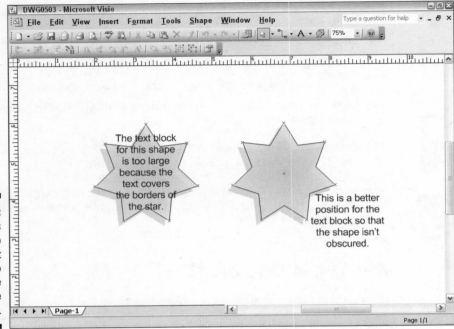

Figure 5-3:
Sometimes
you need to
move a text
block to
make the
shape more
visible.

5. **Click the Pointer Tool button to bring back your normal mouse pointer.**

Even if you move a text block halfway across a drawing page, it's still attached to its shape. If you move the shape, the shape's text block moves with it. If you copy the shape, the text is copied with it. If you paste the shape, the text is pasted with it. And if you rotate the shape . . . well, you get the idea.

Because freestanding text is its own shape, you can move it just like you move any other shape in a drawing. You don't need to use the Text Block button. Instead, just use the Pointer Tool button. Follow these steps:

1. **Click the Pointer Tool button (refer to Table 5-1) on the Standard toolbar.**

2. **Click the text-only shape that you want to move.**

   The green selection handles and frame appear.

3. **Drag the text to a new location and release the mouse button.**

Resizing a text block

Most shapes come with a text block of a reasonable size; that is, the text block usually fits the shape. If you don't like the size of a text block, it's possible to resize it. But it's questionable whether you should spend your time doing that, because text blocks automatically resize themselves if you enter too much text!

So, does that mean resizing a text block is irrelevant? Not necessarily. You can still set the size of a text block as a *guideline* for when you enter text. As soon as you begin overfilling the text block, you'll see it resize right before your eyes. That's your cue to stop typing or change to a smaller font size if you need to enter more text.

Use these steps to resize a text block:

1. **Click the Text Block button on the Standard toolbar.**

   When you move the mouse pointer over the text in the text block, the pointer changes to a double rectangle.

2. **Click the shape.**

   The green text block frame and handles appear. See Figure 5-4.

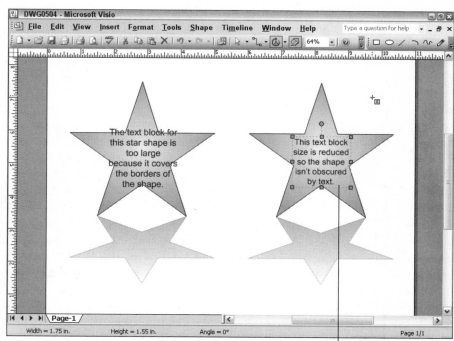

Figure 5-4:
The text frame for the star on the right is resized to fit within the star.

Text frame

3. **Move the mouse pointer over a side handle to resize the shape's width or over a top or bottom handle to resize the shape's height. Or choose a corner handle to resize in both directions at once.**

   The mouse pointer changes to a double-headed arrow.

4. **Drag the handle to resize the text block, and then release the mouse button.**

5. **Click the Pointer Tool button to bring back the standard mouse pointer.**

Changing alignment

Whenever you create text in a drawing, you need to pay attention to how the text is aligned. *Horizontal alignment* refers to the way characters line up left to right in the text block. Vertical alignment refers to the way text lines up top to bottom in the text block.

In many shapes, the default horizontal alignment is left alignment. However, center, right, and justified alignments have their place and are sometimes more appropriate. Figure 5-5 shows an example of each style.

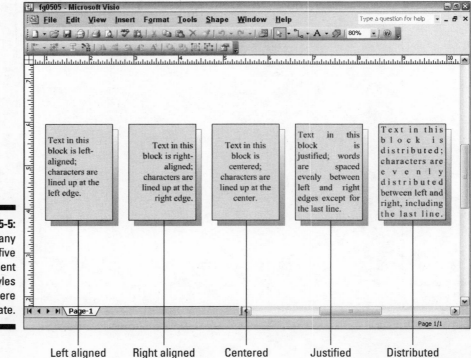

Figure 5-5:
Use any of five alignment styles where appropriate.

Left aligned   Right aligned   Centered   Justified   Distributed

To change the alignment of text, you could use menu commands, but it's much faster to use the toolbar. Toolbar buttons for text alignment appear on the Formatting and Format Text toolbars.

Table 5-2	**Toolbar Buttons for Formatting Text**		
Button	*Name*	*Toolbar*	*What It Does*
	Align Left	Formatting	Lines up text on the left side of the text block
	Align Center	Formatting	Lines up text around the center point of the text block
	Align Right	Formatting	Lines up text on the right side of the text block
	Justify	Formatting	Lines up text on both the left and right sides of the text block by adding spaces between words
	Distribute	Formatting	Lines up text on the left and right sides of the text block by adding spaces between characters and words
	Align Top	Format Text	Aligns the first line of text with the top of the text block
	Align Middle	Format Text	Aligns the first line of text with the middle of the text block
	Align Bottom	Format Text	Aligns the last line of text with the bottom of the text block
	Decrease Indent	Formatting and Format Text	Moves text left to the previous indent point
	Increase Indent	Formatting and Format Text	Moves text right to the next indent point

(continued)

Table 5-2 *(continued)*

Button	Name	Toolbar	What It Does
	Decrease Paragraph Spacing	Formatting and Format Text	Brings lines of text in a paragraph closer together
	Increase Paragraph Spacing	Formatting and Format Text	Spreads lines of text in a paragraph farther apart

To change the horizontal alignment of text in a text block, follow these steps:

1. **Click the Text Tool button (refer to Table 5-1) on the Standard toolbar.**

2. **Click the shape that contains the text you want to change.**

   Visio displays the text block.

3. **Select the paragraph that you want to align.**

   If you want to align all the text in the text block, you don't need to select anything.

4. **Click the Align Left, Align Center, Align Right, Justify, or Distribute button (refer to Table 5-2) on the Formatting toolbar.**

   Visio reformats the selected text.

Note in Step 3 that because horizontal alignment applies to each paragraph individually, you can align separate paragraphs differently in the same text block. If you want to align all text the same way in the text block, you don't need to select anything; Visio formats all paragraphs the same way.

I recommend that you use the tools in the preceding steps because they're faster than choosing menu commands. If you prefer using menu commands, however, you can find alignment settings by choosing Format➪Text, clicking the Paragraph tab in the Text dialog box, and then selecting the check box of the alignment option that you want.

Vertical alignment refers to the alignment from top to bottom in a text block. When you work with a text document, you don't usually think about vertical alignment because your text typically starts at the top and fills the page to the bottom. However, when your text is contained in a text block (which is really nothing more than a box), you can choose to align the text with the top or bottom of the box, or you can center the text in the box, as shown in Figure 5-6.

To justify or distribute — that is the question!

Most people are familiar with left, center, and right alignment but are stumped by justify and distribute. Justify fills the space between the left and right borders of a text block (except for "incomplete" lines, which often occur at the end of a paragraph) by adding spaces between words. Distribute fills the space between left and right borders (including short lines at the end of a paragraph) by adding spaces between words and characters. (I think Distribute looks awkward, but I suppose it has its place.)

To change vertical alignment, you use the Align Top, Align Middle, and Align Bottom buttons on the Format Text toolbar.

To set vertical alignment of a text block, follow these steps:

1. **Click the Text Tool button on the Format Text toolbar.**
2. **Click the shape that contains the text that you want to change.**

   Visio displays the text block.

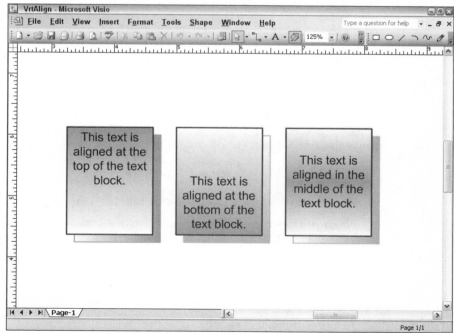

Figure 5-6:
Vertical alignment places your text at the top, bottom, or middle of a text block.

3. **Click the Align Top, Align Middle, or Align Bottom button (refer to Table 5-2).**

   Visio adjusts your text.

To set alignment, I recommend that you use the alignment buttons provided on the Format Text toolbar. If you prefer using menu commands, alignment settings are available by choosing Format⇨Text, clicking the Text Block tab in the Text dialog box, and selecting an option on the Vertical Alignment drop-down list.

Note that unlike horizontal alignment, vertical alignment applies to *all* the text in a text block.

Adjusting margins

Text block margins define the white space that surrounds text in a text block. Visio sets very narrow text block margins — about 1/18 inch. In most cases, these narrow margins are fine, because the outline of the text block usually isn't visible. But if you decide to outline a text block with a frame, these margins can be so narrow that the text doesn't look right. For example, Figure 5-7 shows two text blocks. The text block on the left uses standard margins. The margins for the text block on the right were increased to 1/2 inch. Not only does the text block on the right look better, the words are more readable. And you don't get that claustrophobic feeling looking at it!

Visio uses *points* as the default units of measurement for text blocks and text block margins. Text block margins are set to 4 points. Because 1 inch is equivalent to 72 points, 4 points is equal to about 1/18 inch.

If you prefer to have Visio measure text and margins in inches, you can change the default setting. Just choose Tools⇨Options, click the Units tab, and then change the Text setting. The drop-down box lists all the choices for units.

To change a text block's margins, follow these steps:

1. **Click the Text Block button (refer to Table 5-1) on the Standard toolbar.**

   When you move the mouse pointer over the text in the text block, the pointer changes to a double rectangle.

2. **Click the shape that has the text block you want to change.**

   The green text block frame and handles appear.

3. **Choose Format⇨Text or right-click and choose Text.**

   The Text dialog box appears.

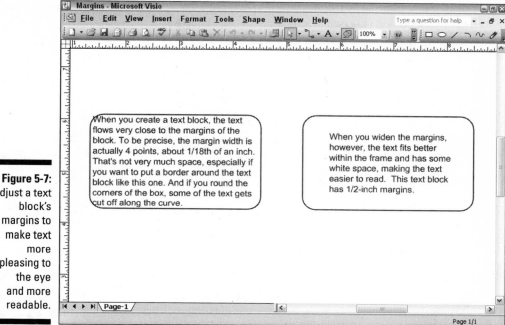

Figure 5-7:
Adjust a text
block's
margins to
make text
more
pleasing to
the eye
and more
readable.

4. **Click the Text Block tab, as shown in Figure 5-8.**

5. **In the Top, Bottom, Left, and Right boxes, type a number.**

   Visio measures margins in points (72 points = 1 inch). If you prefer to use inches, enter them as decimal numbers and type **in** after the number (such as .5 in).

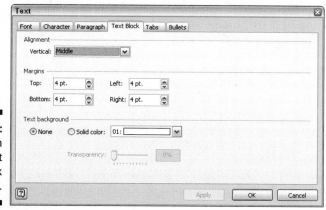

Figure 5-8:
You can
reset text
block
margins.

6. **Click the Apply button if you want to make more changes in the Text dialog box.**

7. **Click OK.**

Using tabs in a text block

Some types of text call for a tabular format, even in a drawing. You may want to include a simple table in a drawing, with items aligned in rows and columns. To create this type of layout, you need to set *tab stops* (or just *tabs*) — the points where you want your cursor to jump when you press the Tab key.

You can set tabs to be left aligned, right aligned, centered, or decimal aligned. You can see examples of each in Figure 5-9. When you use a decimal-aligned tab, be sure to type the decimal point in your entry. If you don't enter a decimal point, the entry is left aligned.

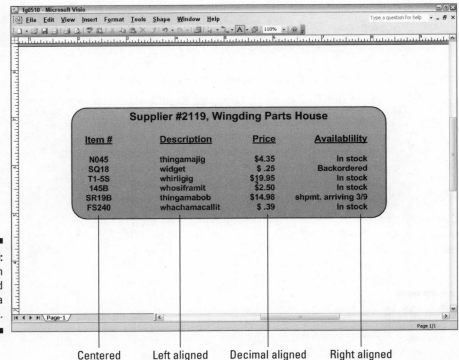

Figure 5-9: Tabs can be aligned within a text block.

The quickest and easiest way to set tabs is by clicking them onto the Text Block ruler. Here's how:

1. **Click the Text Tool button on the Standard toolbar.**

2. **Click the shape with the text that you want to alter.**

   Visio displays the shape's text block.

3. **Right-click the text block and choose Text Ruler.**

   Visio displays a special ruler just for the text block. At the far left end of the ruler is a sample tab for a left-aligned tab as shown in Figure 5-10.

4. **Choose the tab type (left, centered, right, or decimal aligned) by click-ing the sample tab until the type you want is displayed.**

   A left tab looks like an L, a center tab looks like an upside-down T, a right tab looks like a backwards L, and a decimal tab looks like an upside-down T with a decimal point (.) in it.

Sample tab

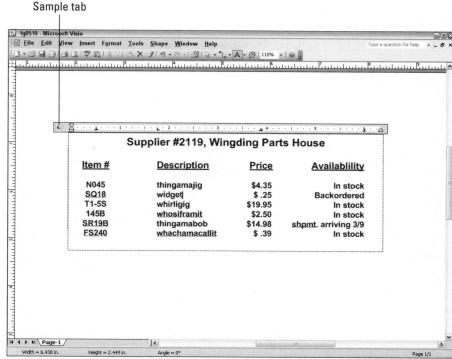

Figure 5-10:
Set tabs on the text block ruler by clicking directly on the ruler.

5. **Click directly on the ruler at the point where you want to set a tab.**

6. **Repeat Steps 4 and 5 to choose additional tabs.**

Now you can type text in the text block. Press the Tab key when you want the cursor to jump to a tab position.

To remove tabs, just drag them right off the ruler.

If you prefer to use a dialog box to set tabs rather than setting them on the text block ruler, use these steps:

1. **Click the Text Block button on the Standard toolbar.**

   When you move the mouse pointer over the text in the text block, the pointer changes to a double rectangle.

2. **Click the shape that has the text that you want to alter.**

   The green text block frame and handles appear.

3. **Choose Format⇨Text, or right-click and choose Text.**

   The Text dialog box appears.

4. **Click the Tabs tab, which is shown in Figure 5-11.**

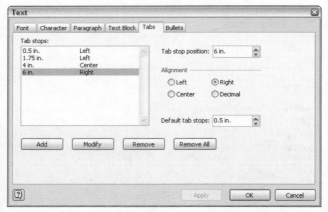

Figure 5-11:
Set tab positions here.

5. **In the Tab Stop Position box, type a number (or click the up or down arrow) and then click the Add button.**

6. **In the Alignment box, choose an alignment style (Left, Center, Right, or Decimal).**

7. **To add more tabs, repeat Steps 5 and 6.**

8. **When you're finished adding tabs, click OK.**

   The Text dialog box closes and you're returned to your drawing.

To remove tabs using the same dialog box, highlight the tab to remove in the Tab Stops area and then click the Remove button.

Creating bulleted lists

Bulleted lists are common in drawings and diagrams — probably because they help summarize and separate material. Fortunately, creating bulleted lists in Visio is easy because Visio does it for you automatically.

You can set up a bulleted format for text that you already typed or for a blank text block. If you set up a bulleted list in a blank text block, Visio inserts and formats the bullets as you type the text.

Use these steps to create a bulleted list:

1. **In the text block, select the text that you want to format with bullets. If the text block is empty, select the text block itself.**

2. **Choose Format⇨Text or right-click and choose Text.**

   The Text dialog box appears.

3. **Click the Bullets tab to display the bullet options, as shown in Figure 5-12.**

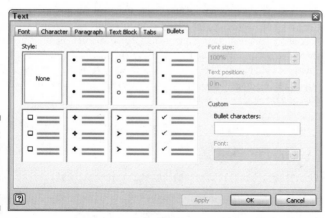

Figure 5-12: Choose from several bullet styles and formats.

4. **Click a bullet style.**

5. **If you want to change the bullet character size, enter a percentage in the Font size box:**

    • To make the bullet character larger than the font text, enter a percentage greater than 100.

    • To make the bullet character smaller, enter a number smaller than 100.

6. **In the Text Position box, enter the amount of space you want separating the bullet from the text (such as .25 in.).**

7. **If you want to use special characters for the bullet:**

    a. **In the Bullet Characters box, type the character or characters you want to use for the bullet.**

    b. **In the Font box, choose a font.**

    This is especially important when using a special font such as Wingdings or another special character font.

8. **When you have made all your choices, click OK.**

    Visio returns to your drawing. If you selected text in Step 1, it formats the text instantly.

If the text block is empty, the bullets will appear automatically when you begin typing. Press Enter at the end of a line to begin a new bullet point.

Creating numbered lists

The process for creating numbered lists is a bit more complicated than the process for creating bulleted lists. Visio doesn't add numbers automatically the way it does with bullets, so you need to type numbers and your text. I think it's easier to format the text block for a numbered list before you enter the text and numbers. (It isn't required, however.) The following steps show you how to set up the indentation for a numbered list; keep in mind that you may want to alter the steps slightly for your particular text.

Follow these steps to set up an empty text block for a numbered list:

1. **Select an empty text block.**

2. **Choose Format⇨Text or right-click and choose Text.**

    The Text dialog box appears.

3. **Click the Paragraph tab, as shown in Figure 5-13.**

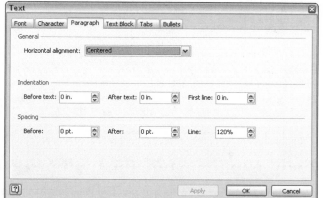

Figure 5-13:
Set up the
format for a
numbered
list.

4. **In the Horizontal Alignment box, choose Left.**

5. **In the Indentation Before Text box, type a measurement such as .5.**

   This sets the indentation from the left margin.

6. **In the Indentation First Line box, type a measurement such as −.5.**

   This sets the position where you type the number for the numbered list.

   The .5 measurement is a standard measurement, but you aren't required to use that measurement. You can just as easily use, say, .2 or 1.2. Just make sure you use the same number for the Before Text and First Line options, with the Before Text number positive and the First Line number negative.

7. **If you want to indent the right side of the paragraph, enter a measurement in the Indentation After Text box.**

8. **Click OK.**

   Visio returns to your drawing.

In case you're wondering what you just did in these steps, you created a *hanging indent.* (The first line where the numbers begin *hangs* out to the left of the rest of the paragraph.) You set the *wrap* point (the point where text wraps on the second, third, and following lines) to .5 inches.

1. **Type the number for the first item (such as 1).**

2. **Press the Tab key.**

   This tab becomes the text wrap point if your text is longer than one line.

3. **Type the text for the first item.**

4. **Press Enter.**

5. **Repeat Steps 1-4 for all the items in the list.**

   You must follow this process for each numbered item to format the text correctly.

If you want to reformat existing text to a numbered list, use the same steps outlined previously to set up numbered list formatting for the text block. The difference is that you need to *insert* the item numbers in the existing text and then be sure to press Tab between the number and the text.

Setting the indentation and spacing of text

To set the indentation for a paragraph, you use the Paragraph tab in the Text dialog box. Indenting is like widening the margins on the left side, right side, or both sides of a paragraph. For example, you may want to indent a particular paragraph half an inch on the right and left sides to give it emphasis. You can also make the first line of a paragraph stand out by indenting only that line.

The Paragraph tab in the Text dialog box also lets you adjust line spacing. For example, you can automatically add space before or after paragraphs. Or you can increase (or decrease) the spacing between lines within a paragraph. Like margins, line spacing is measured in points unless you change the unit of measurement by using the Tools⇨Options command. (See the "Adjusting margins" section earlier in this chapter for more about margins.) For extra space before or after a paragraph, type a number in the Before or After box (see Figure 5-13).

To set the indentation and line spacing for a paragraph, follow these steps:

1. **Click the Text Tool button on the Standard toolbar.**

   The mouse pointer changes to look like a sheet of paper with text.

2. **In the text block or text-only shape, select all or part of the paragraph that you want to indent.**

3. **Choose Format⇨Text or right-click and choose Text.**

   The Text dialog box appears.

4. **Click the Paragraph tab.**

5. **To set the indentation for the paragraph you selected, type a number (measured in inches or decimal inches) in the Before Text, After Text, and First Line boxes.**

6. **To set line spacing for the selected paragraph, type a number (measured in points) in the Before, After, and Line boxes.**

   The Before and After boxes set the number of spaces preceding and following the paragraph; the Line box sets the spacing between lines in the paragraph.

7. **Click OK to return to your drawing.**

A quick way to indent a paragraph on the left side is to use the Increase Indent button on the Formatting toolbar (refer to Table 5-2). Highlight your paragraph, and then click this button. Visio automatically indents the entire paragraph ¼ inch each time you click the button. To take away the indentation, click the Decrease Indent button (also shown in Table 5-2).

Changing the Way Your Text Looks

When you draw a text block and enter text, Visio automatically displays the text as 8-point Arial black characters on a transparent background. Simple. Sedate. Readable. Nothing dramatic. Are Visio shapes set up to display anything more dramatic? Not typically. You might find some variation — maybe 12-point Arial instead of 8-point — but nothing to get excited about.

If you want more pizzazz in your text, it's up to you to create it. You have the option of changing the font, size, color, and style of text. You can also designate a case, position, and language. (No, Visio won't translate English into Portuguese for you!)

Changing the font, size, color, and style of text

The quickest way to make changes to the look of text is by using toolbar buttons. Select the text that you want to change and click one of the toolbar buttons on the Format or Format Text toolbars (see Table 5-3). Some tools change the selected text immediately; others display a drop-down box where you can choose an option for changing the attributes.

Table 5-3	Toolbar Buttons for Changing the Look of Text		
Button	**Name**	**Toolbar**	**What It Does**
Arial	Font	Formatting	Lets you choose a font style
12pt.	Font Size	Formatting	Lets you choose a font size
B	Bold	Formatting	Changes the selected text to bold
I	Italic	Formatting	Changes the selected text to italic

(continued)

Table 5-3 *(continued)*

Button	Name	Toolbar	What It Does
U	Underline	Formatting	Underlines the selected text
A	Text Color	Formatting	Changes the color of the selected text
(fill color icon)	Fill Color	Formatting	Changes the fill color of a shape
Normal	Text Style	Format Text	Changes the selected text to a saved style (usually defined by a template)
A⁺	Increase Font Size	Format Text	Increases the font size incrementally (rather than selecting a specific size)
A⁻	Decrease Font Size	Format Text	Decreases the font size incrementally (rather than selecting a specific size)
abc	Strikethrough	Format Text	Adds a strikethrough character to the selected text
ABC	Small Cap	Format Text	Converts the selected text to small caps
x^2	Superscript	Format Text	Raises the selected text to superscript level
x_2	Subscript	Format Text	Lowers the selected text to subscript level

The buttons you use to format text appear on two toolbars. Some are on the Formatting toolbar, some are on the Format Text toolbar, and some are on both toolbars. What's the reasoning behind this? Your guess is as good as mine! Just learn to look for the icon that represents the button you want. And when you're going to be formatting a lot of text, display the Format Text toolbar on your screen right away so you don't have to hunt for the buttons.

If you want, you can use the Text dialog box to change the text attributes listed in Table 5-3. To use the Text dialog box, follow these steps:

1. **Select the text that you want to change.**

2. **Choose Format➪Text or right-click and choose Text.**

   The Text dialog box appears, as shown in Figure 5-14.

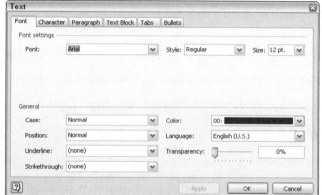

Figure 5-14:
You can
change the
look of text.

3. **Click the drop-down box of the attribute that you want to change:**

   • **To change the font:** Click the Font drop-down list and choose a font style. Unfortunately, the Font tab of the Text dialog box doesn't show you a preview of the font, so you can't see how a font looks before you choose it. The next best thing is to move the dialog box out of the way so that you can see your selected text. This way, when you click the Apply button, you can see how the text looks without closing the dialog box and starting all over again.

   • **To change the text style:** Click the Style drop-down list and choose Regular, Italic, Bold, or Bold Italic.

   • **To change the text size:** Click the Size drop-down list and choose a point size for the selected text.

   • **To change the case:** Click the Case drop-down list and choose Normal (the default setting), All Caps, Initial Caps, or Small Caps.

   • **To change the position of the text:** Click the Position drop-down list and choose Subscript or Superscript.

   • **To underline:** Click the Underline drop-down list and choose Single or Double.

   • **To add strikethrough:** Click the Strikethrough drop-down list and choose Single or Double.

   • **To change the text color:** Click the Color drop-down list and choose a color for the selected text.

- **To change the language used by the Spell Checker:** Click the Language drop-down list and choose a language other than English.

- **To change the transparency of the text:** Drag the slider arrow along the bar until you find the transparency you want.

4. **Click Apply.**

5. **Repeat Steps 3 and 4 if you want to try other settings.**

6. **Click OK.**

    Visio returns to your drawing and reformats the selected text.

Choosing a background color for a text block

If you aren't satisfied with colorful characters alone, you can change the background color of a text block as well. Just think of all the wonderful color combinations you can come up with! Remember, though, your text needs to be *readable*. The more contrast between the text and background colors, the better. (Text blocks are transparent by default.)

To change the background color of a text block, follow these steps:

1. **Click the Text Tool button on the Standard toolbar.**

2. **Select the text block that you want to change.**

3. **Choose Format⇨Text, or right-click the text block and choose Text.**

    The Text dialog box appears.

4. **Click the Text Block tab.**

5. **In the Text Background area, choose a color from the Solid Color drop-down list, as shown in Figure 5-15.**

    To make an opaque background on an unfilled shape, choose white.

6. **Click OK.**

Note: The preceding steps change the background color of a text block. This is not the same thing as filling a shape with a color. The text block and the shape can fill independently of one another. See Chapter 8 for more information about filling shapes.

Painting the formatting to other text

When you use your precious time and energy to set up text with a magenta background, chartreuse text, Elephant font, 38-point font size, underline, bold, italic, and small caps, you don't want to have to do it all over again manually to make a matching text block! This task is much simpler if you just *paint* the format to another shape. Painting the formatting not only saves you time — it ensures consistency. Follow these steps:

1. **Click the Pointer Tool button on the Standard toolbar.**
2. **Click the text block that has the formatting you want to copy.**
3. **Click the Format Painter button on the Standard toolbar.**

   Your mouse pointer now includes a paintbrush.
4. **Click the text block that you want to copy the format to.**

   Visio applies the format instantly.

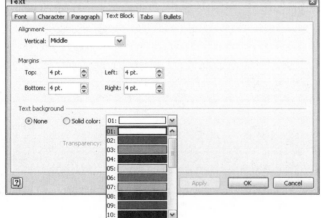

Figure 5-15: You can change the background color.

These steps copy all aspects of the text formatting (font, size, color, bold, italic, underline, and so on). Vertical and horizontal alignment, margin settings, indentation, and tabs are characteristics that belong to the *text block*. These characteristics are copied as well.

Rotating text

One of Visio's most versatile features is its capability to rotate text. For most Visio shapes, the text is oriented horizontally, but sometimes you may need to rotate the text at an angle. Figure 5-16 shows a triangle on the left with a horizontal text block. In the triangle on the right, the text block is rotated and moved so that the text runs parallel to the triangle's side.

To change the rotation of a shape's text block, follow these steps:

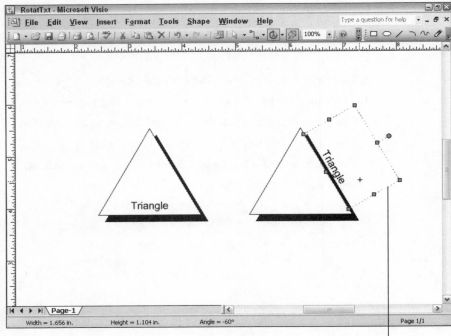

Figure 5-16:
Rotate
text to
complement
the shape
it labels.

Rotated text block

1. **Click the Text Block button on the Standard toolbar.**

   When you move the mouse pointer over the text in the text block, the pointer changes to a double rectangle.

2. **Click the text block.**

   Green selection handles appear, along with round rotation handles at each corner of the frame.

3. **Move the mouse pointer over one of the rotation handles.**

   The mouse pointer changes to two curved arrows in the shape of a circle.

4. **Drag the text in the direction that you want to rotate the text.**

If you want to rotate the text to a specific angle, such as 45 degrees, watch the status bar as you rotate the text. Moving in a counterclockwise direction produces a positive angle up to 180 degrees; moving clockwise displays negative angles up to –180 degrees.

If you want the text to align with a particular part of the shape (such as a border or an outline), it may be necessary to move the text block after you rotate it.

Chapter 6

Connecting Shapes

*I*n this chapter, I unravel the mysteries of two of Visio's most powerful features: glue and connectors. The relationship between glue, connectors, and shapes is a close one. After you understand how each one works, you're on your way to becoming a powerful Visio user.

Discovering Connectors

Connector is a term that is unique to Visio. The simple, nontechie explanation is that connectors are lines between boxes. In the techie world, a *connector* is a special, one-dimensional shape that you use to connect two-dimensional shapes to one another. This technical definition allows for the fact that connectors are not always lines; they can also be one-dimensional (1-D) shapes such as arrows, arcs, hubs, and other specialized shapes (for example, an Ethernet cable) that connect two-dimensional (2-D) shapes to each other.

Where and why do you use connectors? You use connectors to show the following:

✔ The relationship between two shapes

✔ Hierarchy

✔ The path in a process

✔ Two connected shapes (this one seems obvious!)

Some drawings don't make any sense without connectors. Imagine an organization chart without connectors — you might have the president reporting to the copy room clerk! (That doesn't sound like a bad idea, does it?) You find connectors in all sorts of drawings from network diagrams to process flow-charts to Web page diagrams.

In Figure 6-1, the 2-D Executive shape in the organization chart is connected to the 2-D Manager shapes. Manager shapes are connected to 2-D Position shapes. All the connectors are 1-D shapes.

You can always distinguish a 1-D shape from a 2-D shape by the handles the shape displays when you select it. 1-D shapes always have two endpoints — small green squares with an x in the beginning point and a + in the ending point. 2-D shapes always display a dotted green rectangle (the selection *frame*) with green selection handles at corners and sides. (To review shape characteristics, refer to Chapter 4.)

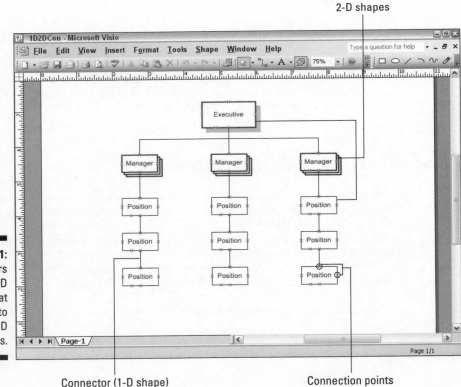

Figure 6-1:
Connectors
are 1-D
shapes that
you use to
bridge 2-D
shapes.

You can create a connector in one of three ways:

- Use the Connector Tool button on the Standard toolbar (to connect shapes automatically as you add them to the drawing)
- Drag a connector shape from a stencil onto a drawing
- Use the Connect Shapes button on the Action toolbar to connect existing 2-D shapes

Visio connectors are more sophisticated than just simple lines or shapes. Some connectors are *dynamic*, meaning they can reconnect to a different point on a shape (if necessary) when you move the shape. Other connectors are *smart*, meaning they can change their form or path around shapes depending on the shapes they're connected to. These features may seem vague and meaningless now, but you'll soon discover how powerful they are.

In this chapter, you work with various tools on the Standard, Action, and View toolbars. These tools are listed in Table 6-1. You might want to display the Action and View toolbar on your screen while working with connectors in a drawing. Just right-click in the toolbar area and select the toolbars you want to display.

Table 6-1	Toolbar Buttons for Working with Connectors		
Button	*Name*	*Toolbar*	*What It Does*
	Pointer Tool	Standard	The standard selection tool that lets you select any shape
	Connector Tool	Standard	Lets you draw connectors between shapes
	Connection Point Tool (below the Connector Tool button)	Standard	Lets you add connection points to a shape
	Connection Point*s*	View	Displays or hides connection points in a drawing
	Connect Shapes	Action	Connects shapes automatically as you drag them into a drawing

You can access the Connection Point Tool button by clicking the down arrow to the right of the Connector Tool button. Or consider adding the Connection Point Tool button to your Standard toolbar (so it's visible all the time) by clicking Toolbar Options (the arrow at the right end of the toolbar) and choosing Add or Remove Buttons⇨Customize.

It's easy to get completely confused between Visio's four different uses of the root word *connect* — that is, *Connect* Shapes button, *Connect*or Tool button, *Connect*ion Point Tool button, and *Connect*ion Points button. As you work through this chapter, try to memorize the icon associated with each button. (The last one, Connection Points, controls only hiding or displaying connection points in a drawing, so I don't mention it again in this chapter.) I can almost guarantee you'll be frustrated at first by trying to keep these four tools straight, but I promise it will become clear with a little practice!

Working with Connection Points

The blue Xs that appear on the sides of each shape are called *connection points* (refer to Figure 6-1). Connection points are the locations on a shape where you can attach a connector. Connection points appear only on your screen; they don't appear on a printout of your drawing.

Adding connection points to a shape

Visio is pretty good about providing ample connection points on its shapes. Sometimes, however, you might run across a shape that doesn't have a connection point where you want it. In that case, add one! Use these steps:

1. **Select a shape.**

2. **Click the drop-down arrow next to the Connector Tool button on the Standard toolbar and choose Connection Point.**

   (Table 6-1 lists these tools.) The mouse pointer changes to an arrow with an X.

3. **Hold down the Ctrl key and click the location on the shape where you want to add a connection point. Then release the Ctrl key.**

You can add as many connection points as you like (but don't get carried away!). You can place them on, inside, or outside a shape.

If you have trouble with Visio tugging your connection points away from where you want to place them, try turning off the Snap function. (Visio turns it on by default.) Snap "pulls" shapes and connectors to the nearest gridline, ruler subdivision, line on a shape, vertex, and so on. Choose Tools⇨Snap & Glue. On the General tab, uncheck the Snap option and then click OK. (To find out more about the Snap function, see Chapter 7.)

Deleting a connection point

Some shapes may have connection points that you don't want to use. Perhaps you added connection points that you no longer need. You can leave them there and just ignore them, or you can delete them.

To delete a connection point from a shape:

1. **Click the drop-down arrow next to the Connector Tool button on the Standard toolbar.**

2. **Click the Connection Point Tool button, which looks like a blue X.**

3. **Click the connection point that you want to remove.**

   The connection point turns magenta.

4. **Press the Delete key.**

   Voilà! The connection point is gone.

Applying Glue (Without the Mess)

Put your sticky white glue away — you don't need it when you use Visio. *Glue,* a feature built into Visio connectors, lets you stick connectors to shapes and keep them there. This may not seem like an important function now, but it's important when you start moving connected shapes all over the place.

Imagine for a minute creating a glueless drawing. Without glue, you have to move a connector each time you move a shape. If the distance between shapes changes, you have to adjust the length of the connector. Then you have to reattach the connector to the shape after you move it. If the path between two shapes changes, you have to reroute the connector. Now multiply those changes about 15 times, because you probably move shapes *at least* that many times in a drawing before it's finished. See? Glue sounds pretty good now, doesn't it? Without glue, creating and editing a drawing is more work than you ever imagined.

Choosing static or dynamic glue

Glue is such a great idea that Visio has two kinds: point-to-point (also known as *static* glue) and shape-to-shape (also called *dynamic* glue). As you see in this section, each one has a different purpose.

Point-to-point glue

Point-to-point glue forms a *static* connection between shapes. This means that if you connect two boxes from points on the top of each box, those connectors don't budge, no matter where you move the boxes! The connectors stay stuck to the top of each box, even if the drawing makes no sense or looks goofy. Point-to-point glue is *static, permanent, unchanging.*

In Figure 6-2, the boxes at the bottom of the figure originally were arranged like the ones at the top — with connectors attached to the tops of the boxes. Each connector uses point-to-point glue. In the bottom of the figure, as you rearrange the boxes, the connectors are *still* attached to the top of each box. And yes, it looks goofy. That's how point-to-point glue behaves. Think of point-to-point glue as stubborn and unyielding.

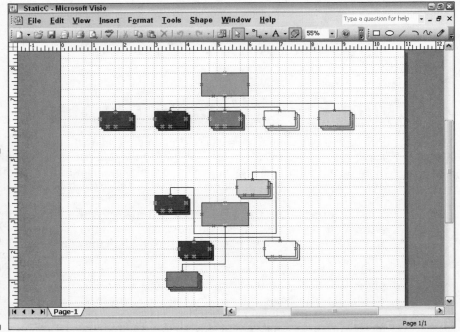

Figure 6-2:
Point-to-point glue keeps connectors attached to the same point, even when you move shapes.

When the way in which shapes are connected is important, or when you want connectors that stay exactly where you put them, use point-to-point glue. Point-to-point glue is also good for drawings you create quickly and for drawings that you aren't likely to change a great deal.

Shape-to-shape glue

Unlike point-to-point glue, shape-to-shape glue is looking for adventure; it loves to travel and find new places to rest! Yet, it's a *sensible* traveler. When you move a shape that has a connector attached with shape-to-shape glue, the connector attaches itself to a different connection point if necessary — one that makes sense in the drawing. (You can always change the connection point if you don't like it.)

Because *shape-to-shape glue* can attach to any connection point on a shape, it forms what are called *dynamic* connections. Figure 6-3 shows the same boxes pictured in Figure 6-2, but the connectors in Figure 6-3 use shape-to-shape glue. If you move shapes connected with shape-to-shape glue, the connectors move to more logical connection points (usually the nearest point) on each box instead of sticking to a specific connection point. Notice in Figure 6-3 that some boxes are now connected at the sides and bottom instead of the top.

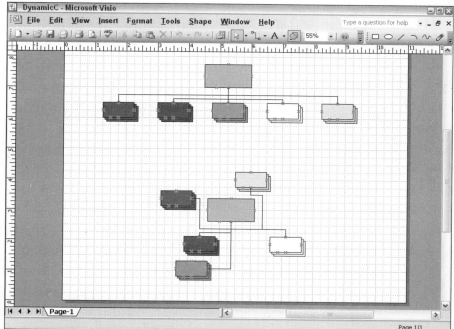

Figure 6-3:
Shape-to-shape glue enables connectors to shift to different connection points when you move shapes.

You want to use shape-to-shape glue when you anticipate moving shapes around a lot, or when it's not important to you that shapes connect at specific points.

Sometimes identical terminology in Visio can be confusing. You already know the popularity of the word *connect* in Visio. Well, they did it again! The term *dynamic* describes glue as well as connectors. Dynamic simply means *changeable. Dynamic glue* attaches a connector to a different point on a shape; a *dynamic connector* changes its shape and path, if necessary.

Identifying glue types

With two types of glue, you need to be able to see in your drawing whether a connector uses shape-to-shape glue or point-to-point glue. After you select a connector (one that's connected at both ends to a shape), look at its endpoints. You see one of two things:

- **When a connector uses point-to-point glue,** the connector's endpoints are dark red squares and are the size of other endpoints and selection handles. The beginning point has an X in it; the ending point has a + in it.

- **When a connector uses shape-to-shape glue,** the endpoints are bright red squares and are larger than other endpoints and selection handles. The endpoint contains no + or X symbols.

Switching from one glue to the other

Before I leave this topic, I want to tell you how to switch a connection from one type of glue to the other. Knowing how to change glue types can be important depending on the type of drawing you create, how much you want to control connections, and how much you may want to change the drawing as you work on it. You might create a connection with shape-to-shape glue and then decide that you want the connector to *always* stay attached to a shape's lower-left corner no matter where you move the shape.

The trick to switching glue types lies in where you point your mouse as you move the connector's endpoint. When you point somewhere inside a shape, you get shape-to-shape glue; when you point directly to a connection point, you get point-to-point glue.

1. **Click the Pointer Tool button (refer to Table 6-1) on the Standard toolbar.**

2. **Select the connector that you want to change.**

3. **Drag either endpoint away from the shape, and then drag the endpoint back toward the shape until a red border appears around the entire shape.**

   You must point somewhere inside the shape, not to a connection point.

4. **Release the mouse button when the red border appears around the entire shape.**

   When you release the mouse button, the endpoint attaches. The endpoint is bright red and slightly larger than other endpoints. This tells you that the connection is now shape-to-shape.

5. **Repeat Steps 2-4 for the other endpoint of the connector so that both endpoints now use shape-to-shape glue.**

When you use shape-to-shape glue, you don't get to choose the connection point; Visio chooses the *nearest* logical point to connect to. If you move the shape that the connector is attached to, the connector might attach to a different point.

Shape-to-shape glue is available only to dynamic connectors. Why? Because dynamic connectors have *elbow joints*: points on the connector at which it can bend. Without them, the connector wouldn't be able to change its path when you move the shape that's attached to it. (This rule makes sense if you think about it.) If you don't see elbow joints, the connector is a *straight* connector, and you can use only point-to-point glue. See the "Drawing connectors using the Connector Tool" section later in this chapter for more information about dynamic connectors and elbow joints.

To change a dynamic (shape-to-shape) connection to a static (point-to-point) one, follow these steps:

1. **Click the Pointer Tool button on the Standard toolbar.**

2. **Select the connector that you want to change.**

3. **Drag either endpoint away from the shape, and then drag the endpoint toward the connection point where you want to attach the connector.**

   A bright red border appears around the connection point only.

4. **Release the mouse button.**

   The endpoint is attached to the connection point. The connection point is a small dark red square, which tells you that the connector is now using point-to-point (static) glue.

5. **Repeat Steps 2-4 with the other endpoint of the connector so that both ends now use point-to-point glue.**

Setting glue options

You might think that connection points are the only areas on a shape where you can attach connectors. In fact, you can attach connectors to guides, shape handles, and shape vertices as well. You also can glue to a shape's *geometry* (anywhere along the lines or curves that define the shape) even without a connection point. You can choose from five options in the Glue To box located in the Snap and Glue dialog box (see Figure 6-4).

Follow these steps to select glue options:

1. **Choose Tools⇨Snap & Glue.**

   The Snap and Glue dialog box appears, as shown in Figure 6-4.

2. **In the Glue To list, click the check boxes of the points to which you want to glue connectors.**

   The Guides and Connection Points options are selected for you automatically. (Guides are lines that you can add to a drawing to help you position shapes accurately. See Chapter 7 for more on guides.)

   If you want to glue connectors to shape geometry, shape handles, or shape vertices, click these check boxes as well. Or you can deselect any of the five options.

3. **Click OK.**

When you choose the Shape Geometry option, you can glue a connector to any point that defines the shape. A circle is a perfect example. A circle typically has five connection points: top, bottom, right, left, and center. When Shape Geometry is *not* selected as a glue option, you can glue a connector to only one of these five points. When Shape Geometry *is* selected, you can attach a connector to any point along the circumference of the circle. The best part is that you can drag the connector clockwise or counterclockwise, and it stays attached to any point you choose along the circumference of the circle.

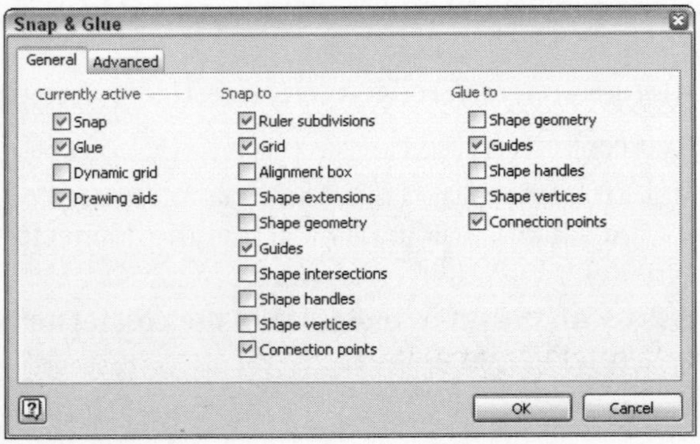

Figure 6-4:
Choose the items you want to glue to from the Snap and Glue dialog box.

Gluing Connectors to Shapes

Visio offers several methods for connecting shapes in a drawing. Some let you connect shapes as you drag them into your drawing, and others let you add connectors later. This section discusses each of the methods for connecting shapes. The method you use pretty much comes down to the type of glue you want to use and personal preference.

Connecting shapes as you drag them

Connecting shapes as you drag them into your drawing is by far the quickest, easiest, no-brainer way to connect shapes. This method is fast because it combines two steps into one.

To connect shapes as you drag them, you use the Connector Tool button on the Standard toolbar. This method uses shape-to-shape glue and dynamic connectors, so if you move shapes later, the connectors reconnect to the closest logical points. Follow these steps to connect and drag shapes into your drawing all in one step:

1. **If necessary, choose File⇨Shapes to open the stencils that you want to use.**

2. **Click the Connector Tool button (refer to Table 6-1) on the Standard toolbar.**

   The mouse pointer changes to the connector tool, which looks like an elbow-shaped arrow.

3. **Drag a shape that you want to use onto the drawing page.**

4. **Drag another shape into the drawing.**

   Visio uses shape-to-shape glue to connect the two shapes automatically with a dynamic (elbow-jointed) connector.

5. **Repeat Step 4 until all the shapes that you want are in the drawing.**

   Visio continues to connect each additional shape to the previous one using shape-to-shape glue.

6. **Click the Pointer Tool button to display the regular mouse pointer.**

As you work through these steps, you may notice that the most recent shape you dragged into the drawing is the one that's selected. After you drag another shape into the drawing, that shape becomes the one that's selected. To turn off this automatic connection feature, click the Pointer Tool button on the Standard toolbar again.

Figure 6-5 shows two boxes that were connected as they were dragged into the drawing. The Connector Tool button is highlighted on the toolbar, the mouse pointer is an elbow-shaped arrow, and the connector glues dynamically.

Dynamic connector

Shape-to-shape connection

Connector Tool mouse pointer

Connector Tool

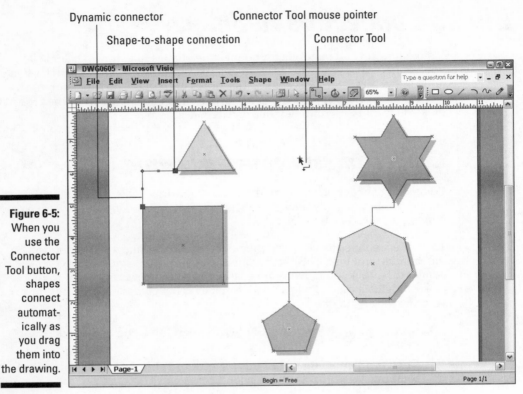

Figure 6-5:
When you
use the
Connector
Tool button,
shapes
connect
automat-
ically as
you drag
them into
the drawing.

If the automatic connection feature isn't working for you, you may be trying
to connect 1-D shapes. This feature automatically connects only 2-D shapes.
(If you need to connect 1-D shapes — which is a rarity — you can draw connectors. See the next section to find out more about drawing connectors.)

Drawing connectors using the Connector Tool

If your drawing already contains 2-D shapes, you can use the Connector Tool
button to go back later and make connections using either point-to-point or
shape-to-shape glue. The Connector Tool button creates dynamic connectors —
that is, incredible, bendable, flexible, elbow-jointed connectors (see Figure 6-6).

To draw a dynamic connector using point-to-point glue, follow these steps:

1. **Click the Connector Tool button on the Standard toolbar.**

   The mouse pointer changes to an elbow-shaped arrow.

2. **Move the mouse pointer over a connection point on a shape.**

   You see a bold red border around the connection point.

3. **Click the connection point and then drag the mouse pointer to a connection point on another shape.**

   You see a bold red border around the connection point on the second shape.

4. **Release the mouse button.**

   The connector is selected and you can see that the endpoints are small dark red squares, indicating a static (point-to-point) glue.

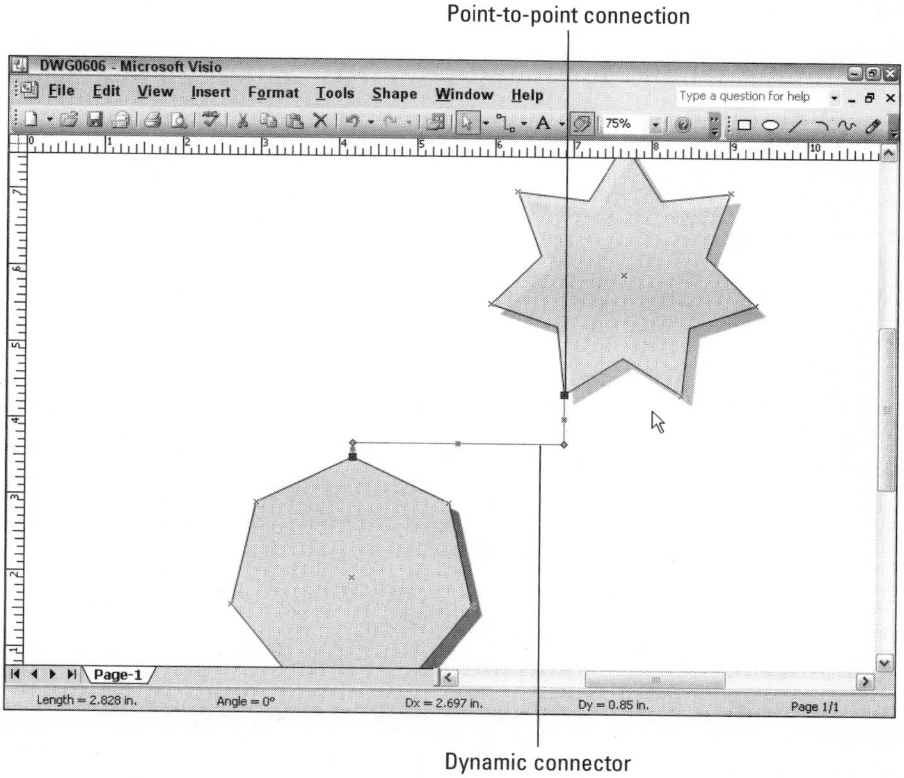

Point-to-point connection

Figure 6-6:
The Connector Tool button creates a dynamic connector that can bend to make connections.

Dynamic connector

If you want to use shape-to-shape glue instead with a dynamic connector, the method is similar but not quite the same as in the preceding steps. Instead of pointing to a connection point, you must point somewhere inside the shape itself. This ensures that the connector uses shape-to-shape glue. Follow these steps:

1. **Click the Connector Tool button on the Standard toolbar.**

   The mouse pointer changes to an elbow-shaped arrow.

2. **Move the mouse pointer over the first *shape* you want to connect. (Be sure to point inside the shape, not at a connector.)**

   You see a bold red border around the entire shape.

3. **Click and then drag the mouse pointer to point to another *shape*. (Be sure to point inside the shape, not at a connector.)**

   When you point to a second shape, you see a bold red border around it. The connector attaches to the most logical point on the second shape automatically using dynamic glue.

Saving time with the Connect Shapes button

The Connect Shapes button is a powerful timesaver. It connects two or more 2-D shapes automatically in the order that you want them connected. This is another good method to use when you have existing shapes that you need to connect.

To use the Connect Shapes button, follow these steps:

1. **Click the Pointer Tool button (which looks like an arrow) on the Standard toolbar.**

2. **Hold down the Shift key and click all the shapes (one by one) in the order that you want to connect them.**

3. **Click the Connect Shapes button (refer to Table 6-1) on the Action toolbar, or Choose Tools⇨Connect Shapes.**

   Visio connects all the shapes automatically using dynamic glue and dynamic connectors (see Figure 6-7).

Choosing a custom connector to connect shapes

A cool variation of the Connect Shapes button lets you connect shapes with the type of connector you choose (something other than a plain line). Suppose, for example, that you want to connect four boxes with block-style arrows or arrow-tipped lines. These are just two examples of 1-D shapes that you can choose from the File➪Shapes➪Visio Extras➪Connectors stencil. If you choose one of these connectors and follow the next set of steps, Visio automatically uses that shape as a connector:

1. **Click the Pointer Tool button on the Standard toolbar.**

2. **Choose File➪Shapes➪Visio Extras➪Connectors.**

   The Connectors stencil appears.

3. **Click the connector that you want to use.**

4. **In the drawing, hold down the Shift key and click all the shapes in the order that you want to connect them.**

5. **Click the Connect Shapes button (refer to Figure 6-7) on the Action toolbar.**

   Visio automatically creates dynamic glue connections between all the shapes that you selected using the connector you chose.

Action toolbar

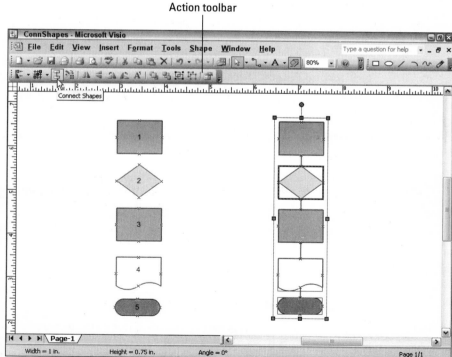

Figure 6-7:
The Connect Shapes button connects a series of shapes automatically.

All connectors are 1-D shapes. Some stencils contain 1-D shapes that Visio calls *connectors*.

Figure 6-8 shows the 1-D Double shape from the Connectors stencil, which serves as the connector between flowchart shapes.

If you try these steps and the "connector" you chose doesn't work, it's probably because it's not a 1-D shape. To act as a connector, a shape must be one-dimensional. A 1-D shape has two endpoints (visible when selected); a 2-D shape has a selection frame and handles. (To review shapes, refer to Chapter 4.)

Dragging connector shapes into your drawing

You can also connect shapes by dragging 1-D connector shapes from stencils into your drawing. The shape you use *must* be one-dimensional, and you can connect only at connection points.

To find 1-D connector shapes, choose File➪Shapes➪Visio Extras➪Connectors. Occasionally other stencils (for instance, the File➪Shapes➪Block Diagram➪ Blocks stencil) might contain a connector or two. When you find one, you can drag it into a drawing and use it as a connector. Here's how:

1. **Click the Pointer Tool button on the Standard toolbar.**

2. **Choose File➪Shapes➪Visio Extras➪Connectors, or choose another stencil that contains 1-D connectors.**

3. **Drag the connector that you want to use into the drawing.**

4. **Do one of the following:**

   • **To make a connection using point-to-point (static) glue,** drag one endpoint of the connector, point to a connection point on the shape, and then release the mouse button.

     First you see a bold red border around the connection point. Then when you release the mouse button, you see the small dark red endpoint (indicating a point-to-point connection).

   • **To make a connection using shape-to-shape (dynamic) glue,** drag one endpoint of the connector, point to an empty area inside the shape, and then release the mouse button.

     First you see a bold red border around the entire shape. Then when you release the mouse button, you see a large red square endpoint (indicating a shape-to-shape connection).

5. **Repeat Steps 3 and 4 to connect more shapes.**

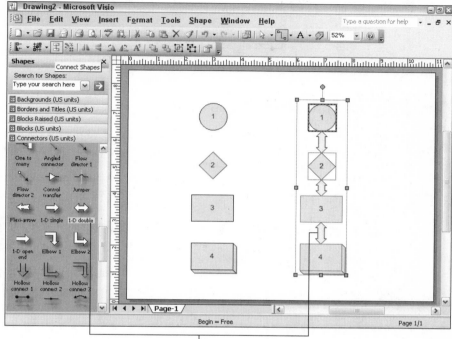

Figure 6-8:
Select a
special 1-D
connector
to connect
shapes.

1-D double connector

Moving connectors

When you want absolute control over where your connectors attach to a shape, you choose point-to-point (static) glue. But if you change your mind about where you attached a connector, you can always move it. Suppose you originally attached a connector to the bottom of a shape, now you want to attach it to the top. You can move the point at which a connector attaches using these steps:

1. **Click the Pointer Tool button on the Standard toolbar (see Table 6-1).**
2. **In the drawing, click the connector you want to move.**

   The connector is highlighted.

3. **Drag the endpoint away from the shape, and then drag it to the connection point on the shape where you want to reconnect.**

   Visio breaks the original connection then outlines the new connection point in red when you point to it.

4. **Release the mouse button.**

   Visio displays the small dark red square at the new connection point, indicating a static glue connection.

Managing Connectors

Some drawings can become quite complex, with connectors running everywhere! You need to have a strategy for making your drawings clearly understood. This section discusses what to do when connectors cross paths and how to route connectors in the direction you want them to go.

Handling connectors that cross paths

In some drawings, such as flowcharts or network diagrams, you might run into problems when connectors cross each other. In a simple drawing, this might not be an issue. But when a drawing is complex, it can be difficult to follow connectors that cross paths.

To solve this problem, Visio adds a *jump* — sort of a wrinkle in a line — to all horizontal connectors in a drawing that cross vertical connectors. The jump makes it easier to see which shapes are connected, as shown in Figure 6-9.

Line jumps are controlled by the settings you choose on the Layout and Routing tab of the Page Setup dialog box (see Figure 6-10). By default, Visio adds an arc-shaped jump to horizontal lines, but you can change the default settings. If you do, the changes apply to all new lines you draw in the current drawing. To make these choices, use the following steps:

1. **Choose File⇨Page Setup.**

2. **Click the Layout and Routing tab (see Figure 6-10).**

3. **In the Add Line Jumps To box, choose the type of lines for which you want to display line jumps.**

4. **In the Line Jump Style box, choose a style.**

5. **To alter the width of jumps, drag the Horizontal Size bar.**

6. **To alter the height of jumps, drag the Vertical Size bar.**

7. **Click Apply to preview the settings in your drawing.**

8. **When all settings are correct, click OK.**

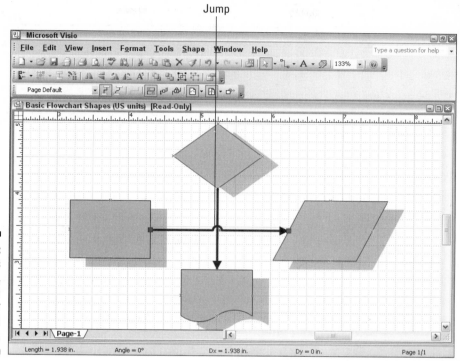

Figure 6-9:
In this drawing, jumps are set for horizontal connectors.

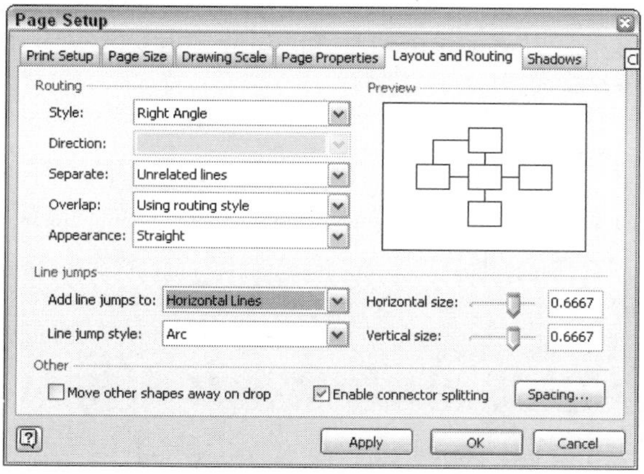

Figure 6-10:
The Layout and Routing tab in the Page Setup dialog box lets you choose line jumps and line jump styles.

If you just want to alter jumps on a case-by-case basis rather than changing the default settings, use the buttons shown in Table 6-2.

Table 6-2		Toolbar Buttons for Adding Line Jumps	
Button	*Name*	*Toolbar*	*What It Does*
	Add Line Jumps To	Layout and Routing	Adds jumps to the selected line. (The tool tip for this button reads No Lines, even though the name is Add Line Jumps To.)
	Line Jump Style	Layout and Routing	Lets you choose a style for the line jump. (The tool tip for this button reads Page Default, even though the name is Line Jump Style.)

To add or remove line jumps and choose a line jump style, follow these steps:

1. **Right-click in the toolbar area and choose Layout & Routing, or choose View⇨Toolbars⇨Layout & Routing.**

   The Layout and Routing toolbar appears.

2. **In the drawing, select the connector or connectors you want to change.**

3. **Click the drop-down arrow next to the Add Line Jumps To button and choose an option.**

   As mentioned in Table 6-2, the tool tip for the Add Line Jumps To button reads No Lines.

   To remove line jumps, choose No Lines.

4. **Click the drop-down arrow next to the Line Jump Style button and choose a style.**

   Again, as mentioned in Table 6-2, the tool tip for the Line Jump Style button reads Page Default.

Note that you can't alter the height or width of jumps using these steps; you must use the File⇨Page Setup⇨Layout & Routing command.

Laying Out Shapes Automatically

Visio provides an automatic layout feature for drawings that typically include connected shapes, such as organization charts, network diagrams, flowcharts, and tree diagrams. This feature saves you the trouble of rearranging shapes manually when you need to make a change in a large drawing. For instance, suppose your company is reorganizing and adding two departments. You need to update the organization chart by inserting new boxes for managers and workers. Inserting is the easy part, but rearranging and realigning is the killer! Visio's Lay Out Shapes feature makes this all a piece of cake.

You can also use Lay Out Shapes when you're in a hurry to create a connected drawing. You can quickly drag new shapes into a drawing without paying too much attention to position or alignment, then let Visio do that part for you. An example of a messy, hastily drawn organization chart is shown in Figure 6-11. Lay Out Shapes can arrange and align all the shapes the way they should be.

Using Lay Out Shapes

To use Lay Out Shapes, you must establish connections between the shapes in the drawing. If you're creating a drawing, the easiest way to do this is by clicking the Connector Tool button before you start dragging shapes into your drawing. (Visio automatically connects one shape to the next when you click the Connector Tool button.) After all the shapes are in the drawing and connected, you're ready to use Lay Out Shapes.

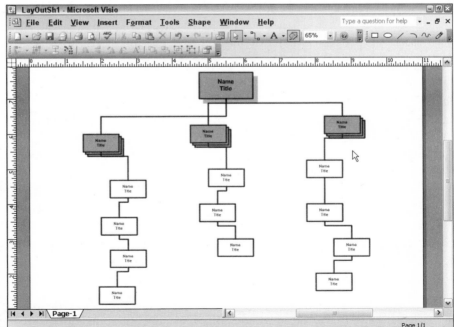

Figure 6-11:
Use Lay Out Shapes to arrange and align the shapes in a hastily drawn chart or diagram.

To use the Lay Out Shapes feature, follow these steps:

1. **Drag all the shapes and connectors into the drawing.**

2. **Choose one of the following:**

    - **To arrange all shapes, click a blank area of the drawing.**

    - **To arrange only certain shapes, drag a selection box around the shapes you want Visio to arrange.**

3. **Choose Shape⇨Lay Out Shapes.**

    The Lay Out Shapes dialog box appears, as shown in Figure 6-12.

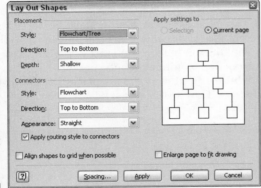

Figure 6-12:
Choose
automatic
layout
settings
here.

4. **In the Placement area, do the following:**

    a. **Click the drop-down arrow next to the Style box and highlight your choice.**

    Visio displays a preview of each style on the right side of the dialog box.

    Note: As you work your way through this dialog box, some of the drop-down boxes listed in these steps may become unavailable based on previous choices you make.

    b. **In the Direction box, make a selection.**

    Check out the preview on the right.

    c. **In the Depth box, make a selection.**

    In an organization chart, for example, choose Deep if the chart contains more vertical shapes than horizontal ones — that is, more positions and fewer managers. If the chart contains more horizontal than vertical shapes (more managers than positions) choose Shallow. If the drawing is pretty evenly weighted, choose Medium.

5. **In the Connectors area, do the following:**

   a. **In the Style box, make a selection.**

   Visio displays a preview to the right.

   b. **In the Direction box, make a selection.**

   You can preview your selection on the right.

   c. **In the Appearance box, choose Straight or Curved.**

6. **Click the following if they apply to your drawing:**

   • Apply Routing Style to Connectors: Applies the routing style you choose in Step 5a to *all* connectors on the page

   • Enlarge Page to Fit Drawing: Enlarges the drawing, if necessary, to adjust the spacing for all shapes during auto-layout

7. **In the Apply Settings To area, choose Selection or Current Page.**

8. **If you want to preview your changes, click Apply.**

   If you don't like the way Lay Out Shapes arranges your drawing, choose Edit⇨Undo or press Ctrl+Z. You can always follow the preceding steps again to make different layout choices.

9. **Click OK.**

   Visio arranges the shapes in the drawing using the settings you select.

Part III
Taking Your Drawings to the Next Level

In this part . . .

Now you start to get into the nitty-gritty of Visio — the stuff that'll make you look like a real pro! You position shapes in a drawing with great precision. Then you have fun creating your own shapes with some cool Visio tools and features. You find out how to work with pages in a drawing and how to keep shapes organized by placing them on different layers. You could get by without knowing these things, but then again, you'd just be getting by.

Chapter 7

Perfecting Your Drawings

*N*o one likes a messy drawing. This chapter shows you how to use Visio's tools to measure, place, and line up elements in a drawing. These tools make "perfecting" tasks easy and save you time. Don't feel that you must use all these ideas. Choose the ones that make the most sense for your particular drawing.

All about Measurements and Placement Tools

This section gives you a preview of the terms used in this chapter. That way, you won't be scratching your head and wondering what the heck I'm talking about:

> ✔ **Alignment and distribution:** *Alignment* refers to shapes lining up evenly. *Distribution* refers to objects being spaced evenly across a given area. When shapes aren't aligned and distributed evenly in a drawing, your eyes sense that something is wrong. Visio helps you automatically align and distribute shapes.

✔ **Grid lines:** These prominent vertical and horizontal lines make the drawing area look like graph paper. The *grid* is a useful tool for measuring and placing shapes. (In many of the figures in this book, I turned the grid off so that you could focus on the topic at hand.)

✔ **Guides:** You can add guide lines and guide points to a drawing to help position and place shapes accurately. If you were to draw a furniture layout on paper, you might lightly sketch lines that represent the boundaries of the room so you could place the furniture precisely. Guides serve the same purpose in Visio.

✔ **Rulers:** These are the objects on the top and left side of the drawing area that look curiously like — well, rulers! Rulers, as you may expect, act as measuring devices.

✔ **Scale:** *Scale* is the ratio of real-life objects to the shapes in your drawing. Remember the last time you looked at a map? The scale was probably 10 miles per 1 inch or something close to that. Unless you can print on life-size paper, you have to scale a drawing when it includes life-size objects!

✔ **Snap:** This feature pulls, or attracts, shapes to any object that you specify such as another shape, a grid line, a guide, or a connection point. This is a terrific feature that helps you place shapes accurately.

As you work through this chapter, it's helpful to have Rulers, Grid, Guides, and Connection Points checkmarked on your View menu. (Just click them.) If they aren't checkmarked, they won't show up on your screen, and you might think I'm just making 'em up (or seeing things)!

You might also find it useful to display the View toolbar (choose View⇨ Toolbars⇨View). The View toolbar buttons are listed in Table 7-1. Each button is a toggle that turns the named feature on or off.

Table 7-1		Toolbar Buttons That Help You Place Shapes	
Button	**Name**	**Toolbar**	**What It Does**
	Rulers	View	Displays or hides rulers at the top and left of the drawing window
	Grid	View	Displays or hides grid in the draw ing area
	Guides	View	Displays or hides guides in a drawing
	Connection Points	View	Displays or hides connection points in a drawing

Another toolbar you might want to display is the Snap and Glue toolbar since I refer to many of its buttons in this chapter. Snap and Glue tools are shown in Table 7-2. All the buttons in Table 7-2 toggle features on or off each time you click the button, so you can turn these features on or off whenever you choose.

Table 7-2   Toolbar Buttons That Help You Snap and Glue Shapes

Button	Name	Toolbar	What It Does
	Toggle Snap	Snap and Glue	Pulls shapes to items you specify in the Snap and Glue dialog box
	Toggle Glue	Snap and Glue	Attaches shapes to items you select in the Snap and Glue dialog box
	Snap to Dynamic Grid	Snap and Glue	Displays dotted lines as you drag shapes into a drawing to help you place the shapes accurately
	Snap to Drawing Aids	Snap and Glue	Helps you draw shapes such as circles, squares, or lines at a particular angle
	Snap to Ruler Subdivisions	Snap and Glue	Pulls shapes to the nearest ruler subdivision
	Snap to Grid	Snap and Glue	Pulls shapes to the nearest grid line
	Snap to Alignment Box	Snap and Glue	Pulls shapes to another shape's alignment box
	Snap to Shape Intersections	Snap and Glue	Pulls shapes to specific points on other shapes (such as the center point, apex of an arc, endpoint, or midpoint of a line)
	Glue to Shape Geometry	Snap and Glue	Attaches shapes to the visible edges of another shape
	Glue to Guides	Snap and Glue	Attaches shapes to guide lines and guide points
	Glue to Shape Handles	Snap and Glue	Attaches shapes to other shapes' handles
	Glue to Shape Vertices	Snap and Glue	Attaches shapes to other shapes' vertices
	Glue to Connection Points	Snap and Glue	Attaches shapes to other shapes' connection points

Using the Drawing Grid

Whenever you create a new drawing, Visio automatically displays a *drawing grid* — horizontal and vertical lines that make the drawing area look like graph paper. The grid helps you place shapes where you want them in a drawing.

Just as you can buy graph paper in different grid sizes, you can set the grid *density* (fine, normal, or coarse) for your drawing. Why would you care about density? If you create a drawing with very small shapes that you want to place precisely, you probably want a finer density — say, lines every ⅛ inch or so. On the other hand, if you use very large shapes in your drawing, a ½-inch grid is more than adequate. See Figure 7-1 for an example of a density set to normal.

Keep in mind that what you see on your screen depends on your monitor and the resolution you use. To figure out what fine, normal, and coarse mean on your monitor, experiment with them by changing the grid density. (The steps to do so appear later in this section.)

The grid in Visio is *variable*. When you zoom in on a drawing, grid lines become more dense; when you zoom out, the grid lines are less dense. This is a great feature when you want to place shapes right on the money.

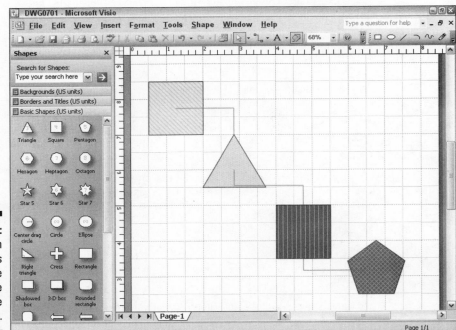

Figure 7-1:
A ½-inch grid is adequate for these large shapes.

If your mouse is equipped with a wheel, the coolest and quickest way to zoom in and out is by holding the Ctrl key as you roll the mouse wheel forward or backward.

Like most settings in Visio, you can turn off the variable grid and instead use a fixed grid (see the steps that follow). If you use a fixed grid, the density stays the same, regardless of the zoom percentage you use. Typically, a grid is evenly spaced horizontally and vertically; when horizontal lines occur every ½ inch, vertical lines do, too. However, you can set an uneven grid if you like, with ½-inch horizontal grid lines and ¼-inch vertical grid lines, for example.

To change grid settings or set a fixed grid, follow these steps:

1. **Choose Tools⇨Ruler & Grid.**

   The Ruler and Grid dialog box appears, as shown in Figure 7-2. Notice that the dialog box includes separate areas for horizontal and vertical grid lines so that you can set the grid scales independently.

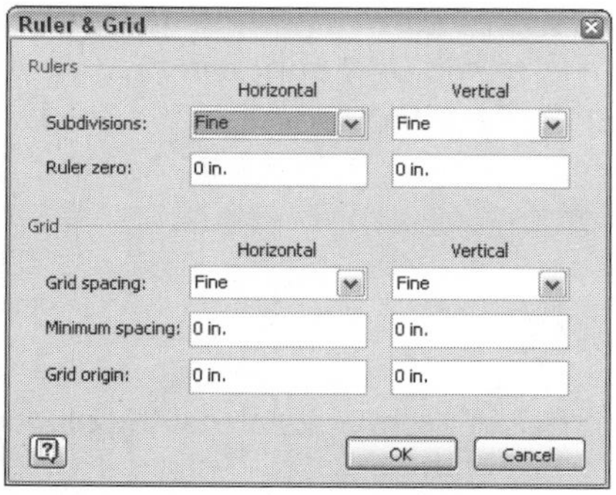

Figure 7-2:
Use the
Ruler and
Grid dialog
box to
set grid
variables.

Ruler & Grid			⊠
Rulers			
	Horizontal	Vertical	
Subdivisions:	Fine	Fine	
Ruler zero:	0 in.	0 in.	
Grid			
	Horizontal	Vertical	
Grid spacing:	Fine	Fine	
Minimum spacing:	0 in.	0 in.	
Grid origin:	0 in.	0 in.	
⟨?⟩		OK	Cancel

2. **Click the drop-down lists for Grid Spacing Horizontal and Grid Spacing Vertical and then click Fine, Normal, Coarse, or Fixed.**

3. **If you want to get picky about the *minimum* spacing to use (for Fine, Normal, or Coarse), type a number (in inches) in the Minimum Spacing boxes.**

4. **Click OK.**

Note: The grid doesn't appear when you print the drawing. It's only an on-screen visual aid.

If you ever want to turn off the drawing grid, click the Grid button on the View toolbar or choose View➪Grid. Turning off the grid helps you see how the drawing will look when you print it.

Using Dynamic Grid

If you create flowcharts or block diagrams, you should check out the dynamic grid feature. The *dynamic grid* helps you position new shapes vertically and horizontally relative to shapes you've already placed in the drawing. How does it work? As you drag a flowchart or block diagram shape into your drawing, horizontal and vertical reference lines appear along with the shape. As you move the shape around the drawing, the reference lines "jump" to show you when the shape is in alignment with another shape close by. When the shape is aligned where you want it, release the mouse button; the reference lines disappear.

Dynamic grid is automatically active when you create a flowchart. To activate dynamic grid for block diagrams or other drawings, click the Dynamic Grid button on the Snap and Glue toolbar (refer to Table 7-2) or choose Tools➪ Snap & Glue and then check the Dynamic Grid option in the Currently Active list and click OK. Each time you click the Dynamic Grid button, the dynamic grid feature toggles on or off.

Setting Drawing Scale

When you create a drawing that doesn't represent a real-life object, such as a flowchart, you don't need to worry about scale. Who cares if your decision shape is 1⅛-inch wide and your process shape is 1¾-inch wide? When you use a template to create a flowchart (or any other type of drawing with abstract shapes), Visio automatically sets the drawing scale to 1:1 (drawing size:actual size).

However, when you create a drawing with shapes that represent any real-life objects larger than a page, the drawing must be *scaled* so that all the objects fit on the page in proper relation to one another. For example, suppose you want to create an office layout. If you choose the Building Plan category and the Office Layout template, Visio automatically sets the drawing scale to ½ inch:1 foot. That is, every ½ inch shown on the printed page represents 1 foot of office space. Terrific — Visio does all the work for you! An example of a ¼ inch:1 foot office layout is shown in Figure 7-3.

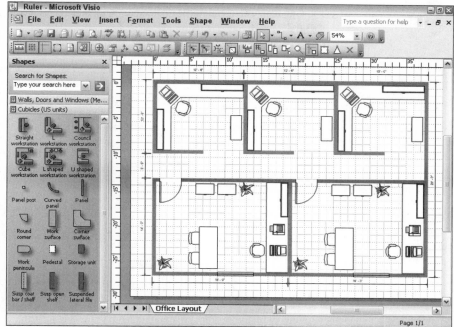

Figure 7-3:
The ¼ inch
per 1 foot
scale works
perfectly for
this office
layout.

If you're not using a template or if you want to adjust the scale set by a template, you can set a drawing scale yourself. Here's the terminology you need to understand first:

- **Page units** represent the measurements on the printed page. For example, in a room layout drawing that uses ¼ inch to represent 1 foot of real-life objects, *inches* are the page units. An 8-foot couch measures 2 inches in page units.

- **Measurement units** represent the real-life measurement of objects in a drawing. For example, in the same room layout drawing that uses ¼ inch to represent 1 foot, *feet* are the measurement units. Therefore, 2 inches on the drawing represents 8 feet of a real-life object.

- **Drawing scale** is the ratio between page units and measurement units.

The larger the spread between page units and measurements units, the larger the area you can illustrate in a drawing. For example, you can represent a much larger area with a drawing scale of ⅛ inch:1 yard than you can with a drawing scale of ¼ inch:1 foot.

TIP

You can set a different drawing scale for individual pages in a drawing.

To set the drawing scale for the current page of a drawing, follow these steps:

1. **Display the drawing page for which you want to set a new drawing scale.**

2. **Choose File⇨Page Setup.**

3. **Click the Drawing Scale tab, which is shown in Figure 7-4.**

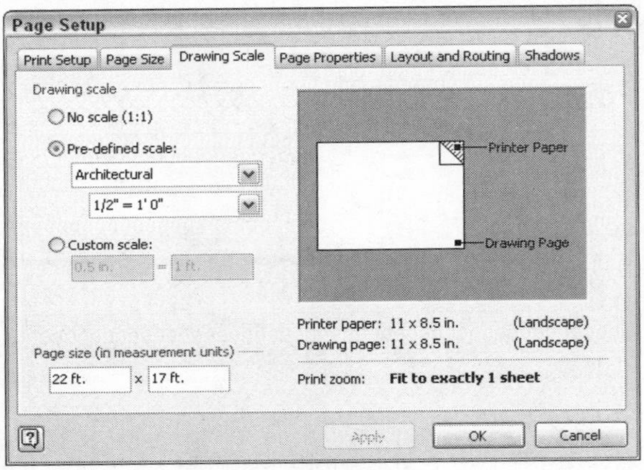

Figure 7-4:
Choose a
predefined
drawing
scale or
enter
measure-
ments for a
custom
scale.

> **Page Setup**
>
> Print Setup | Page Size | Drawing Scale | Page Properties | Layout and Routing | Shadows
>
> Drawing scale
> ○ No scale (1:1)
> ● Pre-defined scale:
>   Architectural
>   1/2" = 1' 0"
> ○ Custom scale:
>   0.5 in.   =   1 ft.
>
>   ┌─ Printer Paper
>   └─ Drawing Page
>
> Printer paper: 11 x 8.5 in.   (Landscape)
> Drawing page: 11 x 8.5 in.   (Landscape)
>
> Page size (in measurement units)
> 22 ft.   x   17 ft.
>
> Print zoom: **Fit to exactly 1 sheet**
>
> Apply   OK   Cancel

4. **Choose a predefined scale or set your own scale:**

   • To choose an architectural or engineering predefined scale, click the Pre-defined Scale option and select a scale from the drop-down list.

   • To set your own scale, click Custom Scale and then type a number and units in the first box for page units and a number and units in the second box for measurement units. For fractional units, enter the decimal equivalent, such as .125 in. for ⅛ inch.

5. **Note the page size, displayed near the bottom of the dialog box.**

   These numbers tell you how large an area you can represent in your drawing. If the area isn't large enough, increase your page units. If the area is too large, decrease your page units. For example, if you need to draw an office plan that's 50 feet x 40 feet and the page size shows only 40 feet x 30 feet, you need to increase page units.

6. **Before leaving this dialog box, click the Page Properties tab.**

   Notice that Visio automatically sets the measurement units for the current page to match the setting you chose in Step 4.

7. **Click OK.**

Visio automatically adjusts the scale in your drawing (as well as the ruler scale) to the new settings you chose.

Snapping Shapes into Place

Snap is a terrific Visio feature. You can't imagine how much time you waste trying to precisely place shapes *without* using snap.

The snap feature in Visio works like a magnet. When snap is turned on, a shape jumps to certain points as you drag it around the drawing area. You can attach a shape to any of the following elements:

- **Ruler subdivisions:** Tick marks that appear on the ruler (1 inch, ½ inch, ¼ inch, and so on).
- **Grid:** Horizontal and vertical graph lines in the drawing area.
- **Alignment box:** A shape's frame (displayed only when a shape is selected).
- **Shape extensions:** Dotted lines that extend out from a shape (such as the horizontal or vertical line of the edges of a rectangle).
- **Shape geometry:** The visible edges of a shape.
- **Guides:** Special lines or points that you add to a drawing to help you align shapes.
- **Shape intersections:** The points at which shapes intersect.
- **Shape handles:** The square green handles on a selected shape that you use to resize the shape.
- **Shape vertices:** The green diamond-shaped points on a shape where lines come together.
- **Connection points:** Blue Xs that appear on shapes when View⇨ Connection Points is checked.

When using snap features, it's helpful to display the Snap and Glue toolbar, which includes the buttons shown in Table 7-2. Note that many of these buttons mirror the Snap and Glue dialog box settings in the preceding list.

Visio turns on snap automatically for ruler, grid lines, connection points, and guides. This means that whenever you drag a shape around the drawing area, the shape jumps (whether you notice it or not!) to align itself to ruler subdivisions, grid lines, guides, or connection points on other shapes. For example, suppose you want to space three rectangles ½ inch apart. As you drag the shapes, they jump to the nearest grid line or ruler subdivision, placing the rectangles exactly ½ inch apart (see Figure 7-5). You could line up these shapes using the rulers and the grid as a visual guide, but why spend more time than you need to when Visio's snap feature helps you do it automatically?

You can choose to have objects snap to any combination of the elements from the list, or you can have them snap to none. Turning on all snap options at the same time can be distracting because your shapes jump every time they get near anything! I recommend that you turn on only the snap options that you really want to use. For instance, you may not want to choose grid and ruler at the same time. Because grid lines rarely correspond to ruler markings, it's not clear where your shape is jumping when both options are selected at the same time.

Along with choosing snap elements, you get to set the *strength* of snap. It's sort of like choosing between a tiny refrigerator magnet and a 10-pound horseshoe magnet. The bigger the magnet, the harder snap pulls. (I doubt you need to set strength; in all the years I've used Visio, I've never noticed snap not pulling hard enough.)

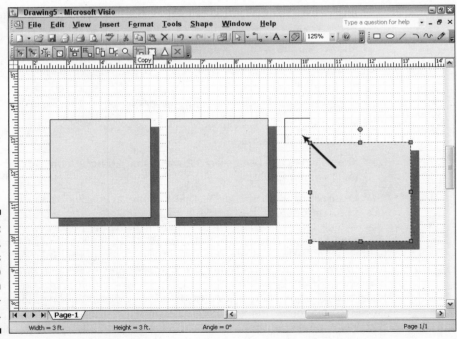

Figure 7-5:
With snap, shapes jump into position automatically.

To change snap settings, use these steps:

1. **Choose Tools⇨Snap & Glue.**

   The Snap and Glue dialog box appears, as shown in Figure 7-6.

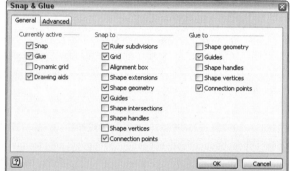

Figure 7-6:
Choose the
elements
you want
shapes to
snap to.

2. **In the Snap To area, click the elements for which you want to activate snap.**

3. **Click OK.**

If you want to turn snap off altogether, click the Toggle Snap button on the Snap and Glue toolbar, or choose Tools⇨Snap & Glue and uncheck the Snap box in the Currently Active area of the dialog box. When you turn snap off, shapes move freely as you drag them around the drawing area. (No more Mexican jumping beans!)

Measuring Up with Rulers

Some drawings don't require rulers. For instance, if your drawing is completely abstract (that is, completely unrelated to real-world shapes), such as a flowchart or an audit diagram, rulers are meaningless. You don't care whether your shapes are 1 inch wide or 1¼ inches wide; it doesn't change the meaning of the information your drawing conveys. The only thing you really care about is whether your drawing fits on the page. When you work with a scaled drawing, however, accurate measurements are essential. By displaying vertical and horizontal rulers in a drawing, you can instantly see the size of a shape and how much space you have on the drawing page.

In unscaled Visio drawings, rulers typically display either inches or centimeters, depending on the template of the drawing type you chose. (Recall that almost all drawing types are available in U.S. units or metric units.) Scaled drawings typically display either feet or meters, but you have many other choices. For example, you might want to use yards for drawings that represent real-life objects, such as landscape plans. If you use the metric system, you might want to switch ruler units to centimeters or millimeters.

Changing the units that the ruler displays does nothing to change the drawing scale. Scale is a *ratio* of units displayed on the page (or screen) to real-life measurements. The ruler changes only the units displayed in a drawing, not their scale.

To change the unit of measure displayed on a drawing page, follow these steps:

1. **Open your drawing and display the page for which you want to change ruler units.**

2. **Choose File⇨Page Setup.**

   The Page Setup dialog box appears.

3. **Click the Page Properties tab.**

4. **Click the drop-down arrow for Measurement Units (see Figure 7-7) and select the unit you want to use for the current page.**

5. **Click OK.**

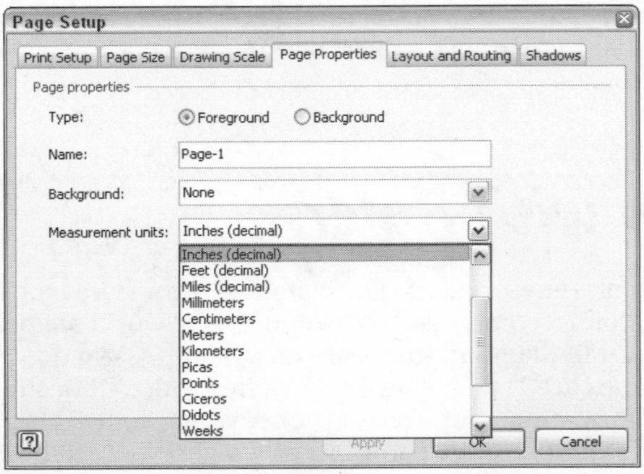

Figure 7-7:
Select the measurement units for the current page.

Visio changes the ruler's measurement units for only the current page. If your drawing contains multiple pages, you can display different ruler units on other pages. Just display the correct drawing page before using the preceding steps, or choose the correct page in the Name drop-down list in the Page Setup dialog box.

The *zero point* for the rulers (the point where 0 appears on a ruler) is generally in the lower-left corner of the drawing page, but you can change this position. If you want a symmetrical drawing, you might move the ruler's zero points to the middle of the page, draw half of a drawing, and then mirror it. Or suppose you're drawing an office layout. You might find the drawing easier to work with if you move the zero points to align with the left and upper walls so you can measure distances from that point (see Figure 7-8).

To change the zero point of both rulers at the same time, follow these steps:

1. **Move the mouse pointer to the gray square where the vertical ruler and horizontal ruler intersect (in the upper-left corner of the drawing area).**

   The mouse pointer changes to a four-headed arrow.

2. **Hold down the Ctrl key and drag the mouse to the new location for the zero point of both rulers.**

   As you move your mouse, watch the faint dotted line that appears on each ruler, marking the position of the mouse.

New zero points

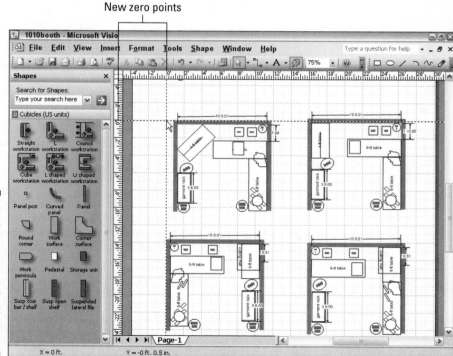

Figure 7-8: The zero point for the rulers is moved to align with the upper and left walls of the floor plan.

 3. **Release the mouse button when the zero point is positioned where you want it.**

If you want to change the zero point of just one ruler, use the same basic procedure, but drag from one ruler only. For example, if you want to place the zero point on the horizontal ruler 2 inches in from the left edge of the paper, follow these steps:

 1. **Point to the vertical ruler until you see the double-headed arrow mouse pointer.**

 That's right. To change the zero point on the horizontal ruler, you point to the vertical ruler.

 2. **Hold the Ctrl key and drag the mouse until the vertical line is positioned where you want the zero point on the horizontal ruler.**

If you prefer not to do all this dragging, you can choose Tools⇨Ruler & Grid. When the Ruler and Grid dialog box appears (refer to Figure 7-2), enter zero points (measured in inches) in the Ruler Zero boxes for Horizontal, or Vertical, or both.

To reset the zero points of both rulers to their default position, just double-click the intersection of the rulers (in the upper-left corner of the drawing area).

This is a good time to use the snap feature, discussed previously in the chapter. Before you adjust the zero point for your rulers, turn on Snap for Rulers if it isn't on already. (The steps are detailed in the "Snapping Shapes into Place" section.) With ruler snap turned on, your mouse jumps to ruler subdivisions so that you can easily place the zero point.

Using Guide Lines and Guide Points

As if you don't already have enough options for positioning shapes in a drawing, Visio gives you two more! *Guide lines* and *guide points* work in combination with snap. Use guide lines when you want a bunch of shapes to line up with each other. Use guide points when you want to pinpoint a shape in an exact location.

To make guide lines and guide points work, you have to turn on snap for guides; otherwise, your guides don't do anything except clutter up your drawing. (See the "Snapping Shapes into Place" section earlier in this chapter to set snap elements.) In Figure 7-9, all the shapes are snapped to the guide line because snap is set to work on guides and shape handles.

Guide line

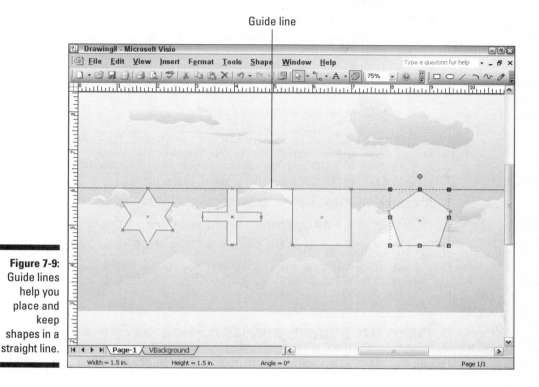

Figure 7-9:
Guide lines
help you
place and
keep
shapes in a
straight line.

To snap shapes to a guide, drag the shape near the guide. The shape snaps automatically to the guide. When you select the shape, the shape's red selection handles clearly indicate that the shape is glued to the guide. (Visio uses dynamic glue, or shape-to-shape glue, to glue shapes to guides. See Chapter 6 for more information about dynamic glue.)

The useful thing about guide lines and guide points is that you can move them. When you do, all the shapes attached to the guides move right along with them.

Creating guide lines

To create a guide line, use these steps:

1. **Move your mouse pointer over the vertical ruler (to create a vertical guide) or over the horizontal ruler (to create a horizontal guide) until the mouse pointer changes to a double-headed arrow.**

2. Drag the mouse pointer.

As you drag, the guide appears as a blue line that runs up and down (or across) the drawing page.

3. When the guide is positioned where you want it, release the mouse button.

The line turns green because it's selected.

Want to create a diagonal guide line? Here's a slick trick. Just create a horizontal or vertical guide and then rotate it. Follow these steps:

1. Select the guide line that you want to rotate.

2. Choose View⇨Size & Position Window.

The Size and Position window appears near the bottom of your screen.

3. In the Angle box, type the degree angle of rotation.

For a diagonal guide, type 45. Visio rotates the selected guide to the angle that you specify.

Creating guide points

When you want to pinpoint a shape in an exact location, create a *guide point*. On the screen, a guide point looks like a circle with cross through it. To create a guide point, use these steps:

1. Move your mouse pointer over the intersection of the vertical and horizontal rulers.

The mouse pointer changes to a four-headed arrow.

2. Drag the mouse.

Two blue lines — one vertical and one horizontal — follow the movement of the mouse pointer on the drawing page.

3. When the intersection of the guides is positioned where you want it, release the mouse button.

The blue lines disappear, and the guide point (a circle with a cross through it) is displayed on the screen.

Guide points work with snap. If snap isn't activated, guide points won't do you any good. When snap is activated, only the activated snap elements will snap to a guide point. (For more information on snap, refer to "Snapping Shapes into Place," earlier in this chapter.) For instance, if you activate snap for shape handles, you can attach a shape's handle to a guide point. If you activate snap for connection points, you can attach a shape's connection points to a guide point. Both of these examples are illustrated in Figure 7-10.

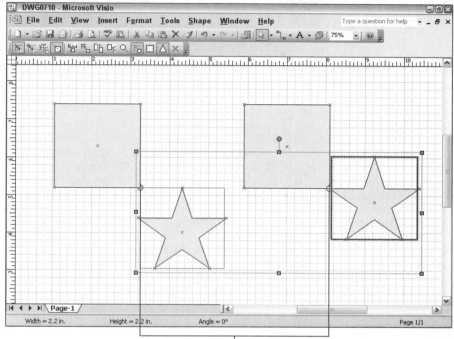

Figure 7-10:
Guide points
let you
place a
shape at an
exact
location.

Guide points

When snap is activated only for shape handles, the square and star on the left side of the drawing can attach to the guide point *only* at their shape handles. On the other hand, when snap is activated also for connection points, you can snap the tip of the star to the guide point, because the star has connection points at each tip (see the square and star on the right side of the drawing).

If you want to use multiple guides spaced evenly across your drawing, here is a great way to create them:

1. **Create the first guide.**

2. **Hold down the Ctrl key as you drag a copy of the guide to the next increment you want — say, 1 inch.**

3. **Press the F4 key.**

   Another guide, 1 inch from the last guide, is created automatically.

4. **Press the F4 key as many times as you want to keep creating guides spaced at the same increment.**

Aligning and Distributing Shapes

Besides using guides, Visio gives you another way to automatically align shapes. Suppose that you create a diagram like the one on the left in Figure 7-11. The shapes aren't lined up, the connectors look goofy, and the whole thing looks like you threw it together in a few seconds. It's okay to create a messy drawing like this because Visio can clean it up for you!

The diagram on the right was aligned with Visio's automatic alignment feature. With the click of a toolbar button (or through a menu command), you can horizontally align the top, bottom, or middle of selected shapes, or you can vertically align the left edge, right edge, or middle of selected shapes. You first select the shape you want other shapes to align to and then select all the other shapes. The first shape you select becomes the reference point for the alignment of other shapes.

To use the alignment tools, display the Action toolbar. The Align Shapes button has a drop-down box, which displays a miniversion of the alignment options available. These options are also available in the Align Shapes dialog box when you choose Tools⇨Align Shapes, as shown in Figure 7-12. (To make this menu command active, you must first select at least two shapes in the drawing.)

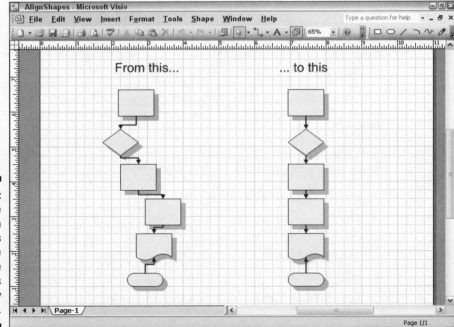

Figure 7-11:
The flowchart on the left is messy. The one on the right is perfectly aligned.

Figure 7-12:
Choose a
vertical or
horizontal
alignment.

To align several shapes horizontally, vertically, or both, use these steps:

1. **Select the shape to which you want the other shapes to align.**

2. **Hold the Shift key and at the same time select all other shapes that you want aligned to the first shape.**

3. **Choose Shape⊅Align Shapes or click the drop-down arrow next to the Align Shapes button on the Shapes toolbar.**

   The Align Shapes dialog box appears (refer to Figure 7-12).

4. **Click the alignment style that you want.**

   If you think you'll be adding more shapes that you'll want aligned with these, consider clicking the Create Guide and Glue Shapes to It option, which is at the bottom of the dialog box.

5. **Click OK.**

   Visio aligns all shapes to the first shape that you selected.

Ever try to space several shapes evenly — say, ½ inch apart — across an area? Doing it manually can be frustrating. Visio refers to the process of spacing shapes evenly as *distributing* shapes. You can distribute shapes using the Distribute Shapes toolbar button (or a menu command, if you prefer). Like the Align Shapes toolbar button, the Distribute Shapes button also has a drop-down box, which displays a miniversion of the Distribute Shapes dialog box shown in Figure 7-13.

Use these steps to distribute shapes across an area:

1. **Select all the shapes that you want to distribute.**

2. **Choose Shape⊅Distribute Shapes or click the drop-down arrow on the Distribute Shapes button on the Action toolbar.**

   The Distribute Shapes dialog box appears, as shown in Figure 7-13.

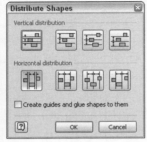

Figure 7-13:
Choose a
distribution
style.

3. **Click the distribution style that you want to use.**

   If you think that you may add more shapes that you'll want to distribute, consider clicking the Create Guides and Glue Shapes to Them option at the bottom of the dialog box.

4. **Click OK.**

   Visio automatically distributes the shapes.

Visio has many time-saving features. Take advantage of the flexibility you have to focus on the content of a drawing, and then use Visio's features to help you perfect your drawing.

Chapter 8

Creating and Customizing Shapes

· ·

In This Chapter

▶ Customizing shapes by using fun Visio tools

▶ Creating your own shapes

▶ Manipulating shapes

▶ Adding character to your shapes

▶ Grouping and stacking shapes

· ·

*B*ecause Visio provides so many shapes in its stencils, you can use the program successfully without ever needing to customize shapes. But if you're adventurous, you might want to use Visio to make shapes *your* way. In this chapter, you discover how to get creative with Visio by changing existing shapes and drawing your own shapes.

Creating Unique Shapes the Fun Way

Near the middle of the Visio Shape menu is a command called Operations. Sounds pretty serious! Well, it's not serious at all. In fact, this command should be called Fun Stuff. After you select the Operations command, Visio gives you a submenu with a list of tools that you can use to create shapes. The following list explains each tool:

- ✔ **Union:** Creates a shape from overlapping shapes by using the perimeter of all the shapes as the new outline.

- ✔ **Combine:** Creates a shape from overlapping shapes by cutting out the areas that overlap.

- ✔ **Fragment:** Breaks shapes into separate shapes along the lines where they overlap.

- ✔ **Intersect:** Creates a shape from *only* the area where two or more shapes overlap (all other areas are deleted).

- ✔ **Subtract:** Cuts away the areas that overlap the first shape you select.

It might take you awhile to remember exactly what each command does. That's okay, just experiment with them! If you don't like the result, choose Edit➪Undo and try another one. The following sections illustrate how each of these commands work — they're easier to see than read about.

I show you how to use a lot of Visio's drawing, formatting, and manipulation tools throughout this chapter, so you might want to open some of the toolbars listed in Table 8-1 now. Unless stated otherwise, use the Pointer Tool button in the instructional steps for selecting shapes.

Table 8-1   Toolbar Buttons for Drawing and Manipulating Shapes

Button	Name	Toolbar	What It Does
	Arc Tool	Drawing	Lets you draw an arc shape
	Bring to Front	Action	Brings a shape to the top of the stack in the stacking order
	Ellipse Tool	Drawing	Lets you draw circles and ovals (ellipses)
	Format Painter	Standard	Lets you apply formatting from one shape to another
	Freeform Tool	Drawing	Lets you draw freehand using curves and lines
	Lasso Select	Standard	Allows you to draw a lasso (an irregular shape) around the shapes you want to select
	Line Tool	Drawing	Lets you draw a straight line
	Pencil Tool	Drawing	Lets you draw lines, arcs, or circles depending on how you move the mouse
	Pointer Tool	Standard	The standard pointer tool for selecting shapes
	Rectangle Tool	Drawing	Draws rectangles and squares
	Rotate Right	Action	Turns a shape 90 degrees to the right
	Rotate Left	Action	Turns a shape 90 degrees to the left
	Send to Back	Action	Sends a shape to the bottom of the stack in the stacking order

Uniting shapes

The Union command does as its name suggests — it *unites* two or more overlapping shapes. The Union command combines these shapes by maintaining the perimeters of all the shapes and erasing their inside boundaries to form one new shape (see Figure 8-1).

To unite two or more shapes using the Union command, follow these steps:

1. **Drag the shapes that you want to unite into the drawing area.**

   If you want to draw shapes, draw them now.

2. **Move the shapes where you want them, making sure each one overlaps at least one other shape.**

3. **Using the Pointer Tool button, select all the shapes that you want to unite.**

4. **Choose Shape⇨Operations⇨Union.**

   Visio unites all the shapes.

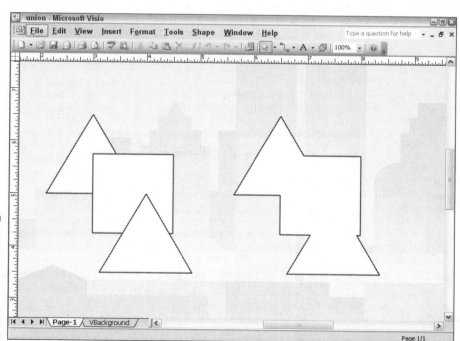

Figure 8-1:
Individual shapes (left) unite to become a single shape (right).

If some of the shapes you select don't overlap, the Union command still unites them anyway, even though they don't appear to be any different. Try selecting one by itself and you'll see that Visio now treats them as one shape. If the first shape you select has any special attributes (such as line color, fill color, or shadow), the second and following shapes take on the same attributes as the first shape.

Union is different from Group in that the borders where shapes overlap are eliminated when you unite them. Grouping simply treats selected shapes as a single shape.

You can click the Undo button on the Standard toolbar to undo a Union command immediately. If you perform other tasks first, however, you can still undo the Union command by selecting the combined shape and then choosing Shape⇨Operations⇨Fragment. This restores your original shapes individually, but it won't return the original formatting to all the shapes.

Combining shapes

The name of the Combine command is a bit misleading. It might be more accurate to call it the Cutout, or Doughnut, command. Notice that on the left side of Figure 8-2, two shapes are placed on top of one another. In the shape on the right, the Combine command uses the outline of the star to cut out the center of the other shape. (You know this is a cutout because you can see the grid through the star.)

Follow these steps to combine shapes:

1. **Draw all the shapes that you want to combine.**

2. **Arrange the shapes so that they overlap.**

3. **Using the Pointer Tool button, to select all the shapes that you want to combine.**

4. **Choose Shape⇨Operations⇨Combine.**

   Visio creates cutouts where the smaller, fully-enclosed shapes overlap the larger ones.

When you combine shapes that don't overlap, there isn't anything for Visio to cut out, but Visio still combines the shapes by treating them as a single shape, just like the Union command does. Also as with the Union command, the second and following shapes take on all attributes of the first shape you select.

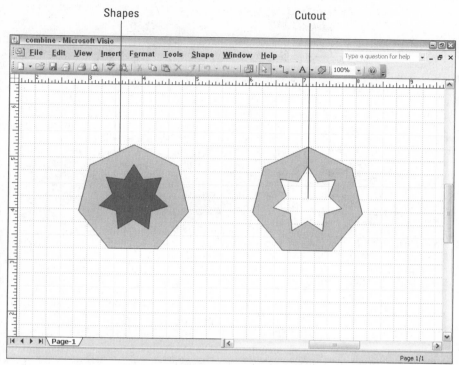

Shapes   Cutout

Figure 8-2:
The shapes
on the left
combine to
create the
shape on
the right.

TIP

You can click the Undo button on the Standard toolbar to undo a Combine command immediately. If you perform other tasks first, however, you can still undo the Combine command by selecting the combined shape and then choosing Shape⇨Operations⇨Fragment. This restores your original shapes individually, but it won't return the original formatting to all the shapes.

In Figure 8-3, you see a more complex array of combined shapes. On the left, each shape is a different shade of gray. After you combine them into a single shape, all the hues convert to that of the triangle — the shape that was created first.

Fragmenting shapes

Fragmenting is fun and a great way to create new shapes from overlapped shapes. The left side of Figure 8-4 shows several overlapped shapes that take on new dimensions when you separate them at their overlap points (right). It's sort of like cutting apart all the pieces where they overlap and making jigsaw puzzle pieces out of them.

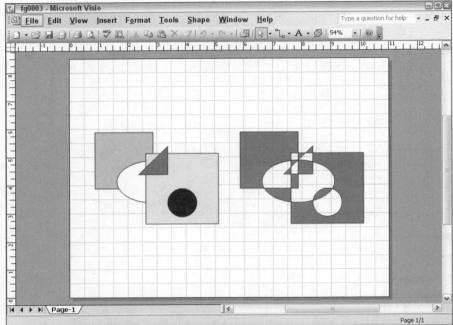

Figure 8-3:
The Combine command lets you create complex cutout shapes.

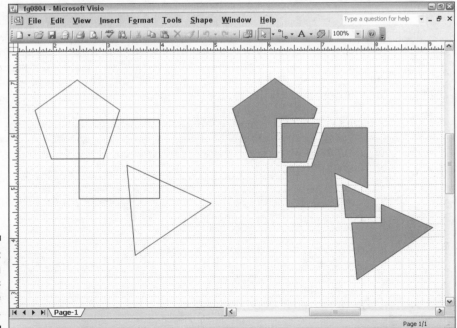

Figure 8-4:
Fragmenting creates jigsaw-like shapes.

To fragment shapes, follow these steps:

1. **Drag all the shapes that you want into the drawing area or draw new ones.**

2. **Arrange the shapes so that they overlap.**

3. **Using the Pointer Tool button, select all the overlapping shapes.**

4. **Choose Shape⇨Operations⇨Fragment.**

   Visio breaks all the shapes into separate shapes along their overlapping lines. You can't control the distance Visio uses to separate the shapes, but you can move the shapes individually after they're fragmented.

Intersecting shapes

The Intersecting shapes command makes a radical change in your shapes! Visio keeps only the parts where *all* the shapes overlap and cuts away the rest. Figure 8-5 shows three overlapping circles on the left. (I drew a dotted line to show the outline of where the shapes overlap.) After you intersect these shapes, the only thing that's left is the triangular portion from the center where all the circles overlap. As with other Operations commands, the resulting shape takes on the attributes (color, line style, and so on) of the first shape you select.

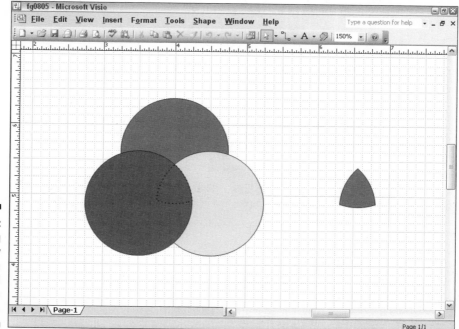

Figure 8-5: Intersecting keeps only the area where all shapes overlap.

To intersect shapes, follow these steps:

1. **Drag all the shapes that you want into the drawing area or draw them.**
2. **Arrange the shapes so that they *all* overlap every other shape at some point.**
3. **Using the Pointer Tool button, select all the shapes that you want to intersect.**
4. **Choose Shape⇨Operations⇨Intersect.**

   Visio leaves only the portion where *all* shapes overlap, removing the extraneous parts. The resulting shape takes on the attributes of the first shape you select.

Subtracting shapes

Subtract is a feature that works just like it sounds: When two shapes overlap, the overlapping part is subtracted, or removed, from the first shape that you select. This command subtracts the *second* shape you select from the *first* shape you select. So the first shape you select is the shape that remains — in part — after using the Subtract command.

Figure 8-6 shows the original shapes — the circle and star — on the left. The partial star in the center is what's left if you select the *star* first. The partial circle on the right is what's left if you select the *circle* first.

Follow these steps to use the subtract command:

1. **Drag the shapes that you want to work with into the drawing area or draw new shapes.**
2. **Position the shapes so that they overlap.**
3. **Using the Pointer tool, select the shape that you want to keep.**
4. **Select the shape that you want to subtract.**
5. **Choose Shape⇨Operations⇨Subtract.**

   Visio removes the shape that you selected in Step 4 and leaves what remains of the shape that you selected in Step 3.

Restacking shapes

Each time you draw or drag a new shape into the drawing area, Visio places it on top of other, existing shapes. (If you don't overlap the shapes, you never notice this.) To understand how Visio keeps track of the order of shapes, pretend that you are drawing each shape on a separate piece of paper. Each time you draw a shape, you drop the paper on your desk. The first one to fall is at the bottom of the stack. Those that fall on top of others clearly overlap one another. Those that don't overlap *still fall in a stacking order*, whether you pay attention to it or not. The last one you drop is at the top of the stack.

Visio has two commands — Bring to Front and Send to Back — to help you rearrange the stacking order of shapes. You can find both buttons on the Action toolbar. You also can go to the Shape menu and find two other commands for restacking: Bring Forward and Send Backward. (You can display the Action toolbar by right-clicking the toolbar area and choosing Action.) What's the difference between all these?

✔ **Bring to Front:** Brings a shape to the top of the stack.

✔ **Bring Forward:** Brings a shape up one level in the stack.

✔ **Send to Back:** Sends a shape to the bottom of the stack.

✔ **Send Backward:** Sends a shape down one level in the stack.

Bring Forward and Send Backward are found only on the Shape menu, but you can add buttons for these commands to the Action toolbar by customizing your toolbar. To find out more about customizing toolbars, refer to Chapter 1.

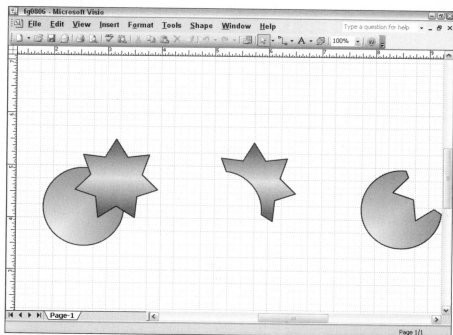

Figure 8-6:
The result of the Subtract command depends on which shape you select first.

In Figure 8-7, the triangle was drawn first, so it's at the bottom of the stack. Suppose that you want to move the triangle above the rectangle but below the ellipse. If you try to move the triangle without changing its order in the stack, it's almost completely hidden by the rectangle. You need to use the Bring Forward command several times to raise the triangle's position in the stack.

To rearrange the stacking order of shapes, follow these steps:

1. **Select the shape that you want to move.**

2. **Determine which command or button you need to use: Bring Forward, Bring to Front, Send Backward, or Send to Back.**

3. **Click the Bring to Front button or the Send to Back button on the Shape toolbar, or choose Shape⇨Order⇨Bring Forward or Shape⇨Send Backward.**

4. **Repeat Step 3 if necessary.**

If you prefer using shortcut keys, press Ctrl+Shift+F for Bring to Front or Ctrl+Shift+B for Send to Back.

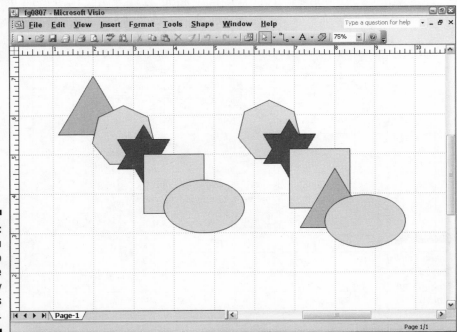

Figure 8-7:
Often you need to rearrange the way shapes overlap.

Drawing Your Own Shapes

As if there weren't enough shapes for you to choose from in Visio, you can make your own, too. You might find that you often make your own shapes, particularly if you work in a specialized field. Visio gives you many buttons on the Drawing toolbar for drawing shapes (refer to Table 8-1).

Drawing with the Line Tool button

You can use the Line Tool button on the Standard toolbar to draw lines or shapes that are made up of straight lines. The points at which you start and stop drawing a line are called *endpoints* (see Figure 8-8). Between the two endpoints is a *control point*, which you use to control the shape of a shape, as discussed later in this chapter. (For more information about working with control points, refer also to Chapter 4.)

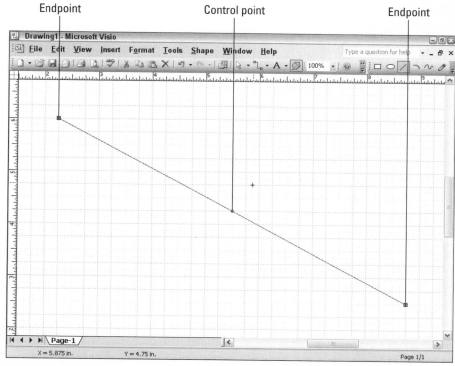

Figure 8-8: Every line has a control point and two endpoints.

It's a bit of a misnomer to call both ends of a line *end*points when one of them is a beginning. The beginning *end*point is marked by a small green square with an X inside; the ending *end*point is marked by a small green square with a + symbol.

To draw a simple line, follow these steps:

1. **Click the Line Tool button (refer to Table 8-1) on the Drawing toolbar.**

   The mouse pointer changes to a line and a plus symbol.

2. **Place the mouse pointer where you want to begin the line; then drag the mouse to the point where you want the line to end.**

   As you drag the mouse, you see a guide line that extends from the starting point to the location of your pointer. The guide line shows you where the line will be drawn if you release the mouse button. Move the mouse around in a circle and you see that the guide line follows your movement. At every 45-degree interval, the guide line shoots out into a ray. This is to help you draw lines at perfect 45-, 90-, 135-, and 180-degree angles from your starting point.

3. **Release the mouse button.**

   The line is selected, and the endpoints appear. (Switch to the Pencil Tool button on the Drawing toolbar if you want to display the control point.)

4. **Click any blank area of the drawing to deselect the line.**

It's not often that you draw a single line by itself. More than likely, you'll want to draw a shape by connecting a series of line segments. The trick here is that you must draw all segments consecutively if you want to create a closed shape. If you don't draw them consecutively, the shape won't be closed, even if the segments appear to be connected.

To connect segments as you draw, follow these steps:

1. **Click the Line Tool button on the Drawing toolbar.**

   The mouse pointer changes to a line and a plus symbol.

2. **Draw your first segment by dragging the mouse and releasing.**

3. **Point to the endpoint of the first segment; then drag the mouse to draw the second segment of your shape.**

   (If you just release the mouse button in Step 2 and don't move the pointer, you'll already be pointing at the endpoint when you're ready to draw the next segment.)

4. **Repeat Step 3 as many times as you want.**

5. **To close the shape, draw another segment from the endpoint of the last segment to the beginning point of the first segment that you drew, and then release the mouse button.**

   The shape becomes a *closed* shape. You see the shape fill with white (or another color, depending on the template you choose). See Figure 8-9.

If your background color is white and your grid is turned off, you can't see the white fill.

Whenever you draw shapes by connecting segments, turn on Snap (Tools➪ Snap & Glue), the feature that pulls shapes into place. Snap helps you connect segments automatically. To find out more about how snap works, see Chapter 7.

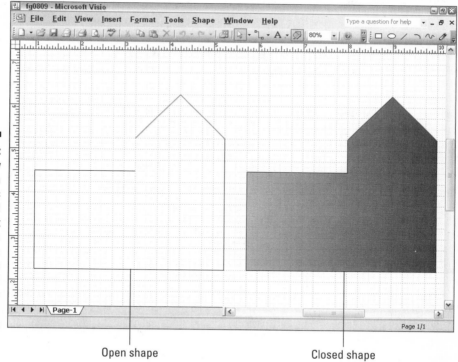

Figure 8-9: You know when a shape is closed because it fills with white or a color (as defined by the template).

Open shape

Closed shape

Drawing with the Pencil Tool button

The Pencil Tool button works almost exactly like the Line Tool button. If you select the Pencil Tool button and move the mouse in a straight line, you draw a straight line. If you move the mouse in a curved direction, you draw a portion of a circle. The size and circumference of the circle depend on how far you move the mouse. Use the Pencil Tool button when you want to draw a shape that includes both curves and lines (see Figure 8-10).

Again, if you want to create a closed shape, you must draw all segments (lines and arcs) consecutively. To draw a shape using the Pencil Tool button, follow these steps:

1. **Click the Pencil Tool button (refer to Table 8-1) on the Standard toolbar.**

2. **Draw the first segment by dragging the mouse and then releasing the mouse button.**

   Drag in a straight line to create a line; drag in a circular direction to create a curve.

3. **Draw the second segment by pointing to the endpoint of the previous segment, dragging the mouse and then releasing the mouse button.**

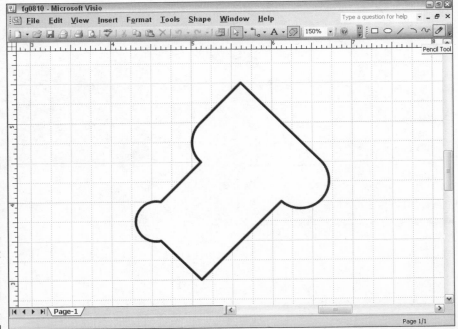

Figure 8-10:
With the Pencil Tool button, you can draw shapes that contain both straight and curved lines.

4. Repeat the motion in Step 3 as many times as you like.

5. Finish the shape by connecting the endpoint of the last segment to the beginning point of the first segment.

Drawing with the Arc Tool button

It might seem obvious that you draw an arc by using the Arc Tool button, but you might be wondering how the Arc Tool button differs from the Pencil Tool button, which also lets you draw arcs. The Arc Tool button lets you draw one quarter of an ellipse, whereas the Pencil Tool button enables you to draw a portion of a circle (not an ellipse and not limited to one quarter). Use the Arc Tool button when you want a less-than-circular curve (such as an oval). Use the Pencil Tool button when you want to draw true circular curves. (See the "Creating shapes with the Ellipse and Rectangle Tool buttons" section later in this chapter to find out how to use the Ellipse Tool button to draw complete circles and ellipses.)

To draw an arc by using the Arc Tool button, follow these steps:

1. Click the Arc Tool button (refer to Table 8-1) on the Standard toolbar.

2. Place the mouse where you want the arc to begin.

3. Drag the mouse in the direction that you want the arc to go.

4. Release the mouse button where you want the arc to end.

Creating irregular shapes with the Freeform Tool button

I call the Freeform Tool button the doodling tool. You use it the same way you use a pencil when you're doodling. The Freeform Tool button (it looks like a squiggly line) obediently displays every curve and scribble you make. Just draw with the Freeform Tool button to create, well, freeform shapes. To create a closed shape like the one shown in Figure 8-11, end your doodling at the point where you began. (The shape in Figure 8-11 is actually a lake drawn for a map!)

If you have a tablet PC or a tablet attached to your computer, the Freeform Tool button is great because it's easier to draw with a pen than with a mouse.

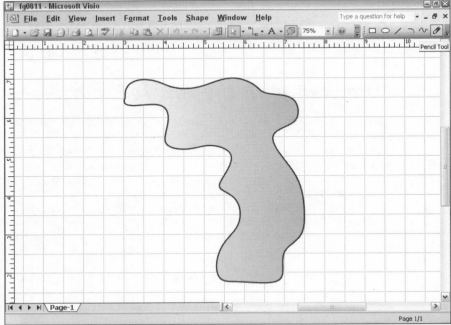

Figure 8-11:
Use the
Freeform
Tool button
to create
curved,
irregular
shapes.

Creating shapes with the Ellipse and Rectangle Tool buttons

You can use the Arc and Pencil Tool buttons to draw curves (elliptical or circular), and you can use either of these buttons to draw four connected segments that form a complete circle or ellipse. But why would you want to do that when Visio gives you a simpler way? Just use the Ellipse Tool button to draw perfect circles or ellipses.

The following steps tell you how to use the Ellipse Tool button:

1. **Click the Ellipse Tool button (refer to Table 8-1) on the Standard toolbar.**

2. **Put the mouse pointer where you want to place the ellipse.**

3. **Drag the mouse in any direction.**

   To draw a perfect circle, hold down the Shift key as you drag the mouse.

4. **Release the mouse button when the ellipse is the size and shape that you want.**

If you want the ellipse to be a particular size, watch the status bar as you drag the mouse. The status bar tells you the exact width and height of your ellipse as you draw. You can also choose Shape⇨Size and Position after you draw the shape and then enter exact dimensions in the Height and Width boxes.

The Rectangle Tool button works in the same way as the Ellipse Tool button. You could use the Line Tool button to create a rectangle by drawing and connecting four segments, but it's easier to draw a rectangle by using the Rectangle Tool button. Follow these four steps to draw a rectangle:

1. **Click the Rectangle Tool button (refer to Table 8-1) on the Standard toolbar.**

2. **Put the mouse pointer where you want to place the rectangle.**

3. **Drag the mouse in any direction.**

   To draw a perfect square, hold down the Shift key as you drag the mouse. To create a rectangle of a specific size, watch the status bar for height and width measurements as you draw.

4. **Release the mouse button when the rectangle is the size and shape that you want.**

Manipulating Shapes

Suppose, for example, that you find a shape in Visio that's almost, but not quite, what you want. You can modify a shape in many ways by tweaking it until it's just what you want.

Moving and adding vertices

With Visio, it's easy to change the form of a shape by dragging part of the shape to a new position. In Figure 8-12, I changed an isosceles triangle by dragging the upper-right vertex to a new place. Remember that a *vertex* appears at the end of every line and at points where lines intersect, which means that you see a vertex at each point of the triangle. Green diamond shapes mark the vertices, but you can see them only when you select the shape by using one of the following buttons on the Standard toolbar (just click the button and then select the shape):

✔ Arc Tool

✔ Freeform Tool

✔ Line Tool

✔ Pencil Tool

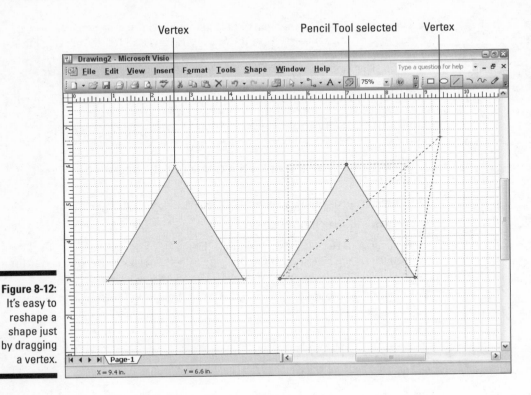

Figure 8-12:
It's easy to
reshape a
shape just
by dragging
a vertex.

To move a vertex, follow these steps:

1. **Select the Pencil, Freeform, Line, or Arc Tool button (refer to Table 8-1).**

2. **Point to the vertex that you want to move.**

   When you're within *selection range* of the vertex, the mouse pointer
   changes to a four-headed arrow.

3. **Click the vertex.**

   The color changes from green to magenta.

4. **Drag the vertex where you want it, and then release the mouse button.**

You also can add a vertex to any shape by following these steps:

1. **Select the Pencil Tool button.**

2. **Select the shape.**

   You see the vertices and control points of the shape.

3. Hold down the Ctrl key, and click a point where you want to add a vertex.

Visio adds the vertex (diamond shape) and a control point (round shape) between the new vertex and the previous one.

4. Repeat Step 3 for as many vertices as you want to add.

When you add a vertex to a shape, you're actually adding a *segment*. That's because Visio automatically adds a control point between the new vertex and the previous one. You can use the control point to change the shape of the segment, as I show you in the "Moving control points" section, later in this chapter.

Why would you want to add a vertex to a shape? Check out the five-pointed star in Figure 8-13. It's not bad, but perhaps you want it to look a little snazzier — maybe with five smaller points between the five existing points. To accomplish this task, you need to add some vertices and move others. Currently, vertices appear at the tip of each point on the star and at each inverted angle of the star. (I know they're small and difficult to see in the figure, but you'll see them clearly on your screen!)

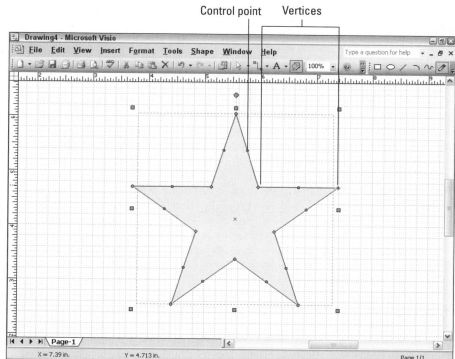

Figure 8-13:
The five-pointed star is a shape from Visio's Basic Shapes stencil.

To create the ten-pointed star (partially shown in Figure 8-14), you pull the inverted angle vertex — let's call it A — out to a point. Before you can do that, though, you need to add new vertices on both sides of A — let's call them B and C. If you pull A without adding B and C, you just make a fatter star with shallower inverted angles. Adding the vertices B and C gives the new tip two new points from which to begin.

Moving control points

Suppose that instead of adding five new points to the star in Figure 8-14, you just want to round out the lines of the star and make it look like one of the stars in Figure 8-15. To do that, you use the *control points*, the round shapes that appear between two vertices.

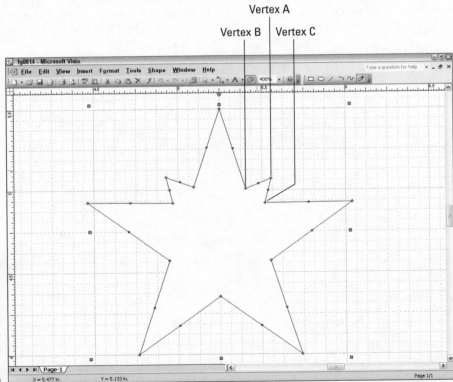

Figure 8-14: Before you can pull on A to create a new point, you must add B and C.

To move a control point, use these steps:

1. **Select the shape by using the Pointer Tool button on the Standard toolbar.**

   You see the selection handles of the shape.

2. **Switch to the Pencil Tool button.**

   You see the shape's vertices and control points.

3. **Point to the control point that you want to move.**

   The mouse pointer changes to a four-headed arrow.

4. **Click the control point.**

   The selected control point switches from green to magenta.

5. **Drag the control point, and then release the mouse button.**

You can make your changes more precise by zooming in on your shape and using the rulers to track the movement of a control point.

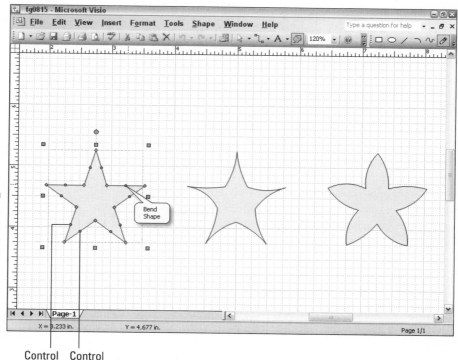

Figure 8-15:
The control points on the legs of each star allow them to be reshaped.

Control   Control
point   point

Rotating shapes

Rotating shapes is something you might need to do frequently. A shape might not be facing the correct angle when you drag it into the drawing. Or it might be easier to draw a shape at one angle and rotate it later.

You can rotate nearly all Visio shapes. If the shape has large, round handles that appear at the corners of its frame, you can rotate the shape. You also see a *rotation pin* (a round handle with a plus (+) symbol) at the center of the shape. This is the point around which the shape rotates. (If a Visio shape can't rotate, it's for good reason — probably because it doesn't make sense to rotate it.)

Visio provides three ways to rotate a shape:

- ✔ **Rotation handles** on a shape let you drag the shape to rotate it. Use this method when you want to change a shape's angle quickly but not necessarily precisely.

- ✔ **Rotate Right and Rotate Left buttons** on the Action toolbar let you rotate a shape 90 degrees at a time (clockwise or counterclockwise). Use this method when you know you want to rotate a shape in 90-degree increments.

- ✔ **The menu command** (View⇨Windows⇨Size & Position) opens the Size and Position window, which enables you to specify a rotation angle. This is the best method to use when the precise angle of rotation is a priority.

Rotation handles

To rotate a shape by using the rotation handles, follow these steps:

1. **Click the Pointer Tool button on the Standard toolbar.**

2. **Click the shape that you want to rotate.**

   The rotation handle, a large green circle, is visible usually somewhere near the top of the shape.

3. **Move the mouse pointer over the rotation handle.**

   The pointer changes to the rotation pointer, which looks like a circular, single-point arrow.

4. **Drag the mouse pointer clockwise or counterclockwise, depending on the direction that you want to rotate the shape.**

   As you drag the mouse, the mouse pointer changes to four arrows in a circular shape. Watch the status bar to see how far (in degrees) the shape is rotating.

5. **Release the mouse button when the shape is in the position that you want it.**

The closer you place the mouse to the rotation pin as you're rotating a shape, the more the rotation angle jumps, sometimes skipping degrees. The farther away you place the mouse pointer from the rotation pin, the more precise the angle of rotation.

Rotation buttons

Figure 8-16 shows how you rotate shapes using the Rotation buttons. You can see the rotation symbol in the figure.

Follow these two steps when you want to rotate a shape 90 degrees at a time:

1. **Click the shape that you want to rotate.**
2. **Click the Rotate Right or Rotate Left button on the Action toolbar.**

You can click the Rotate Right or Rotate Left button repeatedly to continue rotating the same shape in 90-degree increments. This method saves you the trouble of rotating a shape manually or using a menu command.

Rotation mouse pointer (the arrows)

Rotation pin   Rotation handle (the circle)

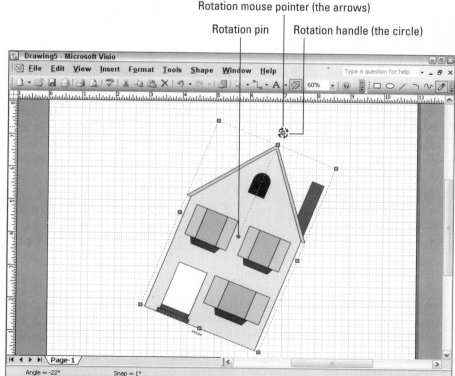

Figure 8-16:
When you rotate a shape, the rotation pin is the anchor around which the shape rotates.

Size and Position window

When precision is important to you, use the menu command to rotate shapes. You can rotate a shape at a precise angle, as little as .01 degree. Use these steps to rotate a shape at a precise angle:

1. **Select the shape that you want to rotate.**

2. **Choose View⇨Size & Position.**

   The Size and Position window appears, as shown in Figure 8-17.

3. **In the Angle box, type a number for the angle of rotation.**

   Type a positive number for a counterclockwise angle of rotation or a negative number for a clockwise angle of rotation.

4. **Click OK.**

   Visio rotates the shape to the angle you specify. Notice that the angle you entered is now reflected on the status bar.

Rotation pin

On most Visio shapes, the rotation pin is right in the center of the shape. If you want a shape to rotate around a different point, you can move the rotation pin. You might need to do this if you want to keep a particular point on

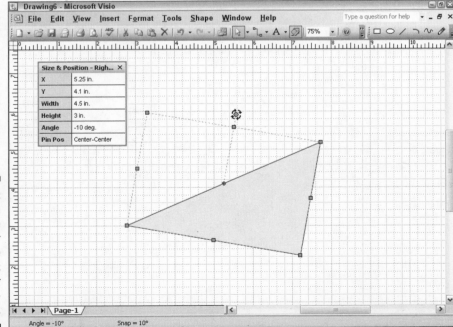

Figure 8-17:
Type a positive number for clockwise rotation; negative for counterclockwise.

the shape anchored. For example, in Figure 8-18, I moved the center of rotation for the triangle from its original position in the center to the upper-right of the triangle. Now the shape will rotate around this point.

You can use also use the Size and Position window to change the location of the rotation pin. After Step 4, choose Top-Left, Top-Center, Top-Right, Center-Left, Center-Center, Center-Right, Bottom-Left, Bottom-Center, or Bottom-Right in the Pin Position box. Or, you can move the pin position manually using tnese steps:

1. **Click the Pointer Tool button (on the Standard toolbar).**

2. **Select the shape.**

3. **If you don't see the rotation pin, move the mouse pointer over the shape's rotation handle.**

   The shape's rotation pin is displayed in a direct line from the rotation handle.

3. **Point to the rotation pin and drag it to a new position.**

4. **Release the mouse button.**

Rotation pin

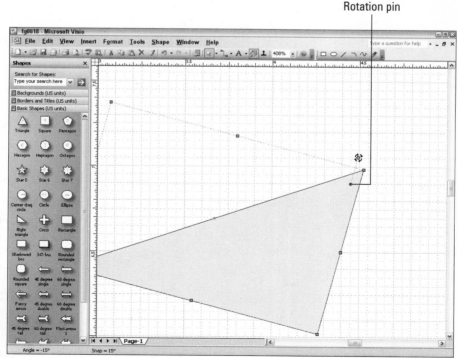

Figure 8-18:
Move the rotation pin to reposition the center of rotation on the shape.

When you move the rotation pin, it helps to zoom in on the shape. Zooming in enables you to place the pin more precisely, and it also displays a finer grid. If you don't want the rotation pin to snap to the grid, turn snap off by choosing Tools⇨Snap & Glue and then clicking the Snap check box to remove the check mark.

To easily return a rotation pin to the center of a shape, choose View⇨ Windows⇨Size & Position. In the Size and Position window, click Pin Pos(ition) and then choose Center-Center.

Flipping shapes

Sometimes you find just the right shape, but it's facing the wrong direction. In that case, you can flip the shape so that it faces the opposite direction. Your choices are Flip Horizontal (which flips a shape right-to-left) or Flip Vertical (which flips the shape top-to-bottom). In Figure 8-19, the first arrow was flipped horizontally, then vertically.

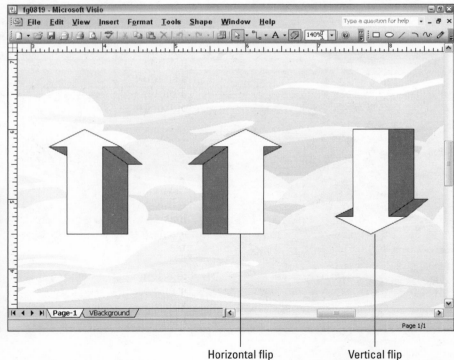

Figure 8-19:
The original arrow on the left was first flipped horizontally, then vertically.

Horizontal flip   Vertical flip

To flip a shape, use the buttons shown in Table 8-2. Select the shape first and then click one of the flip buttons.

Table 8-2	Action Toolbar Buttons for Flipping Shapes	
Button	*Name*	*What It Does*
◢◣	Flip Horizontal	Flips a shape from the left to the right
◢	Flip Vertical	Flips a shape from the top to the bottom

Adding Style to Your Shapes

Although many of the Visio shapes are pretty cool, some are basic — just an outline of something. Not very imaginative. Well, you can jazz up the more basic shapes by adding things such as line color and weight, fill color and pattern, and shadowing. These features are typically referred to as *formatting*.

You usually select a shape first and then apply some special type of formatting to it. If you're formatting one shape, why not format a bunch of them at the same time? This saves you a lot of time when you decide that all 382 whatchamacallits in your drawing should be blue and green checkerboards with a purple outline and a magenta shadow. Select all your shapes (no, don't click each one individually, use the Pointer Tool button to draw a selection box around them or use the Lasso button) and then apply the formatting.

Changing line style

Every shape has an outline, usually a thin black line. Not only can you change the color of the line, you can change the *weight* (thickness) of it as well as the pattern and transparency. You can make it fat and green and dash-dot-dashed, or dainty and pink and dot-dash-dotted. If you decide you don't like square corners, you can round them.

When you work with a 1-D shape like a simple line, you can also add line ends (such as arrows) to the beginning or end of the shape, and determine the size of the line ends. The Line dialog box (shown in Figure 8-20) has a preview window so you can see the changes you make.

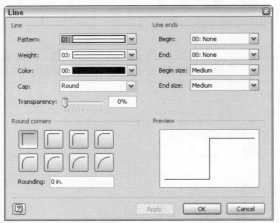

Figure 8-20:
Use the Line dialog box to change many characteristics of a shape's outline or a line itself.

Follow these steps to make changes to a shape's line characteristics:

1. **Select the shape or shapes that you want to change.**

2. **Choose Format⇨Line, or right-click and choose Format⇨Line.**

   Visio displays the Line dialog box, as shown in Figure 8-20.

3. **In the Pattern box, click the down arrow and choose a line pattern.**

4. **In the Weight box, choose a line thickness.**

5. **In the Color box, choose a line color.**

6. **In the Cap box, choose blunt lines (Square) or soft lines (Round).**

7. **To change the transparency of the line, slide the Transparency bar.**

8. **To round the corners of your shape, click one of the rounding styles in the Round Corners area.**

   If you want the rounding to be a specific size (such as beginning ⅛ inch from the corner), type a decimal number in the Rounding box.

9. **If your shape is 1-D, choose line ends and their size in the Begin, End, Begin Size, and End Size boxes.**

10. **View your choices in the Preview area.**

11. **When the shape appears as you want it, click OK.**

In the next section you learn that you can also set the transparency of the fill in a 2-D shape. If you change the shape's fill transparency, it also affects the transparency of the shape's line (whether you change it using the previous steps or not).

Visio provides five buttons, shown in Table 8-3, to apply line style changes without opening a menu. These buttons appear on the Formatting and

Format Shape toolbars, which you can display by choosing View⇨Toolbars⇨ Format and View⇨Toolbars⇨Format Shape. To use any of these buttons, first select the shape or shapes you want to change, and then click the tiny down arrow next to the button to display a list of choices.

Table 8-3		Toolbar Buttons for Changing Line Styles	
Button	*Name*	*Toolbar*	*What It Does*
	Line Color	Formatting	Lets you choose the line color for the selected shape
	Line Weight	Formatting	Lets you choose the line thickness for the selected shape
	Line Pattern	Formatting	Lets you choose the line pattern for the selected shape
	Line Ends	Formatting	Lets you choose endpoints for a line
	Corner Rounding	Format Shape	Lets you choose a line corner style for 2-D shapes

Adding fill color, pattern, and shadow

White, white, white can become monotonous after awhile. Why not add some excitement to your shapes by making them patterned and colorful with shadows? Color and shadows aren't just aesthetic qualities; they also attract attention, hold interest, and help the reader interpret data more easily.

Filling a shape with a solid color is straightforward. Just choose the color and that's that. If you fill a shape with a pattern, however, you have to choose two colors — one for the foreground and one for the background. The foreground color comprises the pattern, such as dots, hash marks, stripes, or crisscrosses. The background color is the one that shows through the pattern. Often, patterns show up in black and white, so you don't even think about the possibility of choosing colors for the foreground and background. You can use black and white in Visio as well, but it's good to know what foreground and background colors are so that you get the results you expect.

A shape's shadow doesn't have to be a solid color. You can choose a shadow style, pattern, foreground color, background color, and transparency for the shadow as well.

Follow these steps to add any of these colorful features to a shape:

1. **Select the shape or shapes that you want to change.**

2. **Choose Format⇨Fill, or right-click and choose Format⇨Fill.**

   The Fill dialog box appears, as shown in Figure 8-21.

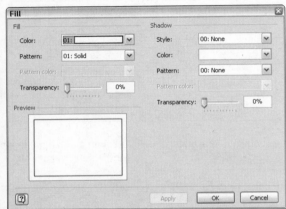

Figure 8-21:
Use the Fill dialog box to change a shape's fill and shadow characteristics.

3. **In the Fill area, choose the color, pattern, pattern color, and transparency.**

4. **In the Shadow area, choose style, color, pattern, pattern color, and transparency.**

   The Preview area shows a sample of the choices that you selected.

5. **Click OK.**

   Visio returns to your drawing and reformats the selected shape.

To make further refinements to the shadow (beyond what's available in the Fill dialog box), choose Format⇨Shadow, which displays the Shadow dialog box. Here you can also change the size, position, offset, direction, and magnification of a shadow. To change these settings, select the shape you want to change, and then choose Format⇨Shadow.

Visio also provides timesaving toolbar buttons for fill color, transparency, fill pattern, and shadow color, as shown in Table 8-4. Select a shape or shapes you want to change, and then click the down arrow next to the button to display a list of choices.

Table 8-4		Toolbar Buttons for Changing Fills and Shadows	
Button	*Name*	*Toolbar*	*What It Does*
	Fill Color	Formatting	Lets you choose a fill color for 2-D shapes
	Transparency	Format Shape	Lets you set a transparency level for the fill and the line
	Fill Pattern	Format Shape	Lets you choose a fill pattern for 2-D shapes
	Shadow Color	Format Shape	Lets you choose the shadow color, the style, and other settings for 2-D shapes

Copying formats

Suppose that you painstakingly format a shape with a purple and red patterned fill, a burgundy and chartreuse shadow, and a 4-point, canary, dotted outline. (No one ever accused you of having an eye for color!) Now you want to apply those lovely colors and styles to another shape. Do you have to set all these features by hand again? Nope. Visio makes it easy for you. Ever notice that paint brush button on your Standard toolbar? It's called the Format Painter button, and it lets you paint a format from one shape to another. This truly is a timesaving feature. Use it often!

Follow these steps to copy a format from one shape to another:

1. **Click the shape that has the format you want to copy.**

2. **Click the Format Painter button (refer to Table 8-1) on the Standard toolbar.**

   Your mouse pointer changes to a paint brush.

3. **Click the shape that you want to apply the format to.**

   Presto! All that beautiful color and style is instantly copied to your shape.

Reformatting a shape

So, you decide that you don't like violet polka dots on an orange background with a green frame and a green and purple crisscross shadow pattern. How do you get rid of it? Unfortunately, you can't click a button that magically removes all the formatting that you add to a shape.

You have to reset line, fill, pattern, and shadow features the same way that you added them: using Format➪Line, Format➪Fill, and Format➪Shadow commands, or using the toolbar buttons. But you can reformat one shape and then use the Format Painter button again to paint a plain style onto other shapes. That's the quickest way to undo what you did.

Managing Shapes by Grouping

Nothing is more frustrating than spending a good deal of time creating a shape out of many shapes, getting everything perfectly aligned, and then messing it all up when you try to move it or resize it. One way to avoid this is to group shapes so that they behave as a unit.

In Figure 8-22, the computer on the left is a *grouped* shape (it's selected as a unit). The computer in the center is not grouped because you can select all the parts individually. On the right side of the figure, the computer's individual parts are spread out so that you can see how complex the shape is.

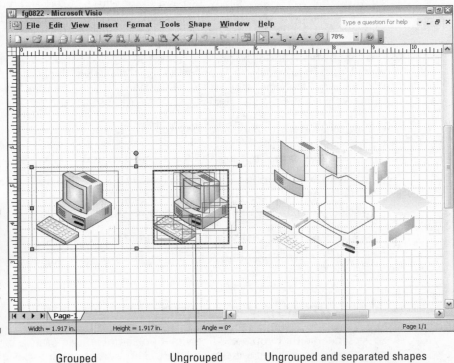

Figure 8-22:
Grouped shapes are often more complex than they appear.

Grouped   Ungrouped   Ungrouped and separated shapes

This figure shows the importance of grouping. Ungrouped, it's easy to accidentally drag the screen off without the monitor. Grouped, there's no chance of that happening. Grouping also enables you to size, rotate, flip, and otherwise treat the whole shape as a unit.

Creating groups

You can group any set of shapes that you select; their proximity to one another makes no difference! (The group you create has to make sense only to you!) The steps that follow specify menu commands as well as toolbar buttons, which are shown in Table 8-5.

Table 8-5	Action Toolbar Buttons for Grouping Shapes	
Button	*Name*	*What It Does*
	Group	Groups all selected shapes
	Ungroup	Ungroups the selected shape

To create a group, use these steps:

1. **Select all the shapes that you want to group.**
2. **Choose Shape⇨Grouping⇨Group or click the Group button on the Action toolbar.**

   Visio reframes the shapes with a single frame and handles.

To ungroup a shape, follow these steps:

1. **Select the grouped shape.**
2. **Choose Shape⇨Grouping⇨Ungroup or click the Ungroup button on the Shape toolbar.**

   Visio separates the grouped shape into its original shapes and selects each one individually.

If you prefer to use shortcut keys, you can press Ctrl+Shift+G for Group and Ctrl+Shift+U for Ungroup.

Editing a group

When you click a group, Visio selects the entire group. Clicking a component shape in that group lets you *subselect* just that component. When you click a group once, you see green selection handles around the entire group. Click again on a member of the group to subselect it. You see green selection handles for only that shape, and the handles that defined the boundaries of the entire group change to a faint line of gray dashes.

This feature of subselecting allows you to easily edit a shape in a group (You don't have to ungroup shapes to edit an individual shape.) After you subselect a shape, you can move it, resize it, reshape it, change its line color, fill it, or make any other changes without affecting other shapes in the group. When you finish making changes, click anywhere outside the group or press Esc to deselect the shape.

If you prefer to have Visio select members of a group with the first mouse click and then select the entire group with a second mouse click, you can set Visio to behave this way. Or maybe you prefer to have Visio select only the group and *never* subselect shapes. This is another option you can set.

To change the way Visio selects groups, use these steps:

1. **Click a grouped shape.**

2. **Choose Format⇨Behavior.**

   The Behavior tab in the Behavior dialog box appears. Look in the Group Behavior area of the dialog box.

3. **Indicate your preference in the Selection drop-down list:**

   • To disable subselecting, choose Group Only.

   • To change back to Visio's default setting, in which you select a group with a single click and individual shapes with a second mouse click, choose Group First.

   • To select members of a group with a single click and the entire group with a second mouse click, choose Members First.

4. **Click OK.**

Adding a shape to a group

Sometimes when you create a group, you'll want to add another shape to the group. Visio has a special command for adding shapes to an existing group. Use these steps:

1. **Select the shape to which you want to add a shape.**

   Visio displays the shape's selection frame and handles.

2. **Select the shape you want to add.**

   Visio adds the shape to the selection frame.

3. **Choose Shape⇨Grouping⇨Add to Group.**

   Visio adds the shape to the group selection frame.

Never create a group, add shapes to it, and then group it again. Adding shapes to an already-grouped group creates what Visio calls a *nested* group. Each time you group a group, the file size increases unnecessarily and performance (load time and save time) declines.

Removing a shape from a group

You can remove a shape from an existing group just as easily as you can add one. Just click the group to select it, and then click the component of the group that you want to remove. Visio displays the selection frame and handles for just that component shape. Choose Shape⇨Grouping⇨Remove from Group. Visio removes the component from the group. The shape remains in the drawing but is now ungrouped from the original group.

Adding text to grouped shapes

Normally if you double-click a shape, Visio displays the shape's text block so you can add or edit text. But you can't double-click a shape in a group to display its text box. To add text to a shape that's part of a group, you need to use a separate window.

Follow these steps:

1. **Select the group.**

2. **Choose Edit⇨Open Group.**

   Visio opens a separate window and zooms in on the group.

3. **In this window, double-click the shape that you want to add text to.**

   Visio zooms in on the shape's text block.

4. **Type the text you want to add to the shape, and then press Esc or click somewhere outside the text block.**

5. **Click the window's Close button.**

   Visio returns to your drawing window, and the text you added appears in the shape.

Chapter 9

Working with Pages

*J*ust about now you may be thinking, "A page is a page; what's to know? Pretty boring stuff." There's a lot to know about pages in Visio! Visio files aren't like documents, where text flows smoothly from one page to the next with a few interesting figures thrown in here and there. Some drawings have only one page; others may have multiple pages. And in Visio, pages are independent animals. You can set a different page size, orientation, drawing scale, background, shadow, and even header and footer for each page in a single Visio file. You can also rotate a page to make drawing angled lines and shapes easier — and then rotate it back again when you've finished drawing. This makes Visio flexible, but it also makes it more complex than your average text editor.

The Role of the Template

A template is designed to make creating a drawing easier because it sets up a drawing scale (such as a typical architectural scale of ¼ inch:1 foot), and it automatically opens the stencils that you need to create a particular type of drawing (such as the Office Layout stencil for creating a space plan). See Chapter 2 if you need a refresher on using templates to create a Visio file.

A template also sets up the size of the drawing page and the printer paper (both usually 8½ by 11 inches) and the orientation of the page (portrait or landscape). You need to be aware of these settings when you work with pages in a drawing. Using a template is a definite advantage because it automatically matches the size and orientation of the drawing page to the size and orientation of the printed page, which ensures that your drawing prints correctly.

Drawing page size refers to the drawing area that you see on the screen, *printer paper* refers to the paper you print on, and *printed drawing* refers to the drawing as printed on paper. (See Chapter 3 for more details on these printing terms.)

Reorienting a Page

Suppose that you're creating a network diagram in portrait orientation, and you realize that the drawing is too wide to fit on 8½-inch-wide paper. You can change the paper orientation to landscape rather than adjust the layout of your drawing. Switching to landscape orientation turns your drawing page 90 degrees so that its width is greater than its length.

When you change the orientation of your drawing page, however, you need to make sure that the printer settings match. Follow these steps:

1. **Choose File➪Page Setup.**

   The Page Setup dialog box appears.

2. **If the Print Setup tab isn't selected, select it now (see Figure 9-1).**

3. **In the Printer Paper area, click either Portrait or Landscape.**

4. **Click the Page Size tab (shown in Figure 9-2).**

   Note that Visio changes the Page Size to the orientation you chose in Step 2. The preview looks identical to the one shown on the Print Setup tab. The printer paper and drawing page orientations match because the Same as Printer Paper Size option is selected by default.

5. **Click OK.**

When you switch page orientation, the shapes in your drawing don't mysteriously disappear or get erased, but it's possible that some of them are either straddling the page borders or are completely off the page (see Figure 9-3).

You just moved the boundaries of the page, but the shapes are placed where they always were (within the old page boundaries — sort of like the Incredible Hulk bursting out of his shirt). Now that you have new boundaries, you need to move your shapes to get them back onto the drawing page.

Choose a page orientation

Figure 9-1:
You can change the orientation for a page on the Print Setup tab of the Page Setup dialog box.

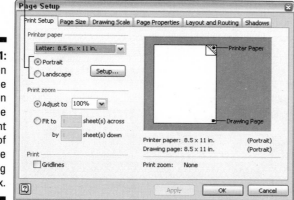

Figure 9-2:
The preview on the Page Size tab shows that the drawing page size and printer paper size match.

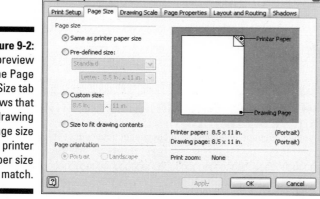

 Choosing Tools➪Center Drawing helps you begin rearranging shapes by placing the drawing in the center of the new page boundaries. You may still need to move some shapes around to fit them on the page, but the Center Drawing option gives you a head start.

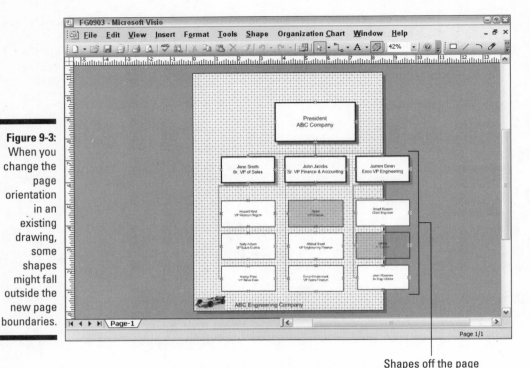

Figure 9-3:
When you
change the
page
orientation
in an
existing
drawing,
some
shapes
might fall
outside the
new page
boundaries.

Shapes off the page

Setting a Page Size

Page size refers to the size of your drawing; it has nothing to do with the paper size in your printer. For most documents, we match our page size (drawing size) to our paper size, whether the paper is standard size (8½ x 11 inches) or legal size (8½ x 14 inches). Drawings, however, are often a different animal from standard text documents. Drawings can come in all shapes and sizes, especially in engineering and architectural fields. Some drawings won't fit on standard-size paper and must be printed across several sheets (unless you're fortunate enough to have a plotter).

Visio lets you determine your drawing page size in the following ways:

- ✔ Using predefined sizes
- ✔ Entering custom measurements
- ✔ Using the drawing content as size boundaries

Letting Visio determine the size based on the drawing content is a good one to choose when you want your drawing to fill the entire page.

Some of the predefined sizes you can choose from include Metric (such as 148 x 210 millimeters), ANSI Engineering (such as 22 x 34 inches), and ANSI Architectural (such as 24 x 36 inches).

Drawing pages are independent, even when they belong to the same Visio file. This means you can make different pages in a file different sizes.

For all three methods of sizing your drawing, you use the Page Size tab in the Page Setup dialog box, as follows:

1. **Choose File⇨Page Setup.**

2. **Click the Page Size tab (see Figure 9-4).**

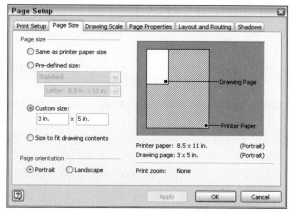

Figure 9-4: Set the size of your drawing on the Page Size tab of the Page Setup dialog box.

3. **Click one of the following options for the page size:**

   • **Same as Printer Paper Size:** Sets your drawing size to the same size as your printer paper.

   • **Pre-Defined Size:** Uses a predefined size in one of the following categories: Standard, Metric, ANSI Engineering, or ANSI Architectural. For this option, you select a category in the top box and then select a size in the category you chose.

   • **Custom Size:** Enables you to set a custom size. Type the width in the first box, followed by the length in the second box. (Type *in* for inches or *mm* for millimeters following the number.)

   • **Size to Fit Drawing Contents:** Sizes the drawing based on its contents.

4. **Click OK.**

Setting a custom size can be useful if you're printing on nonstandard-sized paper. You can also use this option to *position* or *isolate* a drawing on standard-sized paper. For example, suppose that you want to print a 3-x-5-inch Visio drawing in the upper-left corner of an 8½-x-11-inch piece of paper and leave the remaining white space for reviewers to write comments. When you set a unique page size that's smaller than your paper, the drawing prints in the upper-left corner of the page.

Keep in mind that if you reduce the page size of an existing drawing, the shapes in that drawing don't move or change size. If some of the shapes are outside the new page dimensions, you need to move them inside.

You can also change the size of your drawing page dynamically by dragging the page edges with your mouse. (This method saves you the trouble of opening the Page Setup dialog box.) Here's how it works:

1. **Display the drawing page that you want to change.**

2. **Click the Pointer Tool button on the Standard toolbar.**

3. **Press and hold down the Ctrl key and move the mouse pointer over the edge of the drawing page that you want to drag.**

   The mouse pointer changes to a double-headed arrow (horizontal or vertical, depending on the page edge you chose).

4. **Drag the mouse in the direction you want to expand (or contract) the borders.**

   A dotted outline shows the location of the new page dimensions, as shown in Figure 9-5.

   To resize the page's height and width at the same time, move the mouse pointer near (but not directly on) one of the page's corners. The double-headed mouse pointer now points diagonally.

5. **Still holding the Ctrl key, drag the mouse until the page is the size that you want, noting the page dimensions on the status bar.**

To see how your drawing page size differs from the current paper size settings, choose File➪Page Setup. To change the paper size, click the Print Setup tab in the Page Setup dialog box. Refer to Chapter 3 for more information about printing.

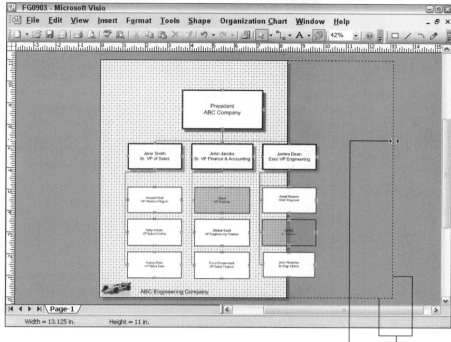

Mouse pointer for resizing   New page
dimensions

Adding and Deleting Pages in a Drawing

When you create a new Visio drawing, it includes only one page. You can add
pages to a drawing. Following are some good reasons for doing so:

- **Keep a set of related drawings,** such as a collection of maps with driving
  directions for your city, on separate pages in one Visio file.

- **Use pages to create overview drawings and detail drawings** of your
  corporate, regional, and branch organization charts, for example. You
  can even add *jumps*, similar to links between Web sites, from one page to
  another. (See Chapter 14 for more on adding jumps.)

✔ **Use pages to keep track of the history and revisions of a drawing,** which can work something like this: Page 1 is the original draft, Page 2 is the second draft, Page 3 is the review drawing, Page 4 is the revised drawing, Page 5 is the second review drawing, and Page 6 is the final drawing.

✔ **Create a mini-slideshow** with a series of drawings on separate pages and present them in full-screen view.

✔ **Include your company name and logo on background pages** so that the logo shows through on every page without being part of your drawing. The icing on the cake is that each page in your drawing can have its own background page, so you can vary the background content from page to page. (Background pages are discussed in detail in the "What's in a Background?" section, later in this chapter.)

You can add as many pages to a drawing as you like. Pages are always added at the end of the drawing, so technically speaking, you can't *insert* pages between other pages (even though Visio uses that terminology). You can, however, reorder pages, as I show you later in the "Reordering pages" section. The new page that you add takes on all the attributes of the page that's currently displayed. If you want to change some of these attributes, you can do so when you create the page or later, using the File➪Page Setup command.

Use these steps to add a page to a drawing:

1. **In your drawing, display the page with the attributes that you want the new page to have.**

   (Of course, that would be the *only* page in your drawing if you haven't added a second page yet!)

2. **Right-click the page tab at the bottom of the drawing window, or choose Insert➪New Page.**

   The Page Properties tab of the Page Setup dialog box appears, as shown in Figure 9-6. Visio suggests a temporary name in the Name box.

3. **For the Type, select Foreground to create a "regular" Visio drawing page.**

   I explain all about background pages later in the "What's in a Background?" section.

4. **In the Name field, type a new name or use the suggested name.**

   At this point, you're free to click the Page Size or Drawing Scale tab to change settings for the new page. However, this isn't necessary if you want the new page to take on the attributes of the page that you displayed in Step 1.

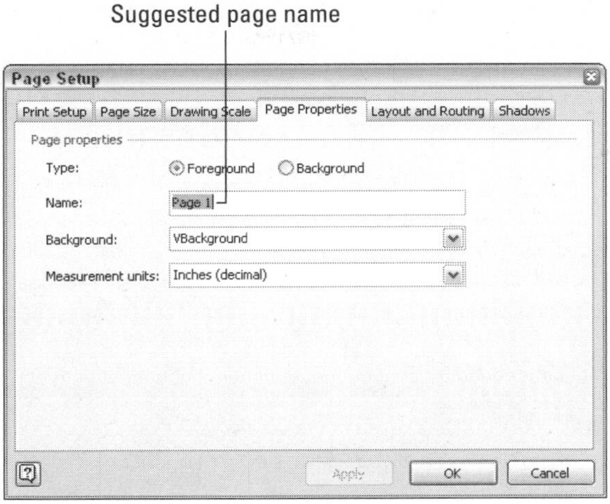

Suggested page name

Figure 9-6:
Set
attributes
for a new
page.

5. **Click OK.**

The new page appears after all the other pages in the drawing, and a tab is added at the bottom of the drawing window.

The precise term for a drawing page is *foreground page*. The foreground page gets its name because it appears in front of the background page. See the "What's in a Background?" section, later in this chapter, for more information about creating and using background pages.

Sometimes after you add a page to a drawing you decide later that you want to delete it. You can delete one page at a time quickly just by right-clicking the page tab and choosing Delete Page. If you have several pages that you want to delete and would rather use a dialog box, follow these steps:

1. **Choose Edit⇨Delete Pages.**

The Delete Pages dialog box appears and lists all the pages in the drawing by name, as shown in Figure 9-7.

2. **Click the page or pages that you want to delete.**

To select a contiguous range of pages, click the first page, and then hold the Shift key and select the last page. To select a noncontiguous range of pages, hold the Ctrl key as you click each page name.

3. **Click OK.**

Visio removes the page or pages from the drawing and closes the dialog box.

Figure 9-7:
Select the
page you
want to
delete.

Working with Multiple Pages

A drawing with multiple pages is more complex than a single-page drawing. You need to know how to get from one page to another and how to rearrange pages, if necessary. You also might find it useful to display more than one page at a time so you can compare pages. Read on to find out how to work with multiple pages in a drawing.

Getting from one page to another

When you add pages to a drawing, Visio creates a tab at the bottom of the drawing area identifying the page. Clicking a page tab is by far the fastest way to switch from one page to another. If your file contains just a few pages, all tabs are usually visible at one time. If your file contains many pages, all the tabs can't be displayed at once at the bottom of the window. In that case, use the scroll buttons to the left of the page tabs to go to the first page, previous page, next page, or last page.

Displaying multiple pages at once

When your drawing contains multiple pages, viewing more than one page at a time lets you compare one page to another quickly and easily. It also lets you edit each page without repeatedly closing one and opening another. Visio opens another page in a separate window. Use these steps to open additional page windows:

1. Choose Edit⇨Go To⇨Page option.

(The Page option is at the bottom of the submenu.) The Page dialog box appears, and lists all the pages in the drawing.

2. Click the page that you want to view.

3. Click the Open Page in New Window option, as shown in Figure 9-8.

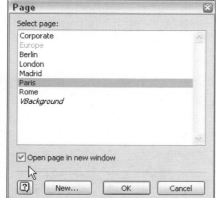

Figure 9-8:
Choose a page to display using the Page dialog box.

4. Click OK.

Visio opens the page in a new window.

5. Repeat Steps 1 through 4 to open additional pages in a new window.

Each time you open a new page, it becomes the current page on your screen, so you still aren't viewing multiple windows yet. You won't see them until you change the way they are displayed.

Choose Window⇨Tile or Window⇨Cascade to arrange the open windows on your screen. The Tile option displays all open page windows next to each other on the screen like tiles on the floor.

The Cascade option staggers the windows so that the title bar of each window is visible. The title bar looks similar to this: *MeetingRoom:1,* where *MeetingRoom* is the file name for the drawing and *1* is the number of the page window you opened. The second page window you opened would be called *MeetingRoom:2.* (Note that the number in the title bar does not correspond to the page number in the drawing; it refers only to the order in which you opened additional pages.)

Reordering pages

When you add pages to a drawing, Visio automatically adds them to the end of the drawing (although the menu name is Insert — go figure). Because Visio doesn't let you insert pages in a drawing (such as between Pages 3 and 4), the only way to put new pages in the order that you want them is to reorder them.

Reordering pages in Visio couldn't be easier! Just drag the page tab (at the bottom of the drawing window) and drop it in the spot you want. As you drag the page tab, the mouse pointer displays a small page and a small arrowhead appears just above the tabs to indicate where the page will be inserted when you release the mouse button (see Figure 9-9).

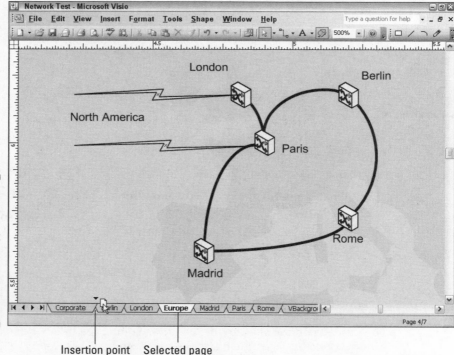

Figure 9-9:
Drag the page tab and drop it where you want to move the selected page.

Insertion point   Selected page

Renaming Pages

If you named a page with your own title when you created it (or even if you didn't), you might decide to change the title later. You can change the title of a page at any time using one of two methods.

The first and easiest is to simply right-click the page tab at the bottom of the drawing window and choose Rename Page. Visio highlights the page name on the tab. Type the new page name right on the tab and press Enter. This method works for both foreground and background pages.

If the page has a background assigned to it, the name change doesn't affect the association between the background and foreground pages. For more information about background pages, see the "What's in a Background?" section, later in this chapter.

If you prefer to use a dialog box to rename a page, use these steps:

1. **Display the page you want to change in the drawing window.**
2. **Choose File⇨Page Setup to display the Page Setup dialog box.**
3. **Click the Page Properties tab.**
4. **In the Name box, type the page's new title.**
5. **Click OK.**

   Visio changes the displayed name on the page tab.

Viewing on the Big Screen

If you want to see how your drawing will look on the printed page, you can always use the Print Preview button on the Standard toolbar (refer to Chapter 3 for information about using Print Preview). But Print Preview is more for checking final details before you print. What if you want to view your drawing pages like a miniature slide show? You can display your drawing using the *entire* screen, without title bars, menu bars, status bars, scroll bars, or any other windows. You can even control the drawing like a slide show, moving forward or backward through the pages.

Using the entire screen is a great way to create a mini presentation for a small group of viewers. Because you don't need a slide projector, you avoid the hassle of setting up special equipment.

Use these steps to view pages in full-screen mode:

1. **Display the first page of your drawing.**

2. **Choose View⇨Full Screen, or press F5.**

   Visio switches to full-screen mode and displays the first page of your drawing.

3. **To move to another page:**

   • To move to the next page, press N, the Page Down key, the right-arrow key, or the left mouse button

   • To move to the previous page, press P, the Page Up key, or the left-arrow key

4. **Press Esc or F5 to return to the Visio screen.**

You can navigate pages also using the pop-up menu shown in Figure 9-10. To display this menu, click the right mouse button. Using the pop-up menu is important if you're on Page 3, say, and want to move quickly to Page 42.

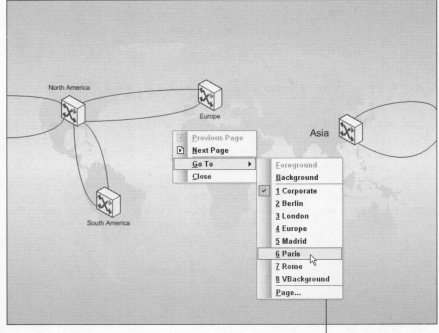

Figure 9-10: In full-screen mode, all of Visio's menus, toolbars, task panes, and other window attributes are hidden.

Shortcut menu for navigation

Hyperlinks — shapes that you click to go to another page — are a cool feature of Visio. If your drawing contains hyperlinks, you can click the hyperlink shape to leap to the link. For details about adding hyperlinks to a drawing, see Chapter 14.

What's in a Background?

As if foreground pages weren't enough, you can also add background pages to a drawing. Why would you want to do that? The best answer is that they offer consistency. If you want to show a file name, a date, a company name, a logo, a page number, or any other information about a drawing — but you don't want it on your drawing page — you can put all that information on a background page. Using a background page is sort of like printing your drawing on a transparency and slipping the background page underneath. The information on the background page shows through the transparency — visible and printable — but the drawing itself isn't mucked up with all sorts of extraneous information.

The technical term for a drawing page is *foreground page*. The foreground page gets its name because it appears in the forefront, or in front of a background page.

You can create as many background pages as you want in a drawing file. What can you do with a background? You *assign* it to a foreground page. Assigning makes the association between the two. You can assign

- A single background page to one or more foreground pages
- A different background page to each foreground page
- A background page to another background page

The most important rule to remember is that you *can't* assign more than one background page to any one foreground page. So what can you do if you want a foreground page to have more than one background? You can piggyback background pages on a foreground page by assigning a background to a background and then assigning that background to a foreground. Clear as mud? Figure 9-11 illustrates how pages can be assigned to one another.

Creating and assigning a background page

Background pages aren't useful by themselves. To use a background page, you must create it and then *assign* it to another page. Unassigned, you can still print a background page, but it prints by itself, without any foreground information.

To create a background page, follow these steps:

1. **Display any page in your drawing.**

2. **Choose Insert➪New Page.**

   Visio displays the Page Properties tab in the Page Setup dialog box. (Refer to Figure 9-6.)

3. **For Type, click the Background option.**

4. **In the Name box, use the default name (Background-1, Background-2, and so on) or type a new name.**

5. **In the Background box, choose None.**

6. **In the Measurement Units box, choose the units you want to use for the background page.**

7. **Click OK.**

That's all there is to creating a background page. Next, you add the information you want the background page to contain. For details on that, see the upcoming "Editing a background page" section.

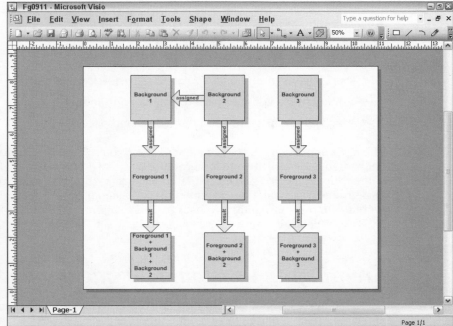

Figure 9-11:
You can assign a background page to either foreground or background pages.

The last step — and it's an important one — is to assign the background page to another page (foreground or background) in the drawing. Until you assign it, it just sits there in the drawing doing nothing.

To assign the background page, follow these steps:

1. **Display the page that you want to assign the background page to.**

   Think of this as the parent page.

2. **Choose File⇨Page Setup.**

   The Page Setup dialog box is displayed.

3. **Click the Page Properties tab.**

   The Name field displays the name of the current page.

4. **Click the Background drop-down arrow.**

   All background pages that you created are listed here. Click the one that you want to assign to the page you displayed in Step 1.

5. **Click OK.**

   Visio creates the association between the two pages, closes the dialog box, and returns to your drawing.

Unassigning a background page

At some point you might change your mind about which foreground page a background page is assigned to. You can always *unassign* a background page. Unassigning breaks the association between two pages. Unassigning doesn't delete the background page; it just leaves it sitting unassigned until you choose to assign it again.

To unassign a background page, display the background page in the drawing area, and then return to the Page Properties tab in the Page Setup dialog box. Choose None in the Background box, and then click OK. In the drawing, the Background page (and page tab) still exist, but unassigned to any other page.

Displaying a background page

When you assign a background page to another page, the content of the background page is displayed on the screen whenever you display its foreground page. This can sometimes be distracting if you're still working on or creating your foreground page. If you don't want the background page content to be displayed while you're working on the foreground page, you must unassign the background from the foreground. See the preceding section to unassign a background page.

Editing a background page

Because a background page is just a drawing page, you edit it just as you do a foreground page. Display the background page by clicking the page tab at the bottom of the drawing window. You can add, delete, move, or format shapes or text on the background page just like on any other page.

Are you driving yourself crazy trying to select a shape that refuses to be selected? That's probably because the shape is on the background page assigned to your foreground page. It just appears to be on the foreground page. It's hard to tell which is which because Visio makes no distinction between foreground and background pages on the screen.

Using a background shape

Visio provides some special shapes designed just for background pages. They are provided to add interest and style to your drawings. Most of the backgrounds are abstract designs, although some represent real-world objects or scenes such as world maps, city scenes, or mountains. Background shapes are usually set to high transparency so that the shapes in your drawing show through easily.

Background shapes reside on their own stencil called Backgrounds. To display them, choose File➪Shapes➪Visio Extras➪Backgrounds. To use a background shape, just open the Backgrounds stencil and drag a shape onto your drawing. An example is shown in Figure 9-12.

Background shapes can't be placed on foreground pages. If you have a simple one-page drawing (without a background page) and drag a background shape into the drawing, Visio automatically creates a background page, places the shape there, and assigns that background to the foreground page.

Background shapes fill the entire page, regardless of the size of your drawing page. So if you start with a page size for your background page of 8½ x 11, and then change it to 3 x 5, the background shape automatically resizes to fill the page.

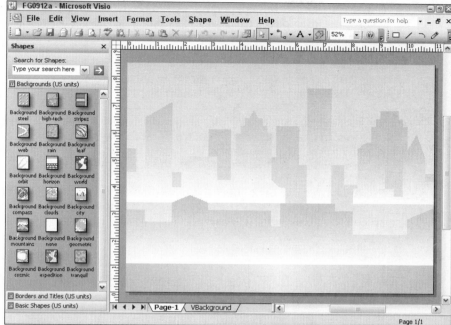

Figure 9-12:
The
cityscape
is a
background
shape.

Rotating Pages

The best computer software programs are designed to work the way you worked before you had the program. Think about the following example. If you were to use a pencil and paper to draw a map of a city in which streets fall at odd angles, you would probably draw all the streets that run parallel to the edges of your paper (or the grid, if you use graph paper) and then *turn the paper at an angle* and draw the angular streets, right? You can work exactly the same way in Visio by rotating a drawing page. The program lets you work the way you work when you're drawing on paper. Pretty cool, huh?

When you rotate a page, the shapes stay in position, just like they do when you rotate a piece of paper. *Guides,* those vertical and horizontal lines you drag into your drawing from the rulers to help you place shapes, also stay in position when you rotate a page. (To review creating and using guides, see Chapter 7.) When you know that you're going to rotate a page, you can use guides as a custom grid.

Unlike on your drawing paper, rulers and the drawing page grid *do not* rotate when you turn a page. This is a good thing — you can always maintain a horizontal and vertical baseline from which to work, regardless of the angle of the paper.

Figure 9-13 shows a city map. I drew the angled streets after rotating the page 60 degrees, then rotated the page back again.

Figure 9-14 shows the same city map rotated 60 degrees. (The angle is noted in the status bar at the bottom of the screen.) Notice that the grid remains parallel to the rulers bordering the drawing area. I didn't need guides to draw the streets because I was able to use the grid as my guide.

Rotating a page doesn't affect the page orientation settings (that is, portrait or landscape) or the way the page prints. Page rotation is simply an on-screen tool to aid you in drawing.

Use these steps to rotate a page:

1. **Click the Pointer Tool button on the Standard toolbar.**

2. **Display the drawing page you want to rotate by clicking its page tab.**

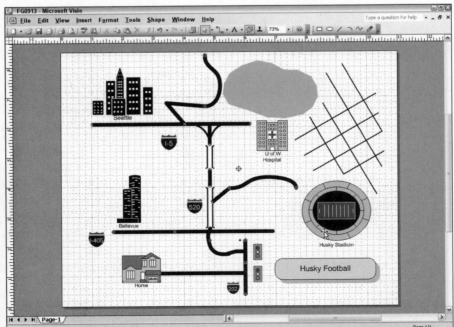

Figure 9-13:
Angled streets would be a challenge to draw without the benefit of page rotation.

Grid is parallel to rulers

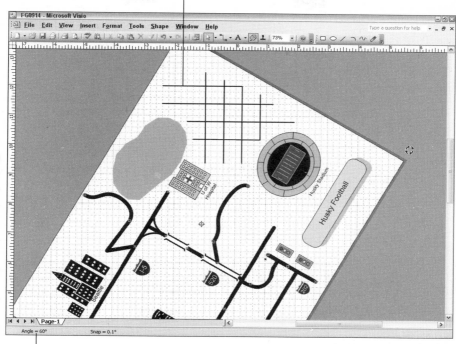

Figure 9-14:
It's easy to draw the angled streets using the grid as your guide when you rotate the drawing at an angle.

Page angle

3. **Press and hold down the Ctrl key and then move the mouse pointer over any corner of the page.**

   The pointer changes to a circular rotation pointer.

4. **Drag the mouse either clockwise or counterclockwise, depending on the direction that you want to rotate the page.**

   To rotate to a specific angle, watch the status bar as you drag the page; it tells you the exact angle (in degrees) of the page as you rotate it.

   The farther you move the mouse pointer away from the page corner, the more precise the angle you can choose.

5. **Release the mouse button and the Ctrl key when the page is rotated to the angle that you want.**

After you try rotating a drawing page, you'll realize how useful this feature is, whether you're drawing street maps or any other type of drawing requiring angled lines.

Chapter 10

Layering Your Drawings

*V*isio defines a layer as a named category of shapes. Huh? How about a more vivid description? When you were a kid, did you ever have one of those cool anatomy books with the transparent sheets? The bottom sheet had the skeletal structure, the next sheet had internal organs, and then you added the nervous system, the muscular structure, and finally the skin? Well, the layer system in Visio works in much the same way. You can create layers in a Visio drawing for the same purpose as your old anatomy book: to show groups or categories of shapes independently of others or as part of the whole.

How can you use layers? In a landscape drawing, you may want to include structural walls and pathways on one layer; grass, ground cover, and small shrubs on another; trees on a separate layer; and ornamental flowers on another layer. Another example is a layout for a building or home in which the walls, doors, and windows appear on one layer, and the wiring, electrical system, plumbing, and HVAC (heating, ventilation, and air conditioning) system appear on individual layers. You can display just one layer to view the shapes in a particular group or display all layers to view the complete plan.

Getting the Essential Facts on Layers and Layering

You need to know the essential facts about layers so that you can make decisions about how and when to use them. Don't let all of these facts scare you off! As you read the following list, try to form a mental picture of what's going on:

- ✔ A Visio drawing can have more than one page.

- ✔ Each page can have its own set of layers.

- ✔ Visio automatically assigns some shapes to predefined layers (based on the template that you choose).

- ✔ A shape can be assigned to (and therefore, appear on) one or more layers. (This is the only point for which our anatomy book example doesn't hold true: A liver or spleen, for example, appears only on the internal organs sheet; you don't find it duplicated on the skeletal structure sheet or the nervous system sheet.)

- ✔ A Visio page (with or without layers) can have one or more background pages.

- ✔ Although similar in behavior, a background page is not the same as a layer! A background page can have its own layers.

Confused yet? It becomes clearer if you keep in mind an image of one transparent sheet as a *layer*, a stack of transparent sheets as a *page*, and multiple stacks as separate pages in a *drawing*. (See Figure 10-1.) Although a Visio background page is also transparent, its purpose is to display repetitive information (such as a company logo or the document's title and date) rather than a category of shapes, as a layer does. If the bottom transparent sheet of the anatomy book had only a title, such as "The Human Body," it would be analogous to a Visio background page. (For information on creating multiple pages and background pages in a Visio drawing, check out Chapter 9.)

When you want to group and display categories of shapes in a drawing, use layers. When you want repetitive information to appear on each page of a drawing, use a background page.

In general, you *assign* shapes to a specific layer or to more than one layer. However, some Visio templates include predefined layers. In these cases, the shapes in the template's stencils are preassigned to a particular layer. (The layers aren't added to your drawing until you use the shapes in your drawing.) When you drag a shape onto the drawing page, Visio automatically creates the layer or layers to which that shape is preassigned. When you drag another shape that's preassigned to a different layer or layers, Visio adds those layers to the drawing.

The Building Plan/Office Layout template is a good example of a template with predefined layers. Some of the layers in this template are

- **The building envelope** (exterior walls, doors, windows)
- **Computer** (all computer-related equipment)
- **Equipment** (fax, copy machines)
- **Furniture** (desks, chairs, tables)
- **Movable furnishings** (plants, lamps, coat racks)
- **Nonmovable furnishings** (corner work surfaces, panels)
- **Wall** (shapes that delineate floor space)

Page

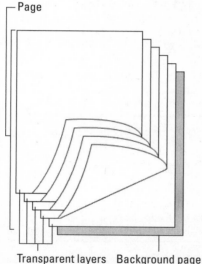

Figure 10-1:
Think of layers as transparent sheets that make up a page.

Transparent layers   Background page

The Building Plan/Office Layout template contains a reasonable number of layers — less than a dozen. Other templates, such as the Building Plan/Space Plan template, contain several dozen layers. The number and type of shapes you include in a drawing determine the exact number of layers that the drawing has.

If you add a page to your drawing, it doesn't contain any layers until you drag into the drawing a shape that's preassigned to a layer or you create a layer, as I describe in the "Adding a layer and removing one" section later in this chapter.

Working with Layers

As you might suspect, there are many different operations for working with layers; adding, naming, deleting, renaming, hiding, activating, assigning shapes, and so on. In this section, you learn the significance and the steps for doing all these tasks. But don't feel you need to do all these at once to work with layers! Just use whatever tasks seem appropriate for your particular drawing.

When you use a Visio template to create a drawing, Visio adds layers automatically as you drag shapes in. You're never *required* to create layers or do anything with existing ones. But they're there if you want to.

Toolbars for working with layers

Two toolbars are helpful when working with layers. The first is the View toolbar. It has a lone button for working with layers, the Layer Properties button, which is shown in Table 10-1.

Table 10-1		Toolbar Buttons for Working with Layers	
Button	**Name**	**Toolbar**	**What It Does**
	Layer Properties	View	Displays the Layer Properties dialog box shown in Figure 10-2
{No Layer}	Layers	Format Shape	Displays the Layers dialog box shown in Figure 10-4, which lists the layer(s) to which a selected shape is assigned

The second toolbar, Format Shape, contains a box called Layers. When you select a shape in a drawing, the layer to which that shape is assigned appears in this box. If the shape is assigned to multiple layers, this box tells you so. If the selected shape is unassigned, this box simply says "No Layer."

To display the View toolbar and the Format Shape toolbar, right-click the toolbar area and choose the toolbar name from the pop-up menu, or choose View➪Toolbars and select their names from the list.

Adding a layer and removing one

When the template you're using doesn't include the layers you want or if you're not using a template at all, you can create layers of your own. Why would you want to? The simple answer is to help you organize shapes.

Suppose your drawing contains a layer called *Computer Equipment*. You might want to refine that further by creating a layer *called Rented Computer Equipment*. That way, you could easily distinguish rented equipment from owned equipment.

Follow these steps to add a layer:

1. **Choose View⇨Layer Properties or click the Layer Properties button on the View toolbar.**

   Visio displays the Layer Properties dialog box, showing a list of layers for the current page, as shown in Figure 10-2.

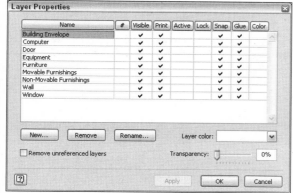

Figure 10-2:
All layers on the current page of the drawing are listed.

TIP

If your Layer Properties dialog box is empty, it doesn't necessarily mean that the template you're using doesn't include predefined layers. The layers appear in the dialog box only after you've dragged preassigned shapes onto your drawing page.

2. **Click the New button.**

   The New Layer dialog box appears, as shown in Figure 10-3.

3. **In the Layer Name box, type the name that you want for the new layer and then click OK.**

   Your new layer is added to the list in the Layer Properties dialog box.

4. **If you want to add more layers, click the Apply button and then repeat Steps 2 and 3.**

5. **Click OK to close the Layer Properties dialog box.**

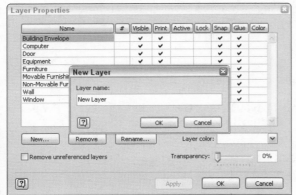

When you add or remove layers, Visio adds or removes them from only the current page. If you want to add or remove layers from multiple pages, you need to do so for each page.

To remove a layer, follow these steps:

1. **Choose View➪Layer Properties or click the Layer Properties button on the View toolbar.**

   Visio displays the Layer Properties dialog box, which shows a list of layers for the current page.

2. **Choose the layer name that you want to remove and then click Remove.**

3. **If your layer contains shapes, reply to the warning, asking whether you really want to remove the layer.**

   If you're willing to sacrifice the shapes on the layer, go ahead and click Yes. If not, click No, then reassign the shapes to a different layer before you remove the layer. (See the "Assigning Shapes to Layers" section later in this chapter.)

4. **Click OK.**

If you respond No to the warning message and then immediately try to remove another layer, beware, Visio will not display the warning message again! If you click Yes for the second layer, Visio deletes it, whether or not it contains shapes. You can restore the layer by clicking the Cancel button before the Layer Properties dialog box closes. If you close the dialog box, you can restore the layer by immediately clicking Undo or choosing Edit➪Undo.

Renaming a layer

You may want to change the name of a layer to something that better describes the shapes that you use or just because you feel like it. It's best to use this option when you're working with layers that you create.

I don't recommend renaming a predefined Visio layer. Here's why: Let's say that Visio adds the Furniture layer to your drawing, and you rename it Leased Furniture. As soon as you drag into a drawing another shape that's preassigned to the Furniture layer, Visio adds the Furniture layer. Now you have both a Furniture layer and a Leased Furniture layer, which can be confusing if you want all your shapes to appear on a single layer.

To rename a layer, follow these easy steps:

1. **Choose View⇨Layer Properties or click the Layer Properties button on the View toolbar.**

   Visio displays the Layer Properties dialog box.

2. **Select the layer that you want to rename and then click Rename.**

   Visio displays the Rename Layer dialog box.

3. **In the Layer Name box, type the new name and then click OK.**

   Visio adds the new layer name to the list in the Layer Properties dialog box.

4. **Click OK.**

Hiding a layer

One of the big advantages of using layers in a drawing is that you can turn them off when you don't want to display their shapes. Consider the office layout example I mentioned earlier in the chapter. Suppose that you want to work on the placement of nonmovable furniture in the building. You'll want to display the layers that contain the building walls (that is, Building Envelope and Walls), but you don't need furniture and other items (Computer, Equipment, Moveable Furnishings, Furniture) cluttering your view.

To hide a layer, follow these steps:

1. **Choose View⇨Layer Properties or click the Layer Properties button on the View toolbar.**

   The Layer Properties dialog box appears.

2. **Find the name of the layer that you want to hide. Click the check mark that appears in the Visible column for that layer.**

The check mark is removed, making the layer invisible.

To display or hide all layers at the same time, click the word *Visible* at the top of the column. (The column header is also a button.) This toggles every item in the column on or off.

3. **If you want to hide another layer, click Apply and then repeat Step 2.**

4. **When you've finished hiding layers, click OK.**

To redisplay a hidden layer, follow the same steps but this time click to add a check mark to the Visible column.

Assigning Shapes to Layers

When you drag into a drawing a shape that isn't preassigned to a layer, the shape goes unassigned. The same is true when you create a shape using the drawing tools or insert a shape from another file, clip art, or a picture. (You can test this by selecting the shape and then choosing Format⇨Layer. The Layer dialog box will show no layers selected for the unassigned shape.) There's certainly nothing wrong with having unassigned shapes, but in many cases you want to assign the shapes to Visio's preassigned layers or to layers you create.

Follow these steps to assign a shape to a layer:

1. **Select the shape to assign.**

   If the shape is part of a group, click the group and then click the shape to select it by itself (it displays its own round green handles with an x inside).

2. **Choose Format⇨Layer.**

   The Layer dialog box appears, as shown in Figure 10-4, displaying a list of all layers in the drawing.

Figure 10-4:
Use the Layer dialog box to assign a shape to one or more layers.

3. **Click the check box for the layer (or layers) to which you want to assign the shape.**

   Yes, you can select more than one layer. If the layer you want doesn't exist, click the New button, type a layer name, and then click OK. Visio adds the new layer to the list shown in Figure 10-4.

4. **If the shape you selected is a grouped shape and its member shapes are assigned to other layers, click the Preserve Group Member Layers box to retain those layer assignments.**

5. **Click OK.**

Visio provides several ways to create a layer, one of which is by clicking the New button in the Layer dialog box shown in Figure 10-4. Refer also to Figure 10-3 for instructions on adding a layer. Either method works.

Technically, you can't move a shape from one layer to another. Instead, you unassign it from one layer and assign it to another. Use the following steps:

1. **Select the shape you want to reassign.**

2. **Choose Format⇨Layer.**

   The Layer dialog box appears.

3. **Click to remove the check mark from the box next to the layer you want to unassign.**

4. **Click to add a check mark in the box for the layer you want to assign the shape to.**

5. **Click OK.**

Determining which layer a shape is assigned to

After you start using layers, your first question will be, how do I tell which layer a shape is assigned to? If it's a preassigned shape, it's not always clear which layer or layers Visio chooses. If you have the Format Shape toolbar displayed (refer to Table 10-1), the layer name appears in the Layer box.

The other way to determine where the shape is assigned is by choosing Format⇨Layer. The Layer dialog box appears, with a check mark next to the layer that the shape is assigned to. If the shape is assigned to more than one layer, check marks appear next to multiple layers.

Selected shape is on this layer   Format Shape toolbar

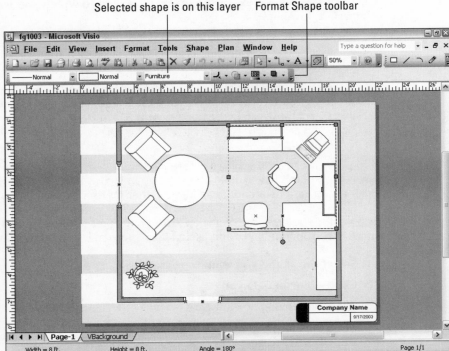

Figure 10-5:
The Format
Shape
toolbar tells
you to
which layer
the selected
shape is
assigned.

Activating layers

Activating a layer causes all unassigned shapes to be assigned to the active layer. You can activate a single layer, or you can activate multiple layers. When you activate multiple layers, the unassigned shapes you use in your drawing are automatically assigned to *all* active layers.

To activate a layer or layers, follow these steps:

1. **Choose View⇨Layer Properties or click the Layer Properties button on the View toolbar.**

    The Layer Properties dialog box is displayed.

2. **In the Active column, click the layer or layers that you want to make active (see Figure 10-6).**

3. **Click OK.**

Using shapes on many layers

Why would you want a shape to appear on more than one layer? One reason is that a shape might belong to more than one category. Suppose that your drawing is a landscape plan and has many layers, among them, Flowering Plants and Shrubs. A plant you assign to the Shrub layer might also be a flowering plant, in which case you would assign it to both layers. What's the advantage? You might want to check your plan for consistency of color among the flowering plants, so you would turn off the Shrubs layer and display only the Flowering Plants layer.

Another reason is that you can track a group of shapes on one layer and component shapes on individual layers. For example, suppose that you're diagramming a computer network that contains components from multiple manufacturers. You might have an IBM layer, an HP layer, a Dell layer, a Compaq layer, and so on. But you would also have a layer called Network Components, which would include shapes from *all* the manufacturer layers. This gives you an easy way to track components in the network or by manufacturer.

Figure 10-6:
All unassigned shapes you drag into the drawing are assigned to the active layer.

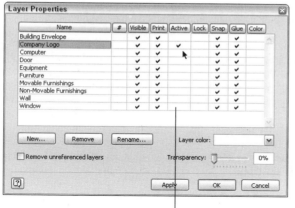

Click here to activate a layer

Using Layers on Background Pages

A background page appears behind another page. Its contents show through the page to which it is assigned. Background pages are designed to contain repetitive information — text or graphics that you want to appear on one or more pages in a drawing. A company name, logo, or document name are examples of information that you may want to put on a background page.

Individual pages in a drawing can have their own or the same background page; you determine to which page (or pages) a background is assigned. (See Chapter 9 for information on assigning and creating background pages.)

Just as foreground pages can have layers, so too can background pages. To create layers on a background page, you first need to create the background page (refer to Chapter 9). Then follow these steps:

1. **Display your background page by clicking the correct tab at the bottom of the drawing area (such as Background-1 or a specific name).**

2. **Choose View⇨Layer Properties or click the Layer Properties button on the View toolbar.**

3. **Click New to display the New Layer dialog box.**

4. **In the Layer Name box, type a new name and then click OK.**

   Visio adds the name to the Layer Properties list.

5. **If you want to add other layers, click Apply and repeat Steps 3 and 4.**

6. **When you're finished adding layers, click OK.**

Protecting Layers from Changes

After you go to all the trouble of defining layers and adding shapes to them, nothing is worse than another user (or yourself) accidentally deleting or changing them. How can you avoid this? You can protect a layer from changes by *locking* it. When a layer is locked, you can't move, change, or delete shapes — you can't even select them! You also can't add shapes to a locked layer.

To lock a layer, follow these steps:

1. **Choose View⇨Layer Properties or click the Layer Properties button on the View toolbar.**

   Visio displays the Layer Properties dialog box.

2. **Locate the layer that you want to lock and then click the Lock column across from the layer name (see Figure 10-7).**

   A check mark appears in the column. This shows that the layer as locked.

   If you want to lock all layers at once, click the word *Lock* at the top of the column. (The column header is also a button.) To unlock all layers at the same time, click the Lock button again.

3. **If you want to lock another layer, click Apply and repeat Step 2.**

4. **When you've finished locking layers, click OK.**

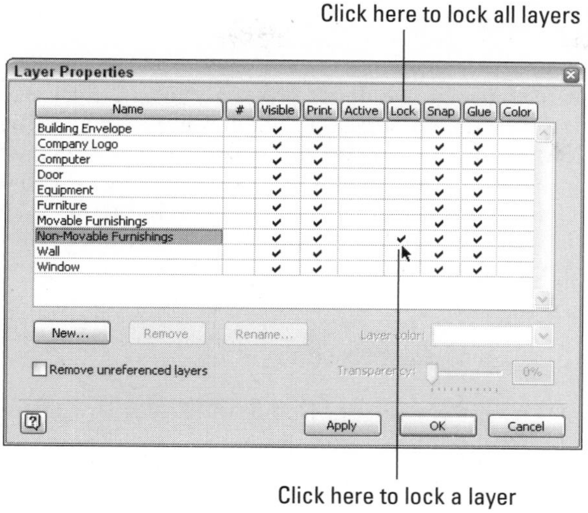

Click here to lock all layers

Figure 10-7:
You can lock
a layer
against
editing
changes,
additions,
and
deletions.

Click here to lock a layer

If you doubt that this method really works, you can test it easily. Just try to move, delete, or copy a shape on the locked layer. You can't do any of these things because Visio doesn't even let you *select* the shape. Also, when you select a different shape in the drawing (one that's *not* on a locked layer) and choose Format⇨Layer, the Layer dialog box (this is the box shown in Figure 10-4) no longer displays the locked layer.

When you're ready to work on the layer again, you can unlock it easily by removing the check mark from the Lock column. The layer will appear again in the Layer dialog box.

For obvious reasons, you can't lock a layer that's marked as an active layer. Not so obvious? Remember that all unassigned shapes are automatically assigned to the active layer or layers. If you could lock the active layers, your shapes wouldn't be assigned to any layer. When you try to lock an active layer, Visio automatically makes the layer inactive.

Locking a layer isn't foolproof protection from changes. After all, you can unlock a layer just as easily as you can lock one. Think of a locked layer as an alert or a reminder — to yourself or other users — that shapes on a locked layer *shouldn't* be changed. If you want a file to be fully protected from changes, open it or distribute it to other users as a read-only file. For more information on creating read-only files, see Chapter 13.

Assigning a Color to a Layer

Why would you want to assign a color to a layer, you ask? Suppose your drawing has a half dozen layers and you're beginning to get confused about which shapes belong to what layer. Assigning a color to each layer lets you determine quickly which shapes belong to a particular layer. You can also assign a color to all locked layers. This reminds you immediately which shapes you can't alter. Or, if you're distributing the drawing to other users for review and comment, you may want to assign a color to the layer that each user may change. Get the idea?

To assign a color to a layer, follow these steps:

1. **Choose View⇨Layer Properties or click the Layer Properties button on the View toolbar.**

   Visio displays the Layer Properties dialog box.

2. **Find the layer to which you want to assign a color, and then click the Color column across from the layer name.**

   A check mark appears in the column.

3. **Make your selection in the Layer Color drop-down list (see Figure 10-8).**

   Visio offers several dozen colors and shades of gray. If these aren't enough options, you can create a custom color using the next set of steps.

4. **Click OK.**

   In your drawing, all shapes on the layer take on the color you chose.

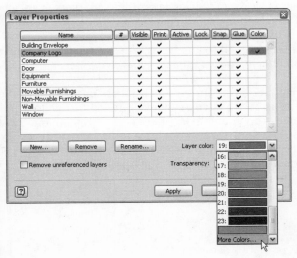

Figure 10-8:
You can create a custom color by clicking More Colors.

When you assign a color to a layer, it affects the printed copy, if you have a color printer. All layers with a color assigned to them print all shapes in that color, regardless of any other custom color formatting applied to the shape. To restore original colors to shapes on that layer, you must remove the color assignment from the layer.

To remove a color from a layer, display the Layer Properties dialog box again and remove the check mark from the Color column.

Removing a color from a layer doesn't remove any custom colors that you created. They are still available in the Color dialog box.

To create a custom color, follow Steps 1 through 3 in the preceding list, and then:

1. **In the Layer Properties dialog box, find the layer to which you want to assign a color, and then click the Color column across from the layer name.**

   A check mark appears in the column.

2. **In the Layer Color box, scroll to the bottom of the list and click More Colors.**

   The Colors dialog box appears, as shown in Figure 10-9.

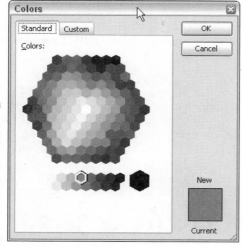

Figure 10-9:
Choose from a wider variety of colors on the Standard tab.

3. **If you want to choose a color on the Standard tab, click the color.**

4. **If you instead want to create a color:**

   a. **Click the Custom tab.**

   b. **Click a shade closest to the color you want to create.**

   c. **To change the intensity of the color, move the small, black arrow up and down the vertical slide bar at the right of the dialog box.**

   d. **To adjust the amount of red, green, or blue in a color, enter a number between 0 and 255 in the appropriate box.**

5. **Click OK.**

   Visio returns to the Layer Properties dialog box and shows the custom color you applied to the selected layer. If you click the Layer Color box, you'll see the custom color you created listed just below color number 23.

Selecting Layers to Print

What good are layers if you can't print them selectively? In a building layout, for example, you probably want to print only the Building Envelope (walls) for the building contractor. Employees don't want or need to see the wiring or HVAC layouts but will probably want to see the layers for the walls, cubicle walls, non-moveable furniture, and possibly the electrical outlets.

Visio automatically assumes that you want to print all layers, but you can change this easily as follows:

1. **Choose View⇨Layer Properties or click the Layer Properties button on the View toolbar.**

2. **For the layers that you don't want to print, click to remove the check mark in the Print column.**

3. **Click OK.**

Don't be deceived by the Visible column in the Layer Properties dialog box! You can't keep a layer from printing by making it invisible. The Print column is the only setting that affects printing; the Visible column affects only what you see on the screen. If a layer isn't visible, but a check mark appears in the Print column, it still prints!

Snap and Glue Options for Layers

If you've followed some of the steps in this chapter, you've seen the Layer Properties dialog box (refer to Figure 10-2), and you're probably wondering about the Snap and Glue columns.

What are snap and glue, you ask? *Snap* is a feature that works like a magnet to let you align and position shapes accurately in a drawing. You can specify that shapes automatically snap to other shapes, grid lines, guide lines, ruler divisions, and more. *Glue* is a feature that keeps shapes connected even when you move them. Connection lines between shapes either stay connected at the same point on the shape or move to a more convenient connection point, depending on the glue options that you specify. See Chapter 6 for more information about the Snap and Glue features.

The following rules apply to the Snap and Glue options in the Layer Properties dialog box:

- ✔ **Snap:** When Snap is checked for a particular layer, shapes on that layer can snap to shapes on other layers and vice versa. (In other words, Snap is enabled in both directions.) When Snap is not checked for a particular layer, shapes on that layer can still snap to shapes on other layers, but not vice versa.

- ✔ **Glue:** When Glue is checked for a particular layer, shapes on that layer can glue to shapes on other layers and vice versa. (In other words, Glue is enabled in both directions.) When Glue is not checked for a particular layer, shapes on that layer can still glue to shapes on other layers, but not vice versa.

By default, Snap and Glue are enabled on all layers in a drawing. If you want shapes on other layers to steer clear of shapes on a particular layer, click to uncheck both options (Snap and Glue) for that layer.

Part IV

Advancing Your Knowledge of Visio

"WELL, SHOOT! THIS EGGPLANT CHART IS JUST AS CONFUSING AS THE BUTTERNUT SQUASH CHART AND THE GOURD CHART. CAN'T YOU JUST MAKE A PIE CHART LIKE EVERYONE ELSE?"

In this part . . .

*I*f you've worked your way through Parts I, II, and III, you should be feeling confident about your Visio skills. You're probably more than a casual user — but there's still more you can do to become the resident expert. In this part, you uncover the real power of Visio: its programmability. You don't have to be a techie programmer-type to benefit from this feature. But you do have to be ready to create your own stencils, master shapes, and templates.

You find out how to store data in shapes, and discover how storing data lets you generate all types of reports. If you work in a group that shares Visio drawings, you'll find Visio 2003's new annotating and reviewing features extremely useful. Then, take advantage of the capability to share Visio drawings with other programs.

Chapter 11

Creating Stencils, Master Shapes, Templates, and Styles

In This Chapter

▶ Creating and editing stencils

▶ Working with master shapes

▶ Creating and saving custom templates

▶ Applying styles to shapes

*Y*ou can use almost any software program as-is successfully without ever taking the time to customize it. But if you use the program a lot, customizing can save you valuable time and keystrokes. Like most software programs, Visio has many features you can customize, or personalize, such as stencils, master shapes, templates, and styles. Perhaps it's more accurate to call these *extensions* because you can actually add things to Visio that make it more useful — for *you.*

Working with Stencils

Chapters 1 and 2 cover the basics of opening and using stencils. This chapter goes beyond the basics and tells you about document stencils, how to customize existing stencils, and how to create your own.

If the template you're using doesn't contain all the shapes you need, choose File⇨Shapes to open additional stencils.

Using the Stencil toolbar

As you work with stencils, I recommend that you use the buttons on the Stencil toolbar, which are listed in Table 11-1. To display the Stencil toolbar, right-click the toolbar area and choose Stencil, or choose View⇨Toolbars⇨Stencil.

Table 11-1		Stencil Toolbar Buttons
Button	**Name**	**What It Does**
	New Stencil	Creates a new stencil
	Show Document Stencil	Displays the document stencil for the current drawing
	Icons and Names	Displays only icons and names for shapes on the current stencil
	Icons Only	Displays only icons for shapes on the current stencil
	Names Only	Displays only shape names for shapes on the current stencil
	Icons and Details	Displays only shape icons and details for shapes on the current stencil

As you work with and create drawings, Visio displays the stencil shape icons and names in the Shapes window. (Note that the Icons and Names button on the toolbar is highlighted.) If you don't care about seeing the names of shapes, or if you want to view more shapes in the Shapes window at one time, click the Icons Only button. (Some stencils contain so many shapes that you need to scroll through them.) If you want names without the pictures (icons), choose Names Only. You can also display the shape tip (the one Visio pops up when you hover over a shape in a stencil) along with the icon and shape name by choosing the Icons and Details button.

An example of each of these stencil options is shown in Figure 11-1. Note that if you have several stencils open, they must all be displayed using the same style.

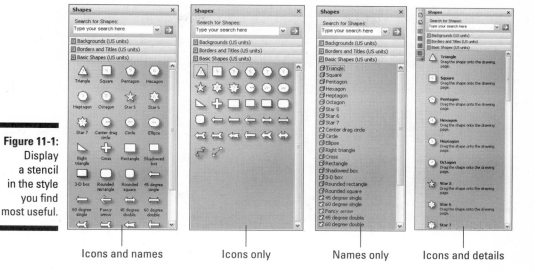

Figure 11-1:
Display
a stencil
in the style
you find
most useful.

Icons and names   Icons only   Names only   Icons and details

Using a document stencil

When you create a drawing, Visio automatically creates a document stencil. You were probably unaware of it until now, unless you discovered it on your own at the bottom of the File➪Shapes menu.

When you're working on an existing drawing, choose File➪Shapes➪Show Document Stencil and see what happens. Visio opens a stencil with the title Document Stencil. (See the lower-left corner of Figure 11-2.) It includes all the shapes that you've used so far in the current drawing. Each time you add a shape from a stencil to your drawing, it's automatically added to the document stencil.

So what's the point of a document stencil? It acts as a log for the shapes in your drawing. Suppose you had to open fifteen stencils to find all the shapes you needed for your drawing. You then closed some of those stencils when you didn't need them anymore. If you want to reuse any of those shapes, you don't have to hunt down the original stencil and reopen it. Instead, you can drag the shapes you need from the document stencil into your drawing.

To close the document stencil, click the stencil's icon and choose Close. Note that a document stencil is always created with a drawing, whether or not you display the document stencil.

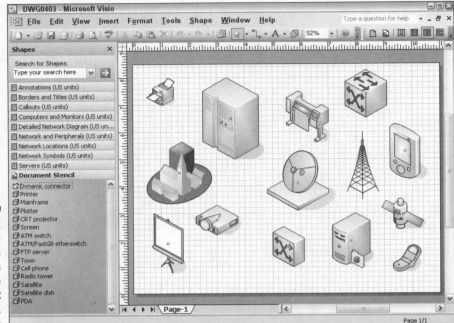

Figure 11-2:
Every shape used in the drawing is listed in the document stencil.

Creating a custom stencil

Do you find yourself using the same shapes from several different stencils over and over? If so, save time and create a custom stencil to store your most frequently used shapes. That way, you won't have to open multiple stencils every time you create a drawing.

The quickest way to create a custom stencil is to base it on an existing stencil or drawing. Follow these steps to create a custom stencil:

1. **Do one or both of the following:**

   a. **Open a drawing that already contains most of the shapes you want to include.**

   If you don't have one, open the next closest thing, or just create a sample drawing and drag all the shapes you want on your custom stencil onto the drawing. (If you make a sample drawing, the order and arrangement of the shapes doesn't matter. You don't really care about the drawing; it's the stencil you want to save.)

    b. **Open a Visio stencil that you want to copy shapes from or open the document stencil (choose File⇨Shapes⇨Show Document Stencil). Arrange the stencils on the screen so you can see all of them.**

2. **Choose File⇨Shapes⇨New Stencil or click the New Stencil button on the Stencil toolbar.**

    A new stencil named Stencil*x*, where *x* is a number, appears on the left side of your screen,. If you create more new stencils, the number is incremented each time. (Don't worry, you'll rename it soon enough.)

3. **Drag a shape onto the custom stencil (see Figure 11-3) using one of these methods:**

    • **From the drawing page,** hold down the Ctrl key (so the shape is copied, not moved) and drag the shape onto the new stencil. (When you hold down the Ctrl key as you drag the shape, you see a plus symbol next to your mouse pointer.) Visio names the shape Master.0 and names subsequent shapes Master.1, Master.2, Master.3, and so on. (You can rename these, as you see later in the "Naming master shapes on a custom stencil" section.)

    • **From the document stencil or from a Visio stencil,** drag the shape onto the new stencil. (You don't need to hold the Ctrl key because Visio automatically copies the shape instead of moving it.) The shape retains its Visio name (such as Rectangle, or Terminal Server, or External Interactor).

4. **When all the shapes you want are on the custom stencil, right-click the icon on the stencil's title bar (at the far left) to display the pop-up menu, and then click Save.**

    Visio displays the Save As dialog box and selects the My Shapes folder, where stencils are stored. This folder already contains a stencil called Favorites, which Visio automatically creates.

5. **In the File Name box, type a name for the stencil.**

    In the Save As Type box, Visio automatically chooses Stencil for the file type (*.vss).

6. **Click the Save button.**

    Visio returns to the drawing screen and the stencil name is now displayed in the title bar.

Now when you choose File⇨Shapes, your custom stencil is listed in the My Shapes category (see Figure 11-4).

New stencil

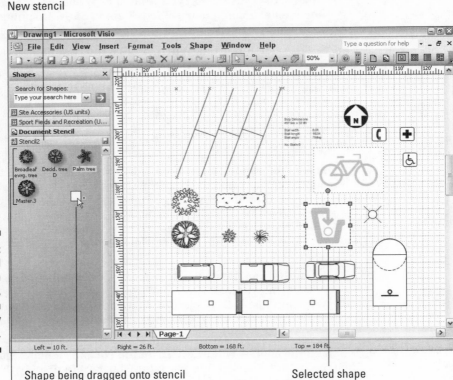

Figure 11-3:
To add
shapes to a
new stencil,
drag them
directly
onto it.

Shape being dragged onto stencil

Selected shape

New shapes in stencil

I assume that most users have shapes (usually in an existing drawing) that they want to include in a custom stencil, so the preceding steps include adding shapes to the stencil. Adding shapes at this time isn't required, however. You can simply choose File➪Shapes➪New Stencil to create a new stencil, and then save it immediately without adding any shapes. You can always come back later and add shapes.

Naming master shapes on a custom stencil

Earlier in this chapter you saw how Visio names shapes on custom stencils Master.0, Master.1, Master.3, and so on as you add them to the stencil. These are intended to be temporary names as you create a custom stencil; your shapes really should have more descriptive, permanent names.

Custom stencils

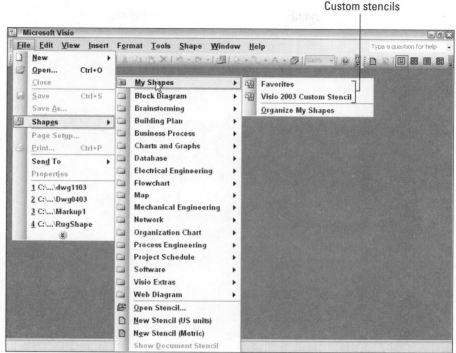

Figure 11-4:
Custom
stencils are
listed under
Shapes⇨
My Shapes.

When you name a shape, you can also type a *tool tip* (a description that pops up when you hover over the shape). In addition, you can store keywords with the shape. Keywords enable Visio to find the shape if you do a search. In the dialog box, type each keyword on a new line in the Keywords box. (Refer to Chapter 4 for help on searching for shapes.)

To rename shapes on a custom stencil, do the following:

1. **Display the stencil that contains the shapes you want to rename.**

2. **Right-click the stencil title bar and choose Edit Stencil.**

   Visio adds a red asterisk to the title bar to indicate that the stencil is in edit mode.

3. **Right-click a shape in the stencil and choose Edit Master⇨Master Properties.**

   The Master Properties dialog box appears, as shown in Figure 11-5.

4. **In the Name field, type a name for the shape.**

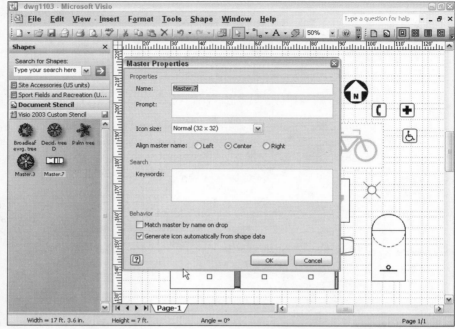

Figure 11-5:
Type a
new name,
prompt,
and key-
words for
the shape.

5. **If you want a tip to appear when you hover the mouse over the shape in the stencil, type the description or instruction in the Prompt field.**

6. **If you want an icon size other than Normal, choose Tall, Wide, or Double in the Icon Size box.**

7. **If you don't want to use Center as the alignment for the shape name, choose Left or Right.**

8. **In the Keywords box, type all the words by which you want to be able to search for this shape.**

9. **Click OK.**

   Visio updates the name of the shape on the stencil.

These steps are the long version for renaming. Use them when you want to edit the prompt and keywords, in addition to changing a shape's name.

If you want to simply rename a shape, do this:

1. **Display the stencil that contains the shape you want to rename.**

2. **Right-click the stencil title bar and choose Edit Stencil.**

3. **Right-click a shape in the stencil and choose Rename Master.**

Visio highlights the current name below the shape in the stencil.

4. **Type a new name for the shape, and then press the Enter key or click a blank area of the stencil.**

Adding master shapes to a custom stencil

You can easily add more shapes to a custom stencil after you create and save it. Just drag shapes from a drawing (remember to use the Ctrl key so you're copying rather than moving) or from another stencil (no Ctrl key needed) onto the custom stencil. Be sure to save your stencil again by right-clicking the title bar and choosing Save.

If you try to add a shape to a Visio stencil, Visio informs you promptly that this is not allowed. I suspect that Visio's intent with this rule is to protect us from ourselves! After all, if you could add a shape to a Visio stencil, you might just as easily delete a shape.

You can add shapes to a custom stencil without having the custom stencil open. This is a good method to use if you're in the middle of creating a drawing and run across a shape that you know you'll want to use in the future but don't need now.

Follow these steps to save a shape without opening the custom stencil:

1. **Display the stencil that contains the shape you want to save.**

2. **Right-click the shape you want to save and choose Add to My Shapes.**

   A menu listing all custom stencils appears.

3. **Click the stencil name where you want to save the shape.**

   Visio saves the shape to your custom stencil.

If the custom stencil is open when you add a shape, Visio adds the shape but doesn't save it right away. Visio asks you later (when you close the drawing or close Visio) if you want to save changes.

Deleting master shapes from a custom stencil

Visio protects its stencils so that you don't accidentally wipe out its shapes. However, you can delete master shapes from a custom stencil anytime you like because you created the stencil yourself. You may find yourself adding and deleting shapes often as your needs change for the types of drawings you create.

Follow these steps to delete a shape:

1. **Open the custom stencil.**

2. **Right-click the stencil title bar and choose Edit Stencil.**

   Visio adds a red asterisk to the title bar to indicate that the stencil is in edit mode.

3. **Right-click the shape you want to delete and choose Delete.**

It's as simple as that. If you change your mind right away, you're in luck because you can choose Edit⇨Undo after you delete a shape to bring it back.

Creating a Custom Template

A *template* is like a model for a drawing; it sets up the page size, orientation, drawing scale, grid, text and font styles for your drawing area. A template also automatically opens up appropriate stencils for the type of drawing that you're creating.

The biggest advantages that templates offer are consistency and efficiency. Companies that rely on Visio often create custom templates that include their name, logo, corporate colors, contact information, and so on. This ensures that every drawing created using Visio has the same look and feel. Even if you're not using corporate information, you might want a custom template for a series of related drawings so that they are consistent from first to last.

It's possible that none of the Visio templates meet your needs exactly, but you can create a custom template that does. You can base your custom template on an existing Visio template or drawing and then change it, or you can create a custom template from scratch.

To create a custom template from a Visio template or an existing drawing, follow these steps:

1. **Select the drawing type that you want to use.**

   Choose File⇨New⇨Choose Drawing Type. If you want to base your new template on an existing drawing, choose File⇨Open to open your file.

2. **Choose File⇨Shapes to open any stencils that you want to include in your new template.**

3. **Choose File⇨Page Setup.**

   The Page Setup dialog box appears.

4. **Click the Print Setup, Page Size, or Drawing Scale tab, as appropriate, to make changes to the template.**

   Refer to Chapter 3 for help with the settings on these tabs.

5. **If you want your template to include a background page, create it now.**

   See Chapter 9 for details.

6. **Choose File➪Save As.**

   The Save As dialog box appears.

7. **In the Save In box, choose the folder in which you want to save your new template.**

   Choose the Visio Solutions folder if you want the template to appear in the Choose Drawing Type dialog box when you start Visio or when you choose File➪New➪Choose Drawing Type.

8. **In the File Name box, type a name for your new template.**

9. **In the Save As Type box, choose Template.**

10. **Click the Save button.**

If you want to create a custom template from scratch, the best way to start is to set up a drawing with all the settings you want the template to have. Choose File➪Page Setup to set the page size, drawing scale, and page property settings that you want for the new template. And don't forget about background pages (see Chapter 9) and layers (see Chapter 10). When the drawing is the way you want it, follow Steps 6 through 10 in the preceding procedure.

Working with Styles

A *style* is a collection of attributes that apply to a shape, such as a green-and-yellow striped fill, a purple outline, a brown shadow, and bold orange text in the Haettenschweiler font. The style has a name — such as Tasteless — and is saved along with a template or a drawing file. (Chapters 4 and 8 talk about working with these elements of a style.)

What's the point of having a style? A style saves you the time of applying all the attributes of Tasteless individually to a shape. You simply apply the style to as many shapes as you want, and — voilà! — you have multiple Tasteless shapes! Using styles not only saves you time but also ensures consistency when you want shapes to be formatted alike.

A style can contain just one attribute or dozens of attributes. It can contain text attributes, line attributes, or fill attributes, or any combination of the three. Most Visio templates contain at least a few predefined styles (with one, two, or all three attributes).

When you work with styles, I recommend that you display the Format Text and Format Shape toolbars on your screen so you don't have to remember the menu commands. (Right-click anywhere in the toolbar area to select these toolbars.)

The Format Text toolbar contains a Text style box; the Format Shape toolbar contains Line style and Fill style boxes. To see how different styles are applied in the drawing, click a shape and look at the style boxes on the toolbar. Now click several other shapes and watch the style boxes each time you click another shape. You see that some shapes have a style assigned to them, but others don't.

In Figure 11-6, you can see that the selected shape (chair) uses the Facilities line style, Facilities text style, and Facilities fill style, all of which are predefined by the Office Layout template.

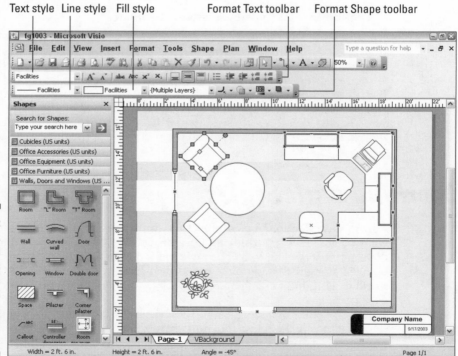

Figure 11-6:
The Text, Line, and Fill style boxes tell you the style that's applied to the selected shape.

Creating and saving a style

You can base a new style on an existing one or create it from scratch. If the style that you want to create is similar to another style, begin with the existing style, make the changes that you want, and then save the new style under a different name.

Use these steps to create a style:

1. **Choose Format⇨Define Styles.**

   The Define Styles dialog box appears, as shown in Figure 11-7.

Figure 11-7: Create the text, line, and fill elements for a new style using the Define Styles dialog box.

2. **In the Name box, type a name for the new style.**

3. **If you're basing the new style on an existing one, select that existing style in the Based On box.**

4. **In the Includes area, check the characteristics that your new style includes:**

   • Text: For font, size, style, and so on

   • Line: For things such as line weight, pattern, and color

   • Fill: For color, pattern, shadow, and so on

I recommend that you check all options here even if you don't use them all right now. You might define them in the future.

5. **For each option that you chose in Step 3, click the appropriate button in the Change box (Text, Line, or Fill).**

   In the dialog box that appears (an example of the Line dialog box is shown in Figure 11-8), choose the attributes that you want and then click OK to close the box. Visio returns you to the Define Styles dialog box.

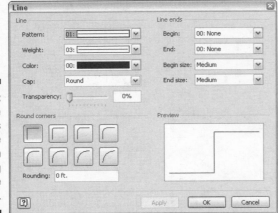

Figure 11-8: Set all line attributes for the custom style using the Line dialog box.

6. **In the Define Styles dialog box, click the Apply button.**

   Visio creates the new style, making it available for use in the current drawing. If you want to see your new style listed, click the down arrow next to the Text Style box on the Format Text toolbar, and the Fill Style and Line Style boxes on the Format Shape toolbar.

You can also use the Define Styles dialog box to rename existing styles or delete styles that you don't want to use anymore. To rename or delete a style, select a shape in the drawing that uses the style, and then choose Format⇨ Styles to display the Define Styles dialog box shown in Figure 11-7. Check to see that the style listed in the Name box is the style you want to rename or delete, and then click the Rename or Delete button, respectively. If you're renaming, Visio displays a dialog box so that you type the new name. If you're deleting, Visio deletes the style without asking you to confirm your choice, so be sure you have the correct style. Click OK to return to the drawing.

Typically when you define a style, that style is available only to the current drawing. However, if you save the style with your template, the style is available to all drawings you create using that template. For more information, see "Creating a Custom Template" earlier in this chapter.

Applying a style to a shape

After you create a style, you simply apply it to a shape to assign all the style's attributes to the shape. You can also apply the style to several shapes at once. Follow these steps:

1. **Select the shape or shapes that you want to apply a style to.**

   To select more than one shape, press and hold down the Shift key as you click the shapes.

2. **Apply text, line, and fill styles:**

   - **Using the Format Style and Format Text toolbars:** Click the down arrow for the style box on the appropriate toolbar (for example, the Fill style box on the Format Shape toolbar). Repeat as needed with the other style boxes.

   - **Using the Style dialog box:** Choose Format⇨Style. In the Style dialog box that appears, choose the appropriate styles from the drop-down boxes and then click OK.

   The styles are applied to the selected shapes.

Copying a style from one drawing to another

Suppose you spend a lot of time creating and applying styles to different shapes in a drawing, and now you want to use those styles in a different drawing. How do you do that when the custom style applies only to the current drawing? Simple — you copy it!

To copy styles to another drawing, follow these steps:

1. **Open the drawing that contains the styles you created.**

2. **Create a drawing and arrange the two drawings side-by-side (or use the Window menu to switch back and forth).**

3. **In the original drawing, select a shape whose style you want to use, and choose Edit⇨Copy (or click the Copy button on the Standard toolbar).**

4. **Go to the new drawing page and choose Edit⇨Paste (or click the Paste button on the Standard toolbar).**

   Visio pastes the shape into the new drawing and the new style appears in the appropriate boxes in the Format Text and Format Shape toolbars.

It doesn't matter whether you really want to use the shape itself in the new drawing. If you don't; just delete it! The style that you copied remains available in the new drawing.

Remember that if you want a style to be available to new drawings, you can define it as part of a template. See the "Creating Custom Templates" section earlier in this chapter.

Chapter 12

Managing Shape Information, Behavior, and Protection

*V*isio is far more sophisticated than it might appear at a quick glance. You might never guess that a Visio diagram or drawing could have all sorts of data stored with it. It might be an even further leap to assume that you could run custom, sorted reports (simple or complex) on that stored data — but you can. Or how about the idea that you can *program* Visio shapes to behave or appear in a particular way or to adjust themselves to changes that you make in a drawing? These are not trivial features. They are part of the sophistication built into Visio that greatly enhances your ability to use the program in many creative ways, as you see throughout this chapter.

Storing Data in Visio Shapes

In Visio, shapes are more than what they appear to be. Some are *smart* — their behavior changes depending on the circumstances in which they're used. Others have sophisticated geometry. Whatever their particular characteristics, *all* shapes can store data.

Why would you want to store data in a shape? Well, you might not if your drawing illustrates a simple workflow process such as Get bills⇨Enter payables⇨ Pay bills⇨Record in register⇨File paperwork. But what if the process is more complex, and costs are associated with each task? You might want to store cost data, the resources required to complete the task, and the duration of time involved in each task.

Now, pretend you're a property manager in charge of distributing and tracking computer equipment for your company. (It may not sound as exciting as whale watching, but it pays!) In an office layout plan, you can store inventory numbers and owner information for each computer component shape shown in a drawing. You might want to store additional information, such as serial numbers, acquisition dates, manufacturer names, or model numbers.

Visio calls any type of custom data that you store in a shape *custom properties data*. You enter the data in a shape's custom property fields. Many Visio shapes have built-in fields for entering custom property data. For example, all office layout shapes include inventory number and owner fields. Flowchart shapes contain fields for recording cost, duration, and resources.

Surprise! Some Visio shapes don't have custom properties fields. (Some shapes are too ordinary for you to care about storing data in them.) To find out if a shape has custom properties, first select or right-click the shape, and then choose Shape⇨Custom Properties. If the shape contains custom properties, Visio displays a Custom Properties dialog box like the one shown in Figure 12-1. If the shape doesn't have custom properties, a message tells you that no custom properties exist and asks whether you would like to define them now. You can just click No to this message.

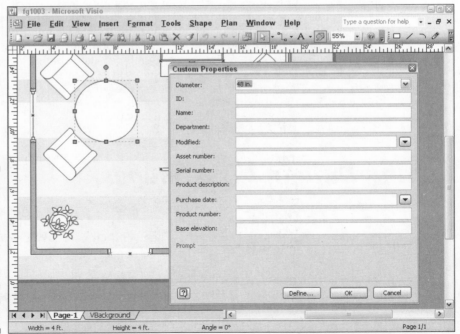

Figure 12-1:
When a shape has custom properties, the data appears in the Custom Properties dialog box.

Another way to display custom properties is with the Custom Properties window, which is shown in Figure 12-2. The nice thing about this window is that it stays on the screen, so you can check custom properties data as you click different shapes in a drawing. Each time you click a shape, that shape's custom properties data is shown. If a selected shape doesn't contain data, the box simply says "No Custom Properties."

You can float the Custom Properties window by dragging it anywhere on the screen, or you can dock it along any edge of the drawing area. When docked, the Custom Properties window, like the Pan and Zoom window, can be rolled up like a window shade — just click the thumbtack icon and then move the mouse away from the window. To make the window reappear, move the mouse over the title bar. For more details, see Chapter 2.

Entering custom properties data

When a Visio shape already contains custom properties fields, it's a cinch to enter the data. Follow these steps:

1. **Open the drawing that contains the shape in which you want to store data.**

2. **Click or right-click the shape, and choose Shape⇨Custom Properties.**

   A Custom Properties dialog box similar to the one in Figure 12-1 appears. All custom properties for the shape are listed in the Properties area at the bottom of the dialog box. In Figure 12-1, for example, some of the properties for the selected shape are Diameter, ID, Name, and Department (among others). A different shape in the drawing might have different properties such as Height, Length, Owner, and Service Date.

3. **In each field, type the data that you want to store.**

4. **Click OK.**

An even quicker way to enter data is by using the Custom Properties window (see Figure 12-2). It isn't just a display box; you can use it to enter data as well. To enter or change data, click the field you want to change and start typing. Press Tab to move between data fields.

Visio stores the data you enter with the shape. Had someone else entered the data, you probably wouldn't even be aware of it because it doesn't make itself visible — unless you ask for it, or want to run a report on it, as you learn later in this chapter.

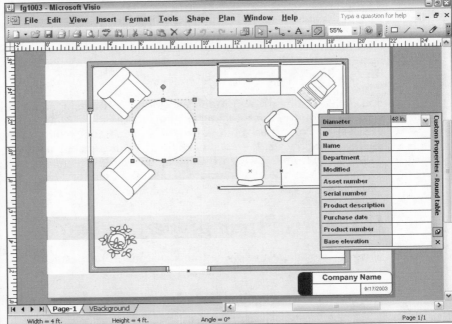

Editing custom properties fields

Suppose you have an office layout drawing that contains office equipment, among other items. You want to store data that tells which employee the equipment is assigned to, the equipment manufacturer's name, and the location of the equipment, in addition to the fields that already exist. Can you add new custom properties? Can you change the name of a custom property?

Well, yes, you can — and you can't. Let me explain:

- ✔ If you want to change or add a custom property for an *instance of a shape* in a drawing, you can.

- ✔ If you want to change or add a custom property for a *master shape on a custom stencil*, you can.

- ✔ If you want to change or add a custom property for a *shape on the document stencil*, you can.

- ✔ But if you want to change or add a custom property for a *master shape on a Visio stencil*, you definitely can't.

I suspect that the reasoning for this rule follows the same line as the one about not adding to or deleting shapes from Visio stencils: Visio wants to protect its shapes and protect you from yourself! If you feel that you *must* change a custom property for a master shape, add the shape to a custom stencil and change it there.

The document stencil applies only to the current drawing. Custom stencils are those you create with whatever shapes you want and are available to use with any drawing. Refer to Chapter 11 for more information on working with stencils.

To add custom properties to a shape in a drawing, use the following steps:

1. **Open the drawing that contains the shape for which you want to add properties.**

2. **Click the shape and choose Shape⇨Custom Properties.**

   If the shape already has custom properties, Visio displays a Custom Properties dialog box. If the shape has no custom properties, Visio displays the message shown in Figure 12-3.

Figure 12-3:
If a shape
doesn't
have custom
properties,
this box
appears.

Microsoft Office Visio

? No custom properties exist.

Would you like to define custom properties now?

[Yes] [No]

3. **Click the Yes button (if the shape has no custom properties) or click the Define button at the bottom of the dialog box (if custom properties are already defined for the shape).**

   The Define Custom Properties dialog box appears, as shown in Figure 12-4. If the shape already has custom properties defined, the first custom property (such as Height or Depth) appears in the Label box. Other custom properties are listed in the Properties area of the dialog box.

4. **Click New.**

   The name in the Label box changes to Property*x*, where *x* is a number. If the shape already has eight properties, for example, the label will be Property9. If the shape doesn't have custom properties defined yet, the name that appears in the Label box is a placeholder called Property1 (because it's the first property you're defining).

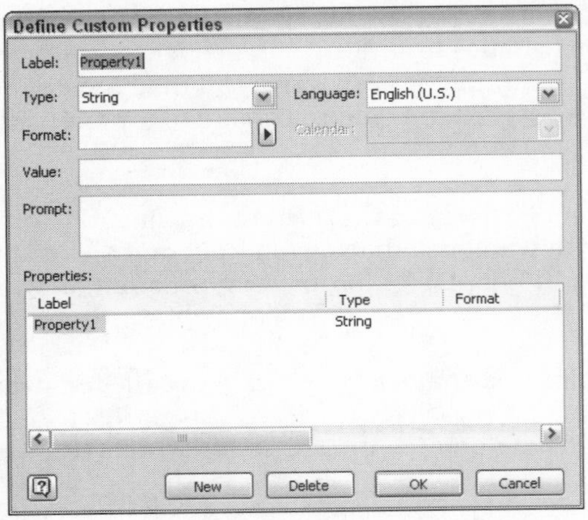

Figure 12-4:
You can
edit, delete,
or create
properties.

5. **Now define your custom property:**

   a. **In the Label box, type a new, descriptive name.**

   As you type, the new label is listed in the Properties area at the bottom of the dialog box.

   b. **In the Type box, choose the type of data that the field will hold (String for text, Number for numeric entries, Currency for money, and so on).**

   c. **In the Format box, choose a format style (such as General, Whole Number, or Fraction).**

   d. **If you want a phrase to indicate the type of input required for this field, type a short phrase in the Prompt box.**

   When using the Custom Properties window, the prompt will appear when you hover the mouse over a custom property label.

   e. **If you want to enter a value for the custom property you just created, type your entry in the Value box.**

   If you prefer to enter data later, refer to the section "Entering custom properties data," earlier in this chapter.

6. **If you want to create another custom property, click the New button and repeat Steps 4 and 5.**

7. **Click OK.**

   Visio returns to the Custom Properties dialog box.

You just added custom properties for a shape in a drawing, but you can also add custom properties to a shape on a custom stencil. When you do, the custom properties apply to every instance of the shape that you drag into a drawing.

To add custom properties to a shape on a stencil, you use similar steps to the preceding ones, but you start from a different point. Here's how:

1. **Open the custom stencil or the document stencil that contains the shape for which you want to edit properties.**

2. **Right-click the stencil's title bar and choose Edit Stencil.**

   A small red asterisk appears on the stencil title bar to indicate the stencil is in edit mode.

3. **In the stencil, right-click the shape you want to edit and choose Edit Master⇨Edit Master Shape.**

   The enlarged shape appears in a separate window.

4. **Right-click the shape and choose Shape⇨Custom Properties.**

   The Custom Properties dialog box appears.

5. **Click the Define button.**

   The Define Custom Properties dialog box appears. In the Label box, Visio displays a property label (such as Height) or a placeholder called Property1.

6. **If the label is for an actual (named) property, click the New button at the bottom of the box.**

   Now the Label box displays Property1.

7. **Define your custom property.**

   (The steps to define your custom property are the same as the ones in the preceding group of steps.)

   a. **In the Label box, type a new name.**

      As you type, the new label is listed in the Properties area at the bottom of the dialog box.

   b. **In the Type box, choose the type of data that the field will hold (String for text, Number for numeric entries, Currency for money, and so on).**

   c. **In the Format box, choose a format style (such as General, Whole Number, or Fraction).**

   d. **If you want a phrase to indicate the type of input required for this field, type a short phrase in the Prompt box.**

      When using the Custom Properties window, the prompt will appear when you hover the mouse over a custom property label.

   e. **If you want to enter a value for the custom property you just created, type your entry in the Value box.**

      If you prefer to enter data later, refer to the section "Entering custom properties data," earlier in this chapter.

8. **If you want to create another new custom property, click the New button and repeat Step 7 (and 8, if desired).**

9. **When you're finished, click OK.**

   The Custom Properties dialog box appears.

10. **Click the Cancel button.**

    Visio returns to the window displaying the master shape.

11. **Click the black X at the far right end of the menu bar to close just this window.**

    Don't click the red X button — that closes Visio!

Whew! That seems like a lot of steps, but *every* time you use this shape, the custom properties are there for you to fill in — if you want to. (You're never required to add data to custom property fields.)

Do you want to test whether your custom property fields have really changed? Drag a shape onto your drawing from the stencil you edited. Right-click the shape and choose Shape⇨Custom Properties. The Custom Properties dialog box appears, and the new custom properties you added are shown.

The previous two sets of steps show you how to add custom properties to shapes. But what if you have a custom property called, say, Source and you want to change it to Supplier? If you want to edit, or change, the name of a custom property, or change any of its attributes (such as Type or Format), you use *basically* the same process — at least, you use the same dialog boxes. Follow these abbreviated steps:

1. **Open the drawing that contains the shape for which you want to edit properties.**

2. **Click the shape and choose Shape⇨Custom Properties, or right-click the shape and choose Shape⇨Custom Properties.**

   The Custom Properties dialog box appears.

3. **Click the Define button.**

   The Define Custom Properties dialog box appears.

4. **In the Properties area of the dialog box, click the property you want to edit.**

   The property you select appears in the Label box.

5. **In the Label box, type a new name for the property.**

6. **If you want to change any other attributes (for instance, the Type, Format, or Prompt) click the appropriate box, make your change, and then click OK.**

Visio returns to the Custom Properties dialog box.

7. Click OK.

Visio returns to your drawing.

Reporting on Data Stored in Visio Shapes

Data sitting in a shape is of limited use as reference information; it's far more useful when you can report on it. Visio provides the tools you need to generate all kinds of reports on your own, or you can choose from a variety — 22, in fact — of predefined reports.

To generate a report, Visio needs a report definition. The report definition is just a simple set of instructions, specifying the following:

- ✔ Which objects you want to report on
- ✔ Which custom properties you want to display as columns in your report
- ✔ Report title
- ✔ Subtotals (if applicable)
- ✔ Sorting guidelines

When you use one of Visio's predefined reports, you don't need to concern yourself with creating report definitions because they're already created for you. Visio allows you to modify them, though, if you want.

Using a predefined report

The type and number of predefined reports available to you depends on the type of drawing you create. Some drawings might have just two and others might have eight or more.

Some predefined reports fall into specific categories. For example:

- ✔ *Count* and *inventory* reports typically count items in a drawing
- ✔ *Flowchart* reports include information on resources, cost, and duration
- ✔ *Asset* reports displays information about asset type, owner, name, and manufacturer
- ✔ *Numeric* reports typically run calculations (totals, averages, maximums, minimums, and the like)

Predefined reports come gratis with the drawing template you choose. Every time you create a drawing using the basic flowchart template, for example, flowchart and inventory reports are predefined for you — whether you use them or not.

To use a predefined report, choose Tools➪Reports to display the Reports dialog box. This dialog box displays whatever report types are applicable to the current drawing type.

To use a predefined report for your drawing, follow these steps:

1. **Open the drawing for which you want to create a report.**

2. **Choose Tools➪Reports.**

   The Reports dialog box appears, as shown in Figure 12-5. Predefined reports are listed in the Report area. The first report is highlighted and a description of it appears in the Description area of the dialog box. You can click different reports to display their description, if you want.

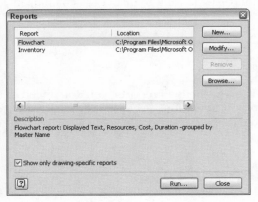

Figure 12-5:
The Reports dialog box displays all available report types for the current drawing type.

3. **Click to select the report you want.**

4. **Click the Run button.**

   The Run Report dialog box appears, as shown in Figure 12-6.

5. **Choose a report format for the results:**

   • Excel generates results in a Microsoft Excel file

   • HTML saves results in your My Documents folder with the name Report_1.html

   • Visio shape inserts results in the current drawing as a shape

• XML saves results in your My Documents folder with the name Report_1.xml

   6. Click OK.

If you chose the Visio shape report format, the results are placed in the current drawing as a shape. Figure 12-7 shows an example of an inventory report shape in a space plan drawing.

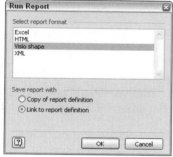

Figure 12-6:
Choose a report format for the output of your report.

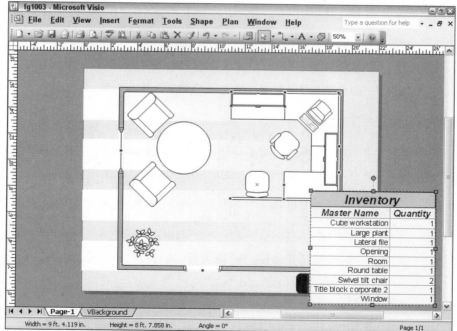

Figure 12-7:
Inventory information is generated by a pre-defined report and added to the drawing as its own shape.

Creating a custom report

Maybe you don't see a predefined report that suits your needs. In that case, you can branch out on your own and create a report from scratch or modify an existing predefined report. Don't let the idea of creating your own scare you off; the process is simple and will give you exactly the results you want.

Suppose that in an office layout drawing, you want a report that lists only the printers in the drawing, not an entire inventory report. That's straightforward; you're asking for only one simple thing: printers. So your report definition has only one requirement:

> Product Description = printer

Or suppose you want something more specific and a little more involved. Maybe there's a recall on a plotter part and you need a count of all the color plotters in the Sales and Marketing departments that were manufactured by ABC Company and have a purchase date of 1999. Generating a report like this requires some simple database-like queries, which you can easily define when you create a custom report. For a report like this, you specify the following:

- Department = Marketing
- Product Description = color plotter
- Manufacturer = ABC Company
- Purchase Date = 1999

The simple rule is that whenever you create a custom report, you do three things:

- Specify which shapes you want to report on
- Choose the custom properties to include in the report
- Choose how you want the report sorted and organized

Visio makes creating a report easy for you by displaying the Report Definition Wizard, which guides you through these choices step by step. Here's how to define a report:

1. **Open the drawing for which you want to create a report.**

2. **Choose Tools⇨Reports.**

   The Reports dialog box appears.

3. **Click the New button.**

   The first screen of the Report Definition Wizard dialog box appears, as shown in Figure 12-8.

Figure 12-8:
Use the first screen of the Report Definition Wizard to choose the shapes you want to report on.

4. **Choose Shapes on all pages or Shapes on the current page.**

5. **To define specific criteria (such as the Marketing Department and a purchase date of 1999):**

   a. **Click the Advanced button.**

      The Advanced dialog box appears, as shown in Figure 12-9.

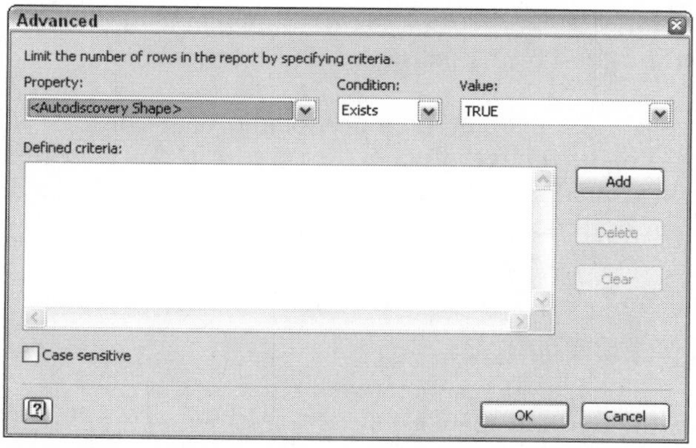

Figure 12-9:
Use the Advanced dialog box to set special conditions in the report definition.

   b. **In the Property box, select a custom property (such as Department).**

   c. **In the Condition box, choose a condition (such as =, <, > <>, <=, >=, or Exists for each custom property you chose.**

      For example, if a custom property is Height, you might choose >= as your condition.

   d. **In the Value box, type a value for the Property and Condition you selected in Steps 6a and 6b.**

> For example, enter 6 if you want to find a shape for which the Height property is >=6.

   e. Click the Add button.

> The condition appears in the Defined Criteria box.

   f. To create additional criteria, repeat Steps b-e.

   g. Click OK.

6. **Click the Next button.**

7. **Click to add a check mark next to each custom property you want displayed in the report (each custom property represents a column in the report), and then click Next.**

8. **In the Report Title box, type a title.**

9. **If you want to include subtotals in your report, click the Subtotals button, choose the options you want, and then click OK.**

10. **To sort by certain criteria and choose the column order, click the Sort button, choose the options you want, and then click OK.**

11. **Click Next.**

12. **In the Description box, type a description for your custom report and then click Finish.**

> Visio returns to the Reports dialog box shown in Figure 12-6. Your custom report is now added to the list of predefined reports.

Run a custom report just like you do a predefined one: Click the Run button in the Reports dialog box and then choose the format for your results. If you find errors in your report definition, simply repeat the preceding steps, choosing different options.

Updating reports

Often after you spend the time creating a report for a drawing, the first thing you do is go back and update your drawing with more shapes! Now your report information is no longer valid. Do you want to re-create a report every time you change your drawing? You probably want to do that about as much as you want a root canal! Fortunately, Visio understands this, so it lets you update existing reports when you change your drawings.

To update a report, use these steps:

1. **In your drawing, right-click the report shape and choose Update Report.**

The Update Report dialog box is displayed and the report type for the current report is highlighted. (This box is nearly identical to the Reports dialog box shown in Figure 12-6 except for the title.)

2. **Click the Run button.**

Visio reruns the report generator and automatically updates the data in the original report shape.

Now wasn't that easy? That's all there is to it — unless you want to modify the report definition itself. If so, repeat the steps shown earlier in the "Creating a custom report" section.

Customizing Shape Behavior

Most Visio shapes are programmed to behave in certain ways, depending on the drawing type and the actions you take in a drawing. For example, the 100-square-foot Space shape (on the Wall, Shell, and Structure stencil used in space plan drawings) adjusts and recalculates its square footage automatically if you resize the shape. Or how about the desk shapes on the Office Furniture stencil that won't let you resize them because they're built to standard industry sizes? These are just two examples of smart behavior in Visio shapes. The average user probably doesn't want to casually mess around with these sophisticated features. (We leave that to the techno-geeks to ponder.)

But what about some simple changes? For instance, what if you want to convert a 2-D shape to a 1-D shape so that it behaves like a connector? That seems like a reasonable task that you might find useful. Or how about customizing the way groups are selected when you click them? If that doesn't interest you, what about determining what a shape will do when you double-click it? These are examples of simple changes that you can make to a single shape in a drawing or to custom shapes on the document stencil or a custom stencil.

Changing a shape from 2-D to 1-D

If you were to take the time to hand-draw an arrow like the one shown in Figure 12-10, you'd probably want it to behave as a connector. Instead, it behaves as a 2-D shape because it is a 2-D shape! That is, it has selection handles that allow you to resize the shape's height and width.

In contrast, connectors are 1-D shapes with endpoints that allow you to connect to other shapes, as shown in Figure 12-11. To use your hand-drawn shape as a connector, you need to convert it from a 2-D shape to a 1-D shape so that it has endpoints.

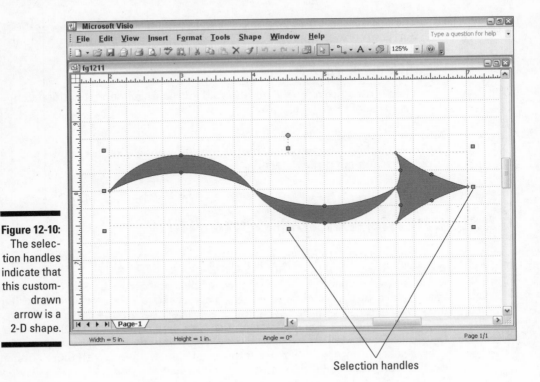

Figure 12-10:
The selection handles indicate that this custom-drawn arrow is a 2-D shape.

Selection handles

Use the following steps to convert a 2-D shape to a 1-D shape:

1. **Create your shape using Visio's drawing tools, or save an existing 2-D shape on a custom stencil.**

2. **Right-click the shape and choose Format⇨Behavior.**

   The Behavior dialog box appears, as shown in Figure 12-12. In the Interaction Style area, the Box (2-Dimensional) option is selected.

3. **In the Interaction Style area, click Line (1-Dimensional).**

4. **Click OK.**

Now return to your drawing and select your shape. You see that its selection handles (that allowed you to resize for height and width) are replaced with endpoints. These endpoints can be connected to shapes at connection points. For more information about connecting shapes, refer to Chapter 6.

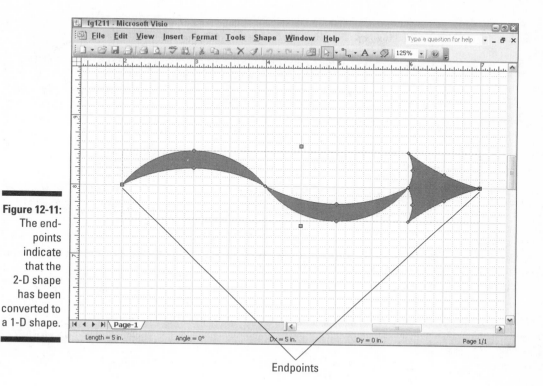

Figure 12-11:
The end-
points
indicate
that the
2-D shape
has been
converted to
a 1-D shape.

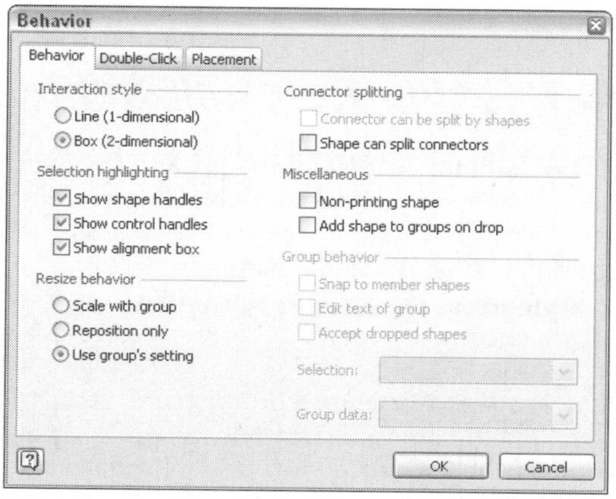

Endpoints

Figure 12-12:
Use the
Behavior
dialog box
to convert
2-D shapes
to 1-D.

Setting a shape's group behavior

A *group* is a set of shapes that behave together as a single unit. Ordinarily when you click a shape that's grouped, the group is selected first. If you click a second time, an individual shape in the group is subselected. But you can choose to swap this selection order and have individual shapes subselected on the first click, or you can choose to have only the group selected (that is, individual shapes are never subselected).

To change the way a group responds when you click it, use these steps:

1. **Open the drawing that contains the grouped shape.**

2. **Right-click the grouped shape and choose Format⇨Behavior.**

   The Behavior dialog box appears.

3. **In the Selection drop-down box (in the lower-right corner) choose one of the following options:**

   - Group Only: Prevents the selection of individual shapes in the group.

   - Group First: Selects the group with one mouse click and a group component with a second mouse click. This is the default setting.

   - Members First: Selects a group component with the first mouse click and the entire group with a second mouse click.

4. **Click OK.**

Setting a shape's double-click behavior

Another cool feature is the capability to set how a shape behaves when you double-click it. By default, a shape's text box opens when you double-click, but a bunch of other choices are available. You can set a shape's double-click behavior to open a grouped shape, display a help screen, run a macro, jump to another page in the drawing, or do nothing at all (like your kids when you announce that it's time for chores!).

Jumping to another page is a way to create a *drill-down* drawing. Suppose that you're diagramming a worldwide communications network. One page of the drawing, called Corporate, shows a worldwide view of the network set on a background of a world map. Network symbols appear on each continent. Understandably, a diagram of this scope shows very little detail. But another page of the drawing, called Europe, shows specific locations where network hubs exist, specifically, London, Berlin, Rome, Madrid, and Paris (refer to Figure 12-13).

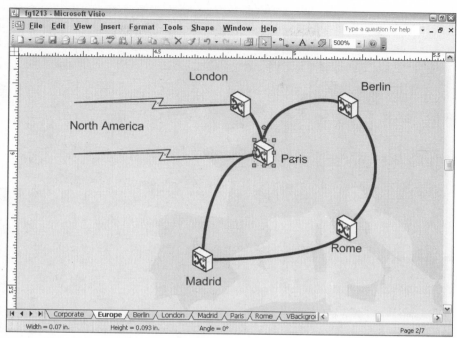

Figure 12-13:
Double-click any city shape to show a detailed map of that city.

The Europe page, however, still doesn't show enough detail. So you create individual pages for each city. In Figure 12-14, you use a city map of Paris as your background (just to add interest) and lay out the network components on top. (You do this on the page you create for each city.)

Now, the question is, how do you get from the high-level Europe map to the detail? You could search through all the page tabs at the bottom of the screen, but a better solution is to set a shape's double-click behavior to *link* to a specific page. On the Europe page, the network shape for each city is set as the link. (Refer to Chapter 9 for more information about working with pages in a drawing.)

Use these steps to set a shape's double-click behavior:

1. **Open the drawing that contains the shape you want to change.**

2. **Right-click the shape and choose Format➪Behavior.**

3. **Click the Double-Click tab, as shown in Figure 12-15.**

4. **Choose one of the options listed:**

   • If you choose Run Macro, click the down-arrow and select a macro from the list. (The topic of macros is beyond the scope of this book.)

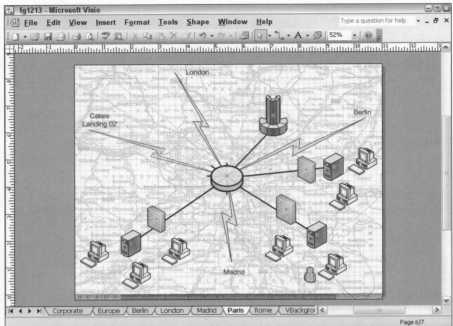

Figure 12-14:
The detail
page of
a city.

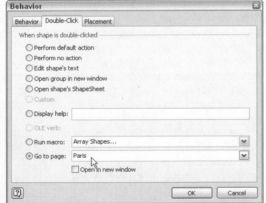

Figure 12-15:
You can set
a shape's
double-click
behavior.

> • If you choose Go to Page, click the down-arrow and select a draw-
>   ing page.

5. **If you want, check the Open in New Window option.**

6. **Click OK.**

To restore a shape to its default double-click behavior (editing text), use the
same steps and choose Edit Shape's Text in Step 3, and then click OK.

Protecting Your Work

When you create drawings that you're going to share with others, you want to protect your work from unwitting destroyers. (Or maybe you need to protect your shapes from yourself!) You can protect entire drawings, grouped shapes, individual shapes, or selected aspects of a shape from being changed. The following sections discuss the several methods available for helping you protect your work.

Preventing shapes from being changed

You use the Format⇨Protection command to protect a shape from changes. This command displays the Protection dialog box, which is shown in Figure 12-16.

Figure 12-16:
You can
choose
specific
aspects of
protection.

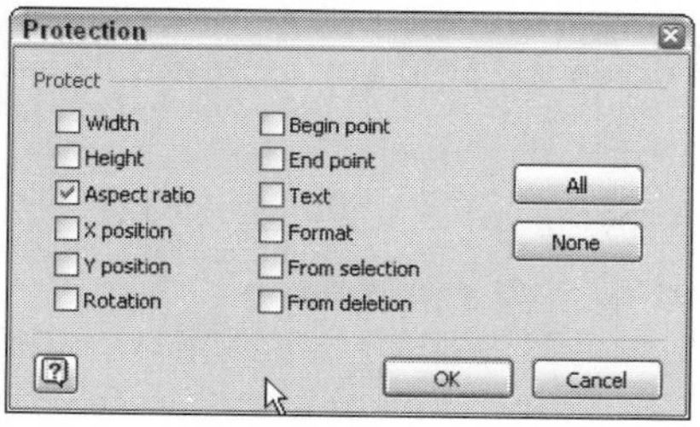

As you can see in Figure 12-16, you can lock several aspects of a shape to prevent it from being changed:

- ✔ **Width:** Prevents anyone from changing the width of a shape or a grouped shape.

- ✔ **Height:** Prevents anyone from changing the height of a shape or a grouped shape.

- ✔ **Aspect ratio:** Prevents anyone from changing the ratio between a shape's width and height, such as 1:1.

- ✔ **X position:** Prevents anyone from moving the shape from its position on the x-axis (horizontal). The shape can be moved up or down but not right or left.

- ✔ **Y position:** Prevents anyone from moving the shape from its position on the y-axis (vertical). The shape can be moved right or left but not up or down.

- ✔ **Rotation:** Blocks anyone from rotating the shape or changing its center of rotation.

- ✔ **Begin point:** Prevents anyone from changing the beginning point of a 1-D shape.

- ✔ **End point:** Prevents anyone from changing the endpoint of a 1-D shape.

- ✔ **Text:** Prevents any changes to a shape's or a grouped shape's text box.

- ✔ **Format:** Blocks changes to any format characteristics.

- ✔ **From selection:** Makes a shape not selectable (To be effective, this selection requires an additional setting, described in the "Keeping drawings secure" section later in this chapter.)

- ✔ **From deletion:** Protects the shape from being deleted.

To lock selected aspects of a shape using the Format➪Protection command, follow these steps:

1. **Open the drawing that contains the shape that you want to protect.**

2. **Select the shape or shapes that you want to protect.**

   You can apply protection to more than one shape at a time. To select more than one shape, hold down the Shift key as you click each shape.

3. **Choose Format➪Protection.**

   The Protection dialog box appears (refer to Figure 12-16).

4. **Click each shape characteristic that you want to lock.**

5. **Click OK.**

If you want the protection to apply to the shape every time you use it, add the shape to a custom stencil and set the protection there. (See Chapter 11 for more information about creating custom stencils.)

If you use the preceding steps to protect a shape from selection, be aware that the shape can still be selected unless you also protect all shapes using the Drawing Explorer window. (It doesn't make sense, but that's how it works.) This feature is described in a later section, "Protecting an entire drawing."

Keeping drawings secure

You have several options for protecting drawings from change. The method you choose depends on the results you want to achieve. All the methods make a drawing readable by others but not changeable (to whatever degree you define).

Locking layers

Locking layers protects parts. If you want other users to be able to edit some layers but not others, *locking layers* is a perfect solution. When a layer is locked, shapes on that layer can't be selected or changed.

If a user knows how to unlock the layer, shapes on that layer *can* be changed. For more secure protection, see "Saving files as read-only," the next section in this chapter.

To lock one or more layers of a drawing, do this:

1. **Open the drawing whose layers you want to protect.**

2. **Right-click the toolbar area and choose View toolbar.**

3. **Click the Layer Properties button (it looks like a stack of pages) on the View toolbar.**

   The Layer Properties dialog box appears.

4. **In the dialog box, put a check mark in the Lock column for each layer you want to lock.**

   In Figure 12-17, for example, the Computer layer is locked.

5. **Click OK.**

When you go back to the drawing and try to select a shape that's on a locked layer, nothing happens. No, really. *Nothing* happens! (It can be quite maddening if you don't remember that you've locked the layer!)

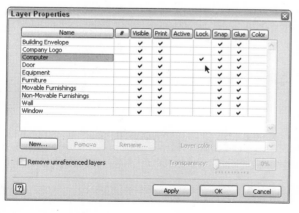

Figure 12-17:
You can lock layers to protect them from changes.

Saving files as read-only

The highest level of protection for a drawing is to save it as a read-only file. This protects every aspect of the file (except viewing, of course!) regardless of any other protections that are set. Setting a file as read-only sends a clear message to your viewers that you don't want them making any changes!

To save a file as read-only, follow these steps:

1. **Open the drawing that you want to save as a read-only file.**

2. **Choose File➪Save As.**

   The Save As dialog box appears.

3. **Highlight the folder where you want to save your drawing.**

4. **In the File Name box, type a name for your drawing.**

5. **Click the down arrow next to the Save button (see Figure 12-18) and choose the Read Only option.**

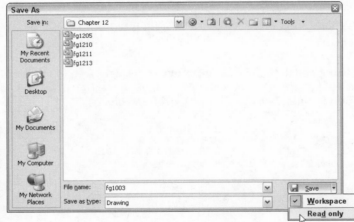

Figure 12-18:
You can save a file as read-only.

If users do want to change the file, they can choose File➪Save As, save a writable version of the file under a different name, and then work in that file. Your original read-only file is still protected.

Protecting an entire drawing

If you don't want to save a file as read-only, you have one more option. You can set protection for certain aspects of the entire drawing using the Drawing Explorer window. Use these steps:

1. **Choose View⇨Drawing Explorer Window.**

   The Drawing Explorer window appears.

2. **Right-click the drawing's path name at the top of the window and choose Protect Document.**

   The Protect Document dialog box appears, as shown in Figure 12-19.

Figure 12-19:
You can apply certain protections to an entire drawing.

3. **Choose any or all of the options shown:**

   - Style: Prevents users from changing, creating, or deleting styles but users can still apply styles.

   - Shapes: Prevents the selection of shapes when shape protection is set on individual shapes. (See the warning in the "Preventing shapes from being changed" section, earlier in this chapter.)

   - Preview: Prevents changes to a drawing's preview image.

   - Backgrounds: Prevents changes or deletion to background pages.

   - Master shapes: Prevents users from changing, creating, or deleting master shapes.

4. **Click OK.**

Chapter 13

Marking Up Drawings for Review

*O*ccasionally you might create simple drawings that are perfect the first time, but chances are this doesn't happen very often! Other drawings you might work on fifteen different times, filing them away while you ponder them, and then coming back to them with fresh ideas or new information. You might even print a copy, scribble some notes to yourself, circle some areas, cross out others, and highlight changes.

Often you want input and opinions from others before your drawing is complete. You might pass out rough drafts to several colleagues and ask them to mark up your drawing, and then incorporate those changes into the final version.

This is the traditional way we edit documents. Word processors such as Microsoft Word have long had the capability of letting you review and edit online rather than the old-fashioned way. Now Visio provides that same capability for your drawings.

Editing, or *annotating*, online has several advantages. First, comments are saved with the file without changing the original. Second, if your colleagues are spread out across the country — or the world — making drawings available electronically saves time and money. Third, electronic editing is orderly and controlled. And fourth, incorporating changes is easy.

In this chapter you discover the techniques for marking up drawings for two audiences: yourself and others. The markup tools you use are the same regardless of the audience.

Discovering Markup Tools

Markup is just another word for *proposed changes* to a drawing. The process of suggesting changes is called *marking up*; the comments themselves are markup. Visio provides two distinct tools for marking up a drawing:

- Comments
- Digital ink

Comments are exactly what you think they are: notes that you add to a drawing that serve as a reminder, ask a question, suggest changes, or add information. Comments appear in a drawing as distinct Visio shapes.

Digital ink is a tool used to mimic handwriting and hand drawing; maybe you want to circle a shape or draw a new one; maybe you want to highlight a title or a text label. If you use a drawing tablet on your computer or have a tablet PC, you can use digital ink to scribble a handwritten note.

Comments and digital ink are bona fide markup tools A third element, *track markup*, is technically not a tool but rather a feature that allows you to use and review proposed changes that others make to a drawing.

Markup tracking is not required for any drawing. But when you choose to track markup, comments and digital ink are displayed differently on the screen. You see this in the examples provided throughout this chapter.

Adding Comments to a Drawing

You can add a comment anywhere in a drawing using one simple command. The comment is saved in a tiny shape that you can place anywhere you like in the drawing, and open and close when needed. That way, you don't have to worry about the comment cluttering your drawing.

Use these steps to add a comment:

1. **Open the drawing to which you want to add a comment.**

2. Choose Insert⇨Comment.

A comment box appears on the screen, with your name and the current date, as shown in Figure 13-1. At the upper-left corner of the comment box is a small box with your initials and a comment number, such as DKW1. The number is incremented with each comment you add.

3. Type the text for your comment, and then click anywhere outside the comment box.

Visio closes the large comment box and leaves the small shape with your initials in it on the screen.

4. Click and drag the comment box to move it to the location in the drawing where it makes most sense; perhaps near a shape that the comment refers to.

To read a comment, click the small comment shape and the box opens to display the text of the comment. To edit a comment, *double-click* the shape. A slightly larger box opens to display the comment so you can edit it.

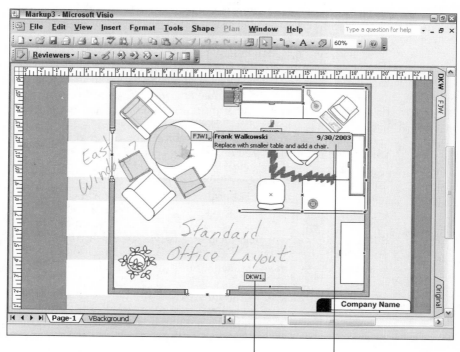

Figure 13-1:
Comment text is hidden until you click it.

Closed comment   Open comment box

What *isn't* visible in Figure 13-1 is the color in which the comment appears on the screen. When you type the comments for your own use (as opposed to tracking other people's proposed changes to a drawing), the comment box is outlined in an olive-green color. When you are tracking other reviewers' changes, a specific color is assigned to each reviewer, and the comment box appears in that color. The next section explains markup tracking in more detail.

How Markup Tracking Works

If you anticipate having one or more people reviewing a drawing, you'll want to use the track markup feature in Visio. Using tracking, reviewers can add comments or suggest changes, and each reviewer's comments are distinct from one another. Here's how it works.

To use the track markup feature, the reviewer must first turn on this feature before they begin reviewing. With tracking on, the reviewer can add comments; add new shapes; change the formatting of new shapes; and draw figures or handwritten notes using digital ink.

The reviewer's proposed changes appear on an overlay on the original drawing — nothing in the original drawing is changed. (An *overlay* is similar to a Visio layer, but overlays are *not* placed on separate layers in a drawing. Think of overlays as on-screen layers only.) If several people review the same drawing file, each reviewer's input appears on a separate overlay.

Overlays are identified by colored tabs on the upper-right side of the drawing window. In Figure 13-2 you can see the tabs (although the distinct colors are impossible to see in grayscale). The Original tab appears in the lower right. You can have each reviewer review a separate copy of the drawing or the original. If reviewers review separate copies, each file will contain your original drawing and one set of reviewer's comments on an overlay. If all reviewers review the same file (the original), each reviewer's comments are assigned a different color and appear as multiple overlays in the drawing file. You can control whether you view all reviewers' comments at once or only those of selected reviewers, as you see later in this chapter.

Even if you, the creator of a drawing, are the only reviewer, you might still want to track markup. Sometimes you're not sure of the changes you want to make right away; you might try out some changes and think about them for a while without altering your original drawing. Markup keeps your original drawing separate from your suggested changes until you incorporate them.

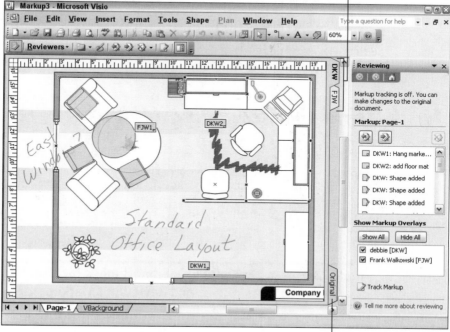

Reviewer overlays

Original document

Figure 13-2:
The reviewers are identified on the tabs by the initials DKW and FJW, and the original drawing appears on the Original tab.

All changes that a reviewer proposes appear on the screen in the reviewer's assigned color, such as red. Even if the proposed changes include adding text, a shape, or a background in a specific color, all changes appear in the assigned color until you incorporate them into the drawing as permanent changes.

Tracking markup in a networked environment

If you work in a corporate environment, you are almost certainly part of a network, whether you access it from your office computer on site or your computer at home. A corporate network often includes file servers, where a single drawing file can be stored and shared by many colleagues. In this environment, anyone who has the proper network permissions can access and review a drawing on the server. Ask your system administrator if file directories are available for you to use to share drawings with colleagues. This is a great way to take advantage of Visio's tracking tools.

Working with Markup

Working with markup encompasses several activities, starting with displaying the proper on-screen tools. From there you can expand your skills to include adding, viewing, and deleting markup, as well as incorporating markup changes into a drawing. I show you how to do all these things in this section.

Using the Reviewing toolbar and the task pane

When you use Visio's tracking feature, I recommend that you display the Reviewing toolbar so that all the tracking tools are close at hand. See Table 13-1. Some of the tools on the Reviewing toolbar appear in the Reviewing pane as well, which you also need to display when tracking and reviewing markup.

Table 13-1	Reviewing Toolbar Buttons for Marking Up and Reviewing Markup	
Button	**Name**	**What It Does**
	Show/Hide Markup	Toggles the display of markup overlays on and off
Reviewers ▾	Reviewers	Lists full names of all reviewers
	Insert Comment	Pops up a new comment box
	Ink Tool	Displays the Ink toolbar
	Previous Markup	Selects the markup entry prior to current selection
	Next Markup	Selects the markup entry after current selection

Button	Name	What It Does
	Delete Markup	Deletes current markup
	Track Markup	Toggles tracking on and off
	Reviewing pane	Toggles displays of the Reviewing task pane on and off

Adding markup to a drawing

It's easy to add markup to a drawing; the hard part is remembering to turn tracking on! If you forget, your changes are incorporated into the original drawing (assuming you have permission to change the file).

You know immediately when tracking is turned on because you see a colored border around the drawing area instead of the overlay tabs, which aren't displayed when tracking is turned on. The Reviewing pane is automatically displayed on the right side of the screen and lists the current reviewer's name. In Figure 13-3, you can see the border around the drawing area and the Reviewing pane to the right of the drawing area. In the drawing, I added shapes, I highlighted an area, and I added handwritten text.

Use these steps to add markup to a drawing:

1. **Open the drawing you want to mark up.**

2. **Click the Track Markup button on the Reviewing toolbar or choose Tools⇨Track Markup.**

   The drawing window is lined in a color border. In the Reviewing pane that appears on the right side of the screen, your name is listed as the current reviewer (refer to Figure 13-3).

3. **Make any of these editing changes:**

   - Use the Text tool on the Standard toolbar to add new text.

   - Drag new shapes into the drawing area and format them as you want.

- Add a comment by clicking the Insert Comment tool on the Reviewing toolbar or in the Reviewing pane, or choose Insert⇨ Comment. Type your text in the comment box that pops up (see "Adding Comments to a Drawing").

- Track Markup doesn't allow you to change or delete shapes in the drawing, so if changing or deleting is your suggestion, add a comment stating that.

4. **Make any of the following suggestions using digital ink (refer to the section "Using Digital Ink" later in this chapter):**

   - Circle or mark areas using ink pens

   - Highlight areas using highlighters

   - Hand-write notes or draw stick figures using digital ink.

5. **When you've finished editing, save the file.**

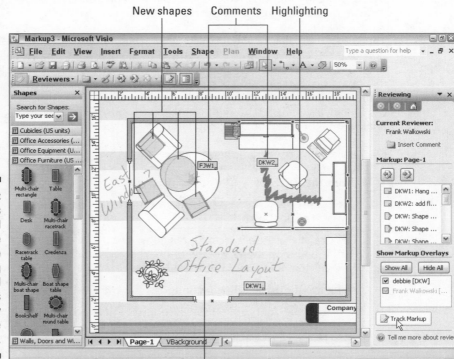

Figure 13-3: Reviewers suggested changes are listed in the Reviewing pane and show up as an overlay on the drawing.

If you are the creator of an original drawing and distribute it for review, but then decide later to make changes to it yourself, you should also use track markup. This makes your proposed changes to the original drawing, your comments, and your questions visible to reviewers. If you don't turn on Track Markup, your changes alter the original drawing.

Viewing markup in a drawing

If you're the originator of a drawing, it's important to be able to view markup from reviewers. But it's important to reviewers as well, especially if multiple reviewers are reviewing the same drawing. If you're a reviewer, your markup is viewable on the screen as you work because Visio creates your personal overlay when you turn on tracking. If others have already reviewed the drawing before you, their markup appears on overlays separate from yours.

Whether you are a reviewer or the originator of the drawing, you have the choice of viewing or not viewing markup.

Tracking markup and *viewing* markup are two separate things. Tracking turns on the feature of creating an overlay for a reviewer; viewing simply displays overlays.

Use these steps to view markup:

1. **Open the drawing file that you want to review.**

2. **Choose View⇨Task Pane or click the Reviewing Pane tool on the Reviewing toolbar to open the Reviewing task pane if it isn't already open.**

   Reviewers comments appear in the Reviewing pane.

3. **If you don't see any markup listed in the Reviewing pane, click the Show/Hide Markup button on the Reviewing toolbar.**

   Markup entries appear in the Reviewing pane and are identified by reviewers' initials and the specific color assigned to them.

4. **Make sure tracking is off.**

   When tracking is off, the first line of text in the Reviewing pane is "Markup Tracking is off" and you see overlay tabs with reviewers' initials along the right edge of the drawing page. The Original tab appears at the lower right.

When tracking is on, the individual reviewers' tabs disappear and a colored border outlines the drawing area. To turn tracking off, click the Track Markup button at the bottom of the Reviewing pane or in the Reviewing toolbar. (The Track Markup button toggles tracking on or off each time you click it.)

5. **To choose the overlays that you want to display, go to the Show Markup Overlays area of the Reviewing pane and do one of the following:**

   • To display all reviewers' overlays (see Figure 13-4), click the Show All button.

   • To turn off the display of all overlays, click Hide All.

   • To display reviewers comments selectively, click the check box next to the names of reviewers' whose overlays you want to display.

6. **In the Markup: Page-# area of the Reviewing task pane, click an entry to highlight the suggested change on the overlay.**

   All markup entries are grouped by reviewer (color-coded and preceded by initials).

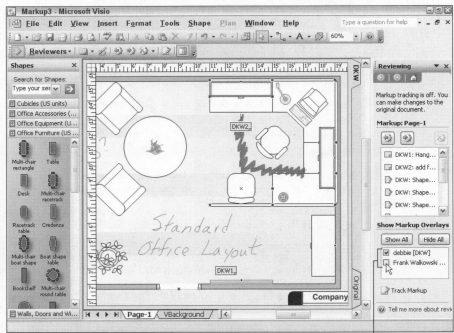

Figure 13-4:
You can choose which reviewers' markup to display in the Show Markup Overlays area.

Reviewers

7. **To move to the reviewer's next suggestion, click the Next Markup button in the Markup: Page-# area of the Reviewing task pane or on the Reviewing toolbar.**

After reviewing all markup, you might want to display only one reviewer's comments at a time when you get ready to incorporate changes.

Incorporating markup changes in a drawing

You might receive many types of suggested changes from reviewers: new or changed text, new or changed shapes; comments; format changes; and more. As the creator of the original drawing, you have control of which proposed changes you incorporate into the drawing.

Many other programs, such as word processors, allow you to accept proposed changes automatically, but Visio doesn't, strangely enough. Even weirder, Visio recommends that you *not* copy changes from an overlay into the drawing because, in some cases, the results can be unexpected (I guess they leave it to your imagination to figure out what *that* means!) I've tested copying changes from an overlay and haven't experienced any unexpected results, but then again, I haven't created every conceivable type of drawing, so . . .

Rather than copying changes, Visio suggests that you re-create the proposed changes. This means drag in new shapes, if necessary, edit text or create text boxes for new text, move or alter shapes as suggested, and apply new formatting as suggested.

To incorporate changes in a reviewed drawing, follow these steps:

1. **Open the drawing file that you want to change.**

2. **Open the Reviewing task pane, if it isn't open already.**

   Choose View➪Task Pane or click the Reviewing Pane tool on the Reviewing toolbar.

3. **If you don't see any markup in the Reviewing pane, click the Show/Hide Markup button on the Reviewing toolbar.**

4. **In the Show Markup Overlays area of the Reviewing pane, click to add a check mark for each reviewers' markup that you want to view.**

   You might choose to view only one at a time.

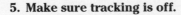

5. **Make sure tracking is off.**

   If you don't see "Markup Tracking is off" in the Reviewing pane, click the Track Markup button on the Reviewing toolbar or at the bottom of the Reviewing pane.

   When Tracking is off, the Original tab is selected automatically. This is where you want to make changes to the drawing. If any other tab is selected, click the Original tab before you begin making changes.

6. **Use the following strategy for making proposed changes:**

   • For a new shape placed correctly by the reviewer, drag the new shape into the drawing and drop it right on top of the reviewer's shape (or place it wherever you like).

   • For minor changes to the text, edit the existing text boxes.

   • For major changes to the text, create text boxes and format them appropriately.

   • For shapes that have special color or formatting suggested by the reviewer, copy and paste the shape to the original so you can see the formatting, and then create your own shape with the same formatting. (Or if you trust Visio to copy and paste the shape without "unexpected results," just use the pasted version.)

7. **As you complete each change, delete the reviewer's entry.**

   This step is optional but recommended. For details on how to delete an entry, see the next section, "Deleting markup."

8. **When you've finished making changes, save your file.**

Deleting markup

Eventually you'll want to delete markup that's been added to a drawing. One strategy, as outlined in the preceding section, is to delete markup entries one-by-one as you incorporate them into your drawing. However, if you prefer, you can delete all markup entries for a specific reviewer.

To delete individual entries as you work, highlight the entry that you want to delete in the list in the Reviewing pane. Then click the Delete Markup button in the Reviewing pane or on the Reviewing toolbar, as shown in Figure 13-5.

Delete Markup button   Delete Markup button

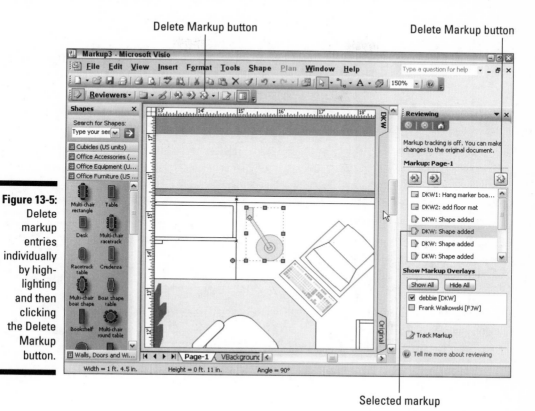

Figure 13-5:
Delete
markup
entries
individually
by high-
lighting
and then
clicking
the Delete
Markup
button.

Selected markup

You can also delete all markup for a specific reviewer or all markup for the entire page. Use these steps:

1. **In the Show Markup Overlays area of the Reviewing pane, click the Show All button.**

   All reviewers are listed.

2. **Click the down arrow next to the Delete Markup button on the Reviewing toolbar, as shown in Figure 13-6.**

   Note: The down arrow does not appear on the Delete Markup button in the Reviewing pane.

Delete Markup button

Reviewers

Figure 13-6:
Delete all
markup for
the current
page,
current doc-
ument, or a
selected
reviewer.

3. **From the drop-down list, choose one of the following:**

   - Delete Markup: Deletes the currently selected markup entry
   - Delete Markup Overlays on Current Page: Deletes all markups on the current page or choose a reviewer's name from the drop-down menu and delete all of his or her markups on the current page
   - Delete All Markup Overlays in Document: Deletes all markups on every page of the drawing

   Visio deletes the markup you selected.

Using Digital Ink

Another great markup tool — and a new feature in Visio 2003 — is called *digital ink*. With the popularity of graphic tablets and tablet PCs, digital ink makes a lot of sense. It lets you annotate a drawing the same way you would on paper. You can circle items, scribble handwritten notes, draw stick figures, and more. And the good news is, if you don't have a graphics tablet or a tablet PC, you can use digital ink with your mouse.

Selecting an ink tool

Visio provides several ink tools on the Ink toolbar (see Table 13-2). Two ball-point pens, a felt-tip pen, and two highlighters should provide plenty of choices for you to mark up a drawing. You also have an Eraser tool close at hand and buttons for adjusting the ink color and line thickness.

To select an ink tool, just click it. The mouse pointer changes to a pen-shaped pointer. The only difference between ballpoint and felt-tip is the point thickness: 1 point for the two ballpoint pens and 1¾ points for the felt-tipped pen. Highlighters draw at a thickness of 10 points, but they behave a little differently — like a real highlighter! They draw transparently, so whatever shape or text you highlight shows through.

1 point is approximately ½2 inch.

You can use any of the pen or highlighter tools as-is, or you can click the Ink Color or Ink Thickness button to change these characteristics. Click the drop-down arrow on the Ink Color button to display a color palette. The arrow next to the Thickness button drops down a list of thicknesses.

Table 13-2	**Toolbar Buttons for Working with Digital Ink**		
Button	*Name*	*Toolbar*	*What It Does*
	Ink Tool	Reviewing	Displays the Ink toolbar
	Ballpoint Pen (1) and (2)	Ink	Lets you draw or write on the screen in two different colors; 1 is blue, and 2 is black
	Felt-tip Pen	Ink	Lets you draw or write on the screen
	Highlighter (1) and (2)	Ink	Lets you highlight areas in a drawing in two different colors; 1 is yellow, and 2 is green
	Eraser	Ink	Lets you erase any markup you've made
	Close Ink Shape	Ink	Closes a selected ink shape
	Ink Color	Ink	Lets you change the color of ink for any pen or highlighter
	Ink Thickness	Ink	Lets you adjust the thickness of pens

Using ink tools

You can use the pens and highlighters from the Ink toolbar to mark up or point out areas in a drawing, or you can use them to design a shape. If you just want to circle something in a drawing, sketch an arrow to draw attention to an item, highlight an area of the drawing, or hand-write a text message, you can use a pen or highlighter the same way you would if you were drawing on paper. Figure 13-7 shows a drawing that has been marked up with handwritten comments, added shapes, and highlighted areas.

Use these steps to add digital ink markings to a drawing:

1. **Open the drawing that you want to annotate.**

2. **Right-click the toolbar area and choose Ink.**

   The Ink toolbar appears (refer to Figure 13-7).

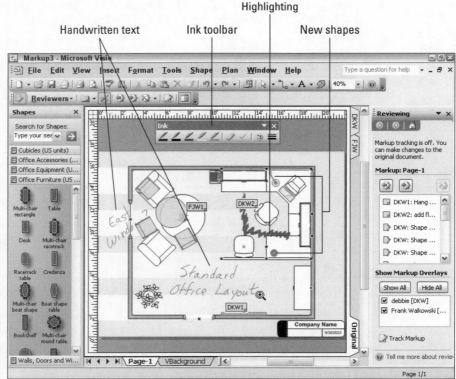

Figure 13-7: Ink works on the screen just like a pen and highlighter on paper.

Handwritten text · Ink toolbar · Highlighting · New shapes

3. **Click one of the Ballpoint Pen buttons or the Felt-Tip Pen button on the Ink toolbar.**

4. **Begin drawing or writing a comment.**

   The mouse pointer changes to a pen-shaped pointer.

   Note: If you're using a mouse rather than a pen on a tablet, hold the left mouse button down as you draw or write. You *can* lift your pen as you draw or write a comment, but you must do it very quickly!

   If you want to fill a shape that you drew using digital ink, you must draw it using only *one* line segment and be sure to close it by joining the end to the beginning. (Zoom in on the drawing area so that you can see the endpoints clearly.) If you use multiple line segments, Visio doesn't recognize it as a closed shape and therefore can't fill it.

5. **When you finish, lift your pen (or release the mouse button) and pause.**

   After a second or two, Visio draws a dotted blue outline with solid corners around the text or shape that you drew. Everything within this border is now considered a shape. (Even if you "drew" text, it's considered a shape right now.)

6. **To stop using digital ink, click the Pointer Tool (or another tool).**

To erase a text or a shape you drew, click the Eraser tool on the Ink toolbar. The mouse pointer changes to an eraser shape. Move the eraser near the text or shape that you want to delete, and it becomes highlighted. Click the mouse button or, if you're using a pen, tap the shape to delete it. The Eraser tool can delete only the entire text or shape, not parts of it.

Changing digital ink shapes to geometry or text

You can convert any shape that you draw using digital ink to *geometry*. This means it becomes an actual Visio shape, just as if you had drawn it using a drawing tool. For example, the rug shape shown in Figure 13-8 was drawn using a digital ink pen. (I suppose I could have drawn it using the freeform drawing tool, but the freeform tool doesn't behave the way the ink pen does.)

Why would you want to convert a digital ink shape to geometry? Because unless you convert it, you can't alter the shape itself or change its formatting, such as line color and style, fill color, transparency, and shadow. (If you don't care about doing these things, converting a digital ink shape isn't necessary.)

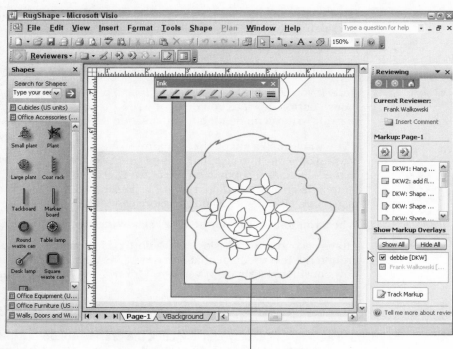

Figure 13-8:
The rug
shape was
drawn using
a ballpoint
pen ink tool.

Hand-drawn shape

To convert a digital ink shape to geometry, use these steps:

1. **Click the Pointer Tool on the Standard toolbar.**

2. **Right-click the digital ink shape you want to convert and choose Convert Ink to Geometry.**

   Visio displays the shape's selection handles, as shown in Figure 13-9. Now you're free to change the characteristics of the shape, such as its line width, line color, fill color, and fill pattern.

Sometimes when you draw a closed shape and then convert it to geometry, you end up with a 1-D shape instead of a 2-D shape. (This can occur if your beginning point and endpoint don't meet.) If you want the shape to be 2-D, right-click it and choose Format⇨Behavior. On the Behavior tab of the Behavior dialog box, choose the Box (2-Dimensional) option and then click OK. Visio converts the shape to a 2-D shape.

A very cool new feature of Visio 2003 is the ability to convert ink to text. If your drawing contains hand-written comments that you created using a tablet PC, you can convert them to text. (Tablet PCs allow you to draw and hand-write text using a stylus.)

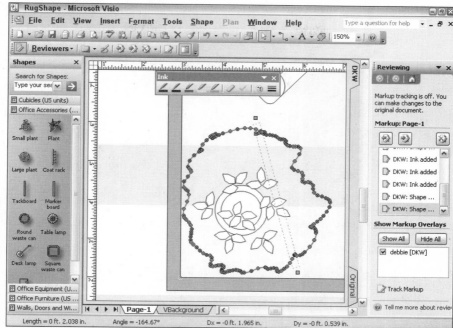

Figure 13-9:
The rug
shape is
converted
to geometry,
or a Visio
shape.

The convert ink to text feature works only for tablet PCs. (If the comment wasn't written on a tablet PC, the menu Convert Ink to Text option appears dimmed, indicating that it's unavailable.) If your drawing contains comments that were created using an attached drawing tablet or the mouse, those comments *can't* be converted.

To convert comments created on a tablet PC to text, use these steps:

1. **Click the Pointer Tool on the Standard toolbar.**

2. **Right-click the digital ink words that you want to convert to text and choose Convert Ink to Text.**

   See Figure 13-10. (This command is available only on a tablet PC.) Visio converts the handwritten words to text, as shown in Figure 13-11.

The conversion of handwriting to text is accurate, for the most part, but be sure to check the spelling and punctuation of the converted text for errors. The closer the handwriting looks to printing, the more accurate the conversion.

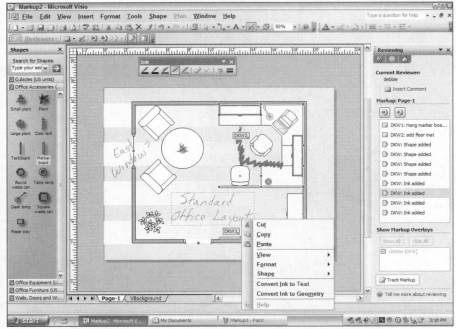

Figure 13-10: The Convert Ink to Text option is available only if you have a tablet PC.

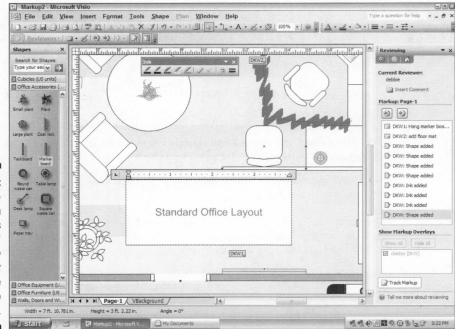

Figure 13-11: The hand-written words *Standard Office Layout* are converted to text.

Chapter 14

Using Visio with Other Programs

Sometimes we can get away with using just one computer program to create a document that stands alone. That's okay for some projects, but others — especially large, mostly text documents — are far more involved. You know if you splash some color, charts, graphs, photos, or tables throughout the document, you're much more likely to keep the reader awake and make your point more effectively.

Sharing data and objects is common with most programs, and Visio is no exception. As a member of the Microsoft Office suite of products, Visio lets you share diagrams and information; and that sharing works in both directions: think of it as inbound and outbound. For instance, you can use Visio diagrams in other documents (outbound), and you can insert data or images (inbound) into Visio drawings. A sophisticated inbound feature of Visio is the capability to use data from other programs to generate Visio diagrams. And, of course, you also have the option of e-mailing Visio drawings to colleagues, or saving drawings in a format that lets you use them as Web pages.

The moral of this story? No document is an island unto itself! Read on to find out how to use these features.

Using Files from Other Programs in Visio

The most common way to share information from other programs in Visio is to paste the information, insert the information, or open a file of another type. You can paste objects from various sources, as you see later in this chapter in the "Exporting and importing shapes and drawings" section.

Using commands on the Insert menu, Visio lets you insert the following:

- Picture (from a file, clip art, or a scanner, or a camera)
- Chart (a simple bar chart you create by entering data)
- Equation symbol
- WordArt
- CAD drawing
- Object

Most of these choices are obvious, except perhaps inserting an object. When you choose the Insert⊅Object command, a dialog box appears, displaying a few dozen different objects (such as a media or video clip, a PowerPoint slide, a Microsoft Address Book View, and an Excel worksheet). Simply select the type of object you want, and insert an existing file, create one, or display an icon for the object rather than the object itself.

If you prefer, you can open a file in Visio. Following are the file types you're allowed to open:

- Drawing, Stencil, Template, Workspace (all Visio file types)
- Scalable Vector Graphics
- AutoCAD Drawing
- Compressed Enhanced Metafile
- Enhanced Metafile
- Graphics Interchange Format (.gif)
- JPEG File Interchange Format (.jpg)
- Portable Network Graphics
- Tagged Image File Format (.tif)
- Windows Bitmap (.bmp)
- Windows Metafile (.wmf)

These file types appear in the Files of Type box in the Open dialog box. When you choose File⊅Open and select a file of one of these listed types, the file is pasted in the current Visio drawing.

The file opened by the File➪Open command replaces any existing shapes in the drawing.

Generating Drawings from Data Stored in Non-Visio Files

Want to save yourself some work? If you have data stored in files you created with other programs such as Microsoft Excel, Microsoft Project, a database, or a simple text file, you can create drawings from your stored data. Why would you want to do that? Check out these three good reasons:

✔ **You can avoid re-entering data.** Maybe you have a lot of data that exists in another program, such as Excel. Do you want to take the time to re-enter the entire database in Visio — just so you can create a drawing? If the data already exists, you can save yourself a lot of time by saving the file in a format that Visio can use to create a drawing for you.

✔ **You can enter the data in the program in which you use it most.** If your data doesn't already exist, sometimes it can be faster to enter the raw data in another program — the program where you really need the data — and have Visio do the work of creating a drawing for you.

✔ **You can share drawings with other Visio users who may not have the same applications that you use to store and compile data.** Suppose that you're a project manager and rely on Microsoft Project to schedule and track large projects. Your site managers, however, don't have Project but do have Visio. You can use Project to generate a daily or weekly Gantt chart (which maps project tasks on a timeline) in Visio and then e-mail them to your site managers. The managers don't need to have Project or know how to use it. All they need to do is open a Visio drawing.

Creating an organization chart from existing data

In a company of any significant size, the information in organization charts — employee names, titles, and reporting managers — is almost surely stored already in a Human Resources database. You don't need to re-key this information just to create an organization chart in Visio; you can use the data you already have.

Obviously, maintaining employee privacy is an issue, but your company's Human Resources department might be willing to provide a subset of non-confidential employee information for you to use.

Visio's Organization Chart Wizard is a fantastic tool that makes all this possible. (A *wizard* is a set of scripted questions that you answer so Visio can do the behind-the-scenes work for you.) The wizard looks for employee data in one of several possible file formats:

- ✔ Microsoft Excel (.xls) format.

- ✔ Microsoft Outlook format.

- ✔ Tab-delimited file (.txt file extension). A tab-delimited file includes a tab character between variables, such as first name, last name, and title.

- ✔ Comma-delimited text file (.csv file extension). A comma-delimited file contains a comma character as the separator between variables. Figure 14-1 shows a text file that uses commas to separate variables.

- ✔ Org-Plus text file (.txt).

- ✔ ODBC-compliant database such as Microsoft Access.

Regardless of the file type, the data must be set up in a format that Visio can work with. For example, the employee data file at a minimum *must* include the following pieces of information (referred to as variables, or *fields*).

- ✔ A unique identifier for each employee, whether a name or an employee number. An employee name can meet the requirement as a unique identifier if each name is unique.

- ✔ The unique ID of the person to whom the employee reports.

Individual records   Field names   Blank field

Figure 14-1:
A comma-delimited file uses commas to separate variables such as name, position, and department.

Notice in Figure 14-1 that the first row of data serves as the column headings for the data fields: Unique_ID, Last_Name, First_Initial, Position, Reports_To, and Department. The fields don't have to appear in any particular order; the wizard finds the data it needs based on the column headings. You also can include more data fields in the organization chart, such as the employee's phone number or physical location.

TIP

To leave a field blank, enter a comma (with no spaces) between the two commas used to separate entries. (In an Excel file, leave the cell blank.)

To create an organization chart from an existing data file, use these steps:

1. **Choose File⇨New⇨Organization Chart⇨Organization Chart Wizard.**

   Visio displays the first screen of the wizard. The option to create the organization chart from information already stored in a file or database is already selected for you.

2. **Click the Next button to go to the second screen of the wizard (see Figure 14-2).**

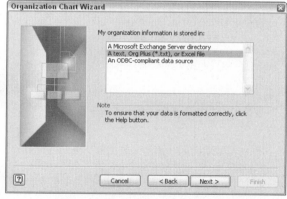

Figure 14-2:
Choose a
data source
for your
organiza-
tion chart.

3. **Choose one of the following sources, and then click Next:**

   • A Microsoft Exchange Server directory

   • A text, Org Plus (*.txt), or Microsoft Excel (.xls) file: This could be any text file formatted like the one shown in Figure 14-1 and containing a unique identifier for each employee and for the person to whom the employee reports.

   • An ODBC-compliant data source: An example is Microsoft Access. Again, the file must contain a unique identifier for each employee and for the person to whom the employee reports.

4. **Locate and select the file that contains the data (click the Browse button if necessary), and then click Next.**

5. **Choose the fields from your data file that correspond to Name, Reports to, and First name, and then click Next.**

6. **Choose the fields you want to include in the organization chart, and then click Next.**

7. **Choose any fields that you want to add to the organization chart shapes as custom property fields, and then click Next.**

   Custom properties contain data stored with a shape (for instance, an employee's telephone number, location, and hire date). For more information about using custom properties, refer to Chapter 13.

8. **On the last page of the wizard, choose how you want to fit information onto the page, and then click Finish.**

   If your organization chart is likely to be larger than one page, you might want to click the option that lets you specify how much data to display on each page. Otherwise, let the wizard decide how to break the chart across pages.

Visio creates the organization chart based on your data file, the fields that you choose to include, and the format you specify. If the chart has some unexpected results, go back, check the format and content of your input file, and then run the wizard again. Each time you run the wizard, it places the new organization chart output on a new page in the same Visio drawing.

 The Info button on most wizard screens is very helpful! If you ever need an explanation of the information that the wizard is looking for, click this button to get help.

A sample of an organization chart generated from data in a text (.txt) file is shown in Figure 14-3. The raw data is there. Now you can add to, format, and spice up the chart as you want. (Refer to Chapter 8 for more information.)

 Sometimes when you use a wizard to create an organization chart, the boxes are too small to hold all the text. You don't want to reduce the font size and make it unreadable, but you don't want to resize each box manually, either! Choose View➪Size & Position to display the Size and Position window. Then select all the boxes you want to resize. (Make sure that you select only the boxes that you want to be the same size.) In the Size and Position window, type new dimensions for Width and Height, and then click anywhere outside the selected shapes. Visio resizes all the selected boxes to the same dimensions.

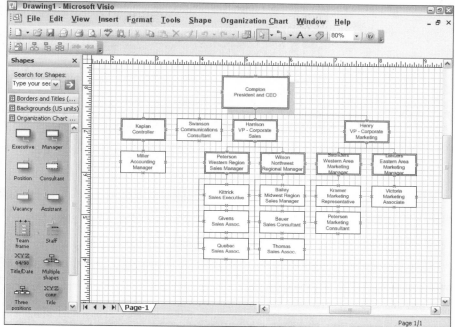

Figure 14-3:
Visio gen-
erates an
organization
chart based
on data in
your text
(.txt) file.

Creating a Gantt chart by importing data

A Gantt chart is a specific type of diagram used for managing a project. A typical *Gantt chart* lists the tasks that you need to complete to accomplish a specific goal, the duration of each task, their dependent tasks, and the resources (people and materials) required to complete each task. It can also show scheduled dates for beginning and completion, as well as the progress made to-date on each task.

If the project data that you want to use exists in a text (.txt) file, the fields must be separated by a tab or a comma (see Figure 14-4). You can also use data from Microsoft Excel (.xls format) or data from Microsoft Project (.mpp or .mpx format), as described later in this chapter. Whatever the file type, the file that contains the data is called the *source* file.

Individual tasks   Empty fields   Field names

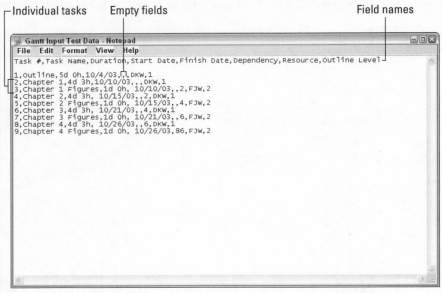

Figure 14-4:
This
comma-
delimited
text file
contains
the correct
data to
generate a
Gantt chart
in Visio.

For all file types, the data must include at least the following fields for each project task:

- ✔ **Unique task number or identifier:** Any number or name that you give to a task to identify it uniquely.

- ✔ **Task name:** The name that you give to a task that's part of a project.

- ✔ **Duration:** The time allowed to complete a task (for example, days, days/hours, hours, weeks).

- ✔ **Start date:** The date when you want a task to begin.

- ✔ **Finish date:** The date when you want a task to be completed.

- ✔ **Dependency (dependent task):** The task that must be completed before the current task can begin.

- ✔ **Resource:** The human resources or materials needed to complete a task.

- ✔ **Outline level:** Highest-level tasks are at outline level 1; subordinate tasks (not dependent tasks) are at outline level 2, and so on.

Importing data from a text file

If you have a text file that contains the data outlined in the preceding section, you can use it to create a Gantt chart using the Gantt Chart Wizard. The wizard guides you through a series of steps and asks you questions about which file to use (your text file is your *source* file), what information you want to include, and how you want the information formatted.

Use these steps to start the wizard:

1. **Choose File⇨New⇨Project Schedule⇨Gantt Chart.**

   Visio creates a Gantt chart drawing and displays the Gantt Chart Options dialog box. Notice also that the Gantt chart toolbar is displayed and that the menu bar now contains a Gantt Chart menu (see Figure 14-5).

2. **Select the options you want (that is, the number of tasks, the units, the duration format, and the start and finish dates), and then click OK.**

   The options you choose here are not set in stone! You can change them at any time. Pay attention to the format for task durations (for example: Days/Hours). It must match the format used in your source file.

3. **Choose Tools⇨Import.**

   Visio displays the first screen of the Gantt Chart Wizard.

4. **Click the Information That's Already Stored in a File option, and then click Next.**

5. **Choose Text File, and then click Next.**

6. **Continue following the steps throughout the wizard. When you get to the last screen, click Finish.**

   Visio creates the Gantt chart for you, inserting your data (see Figure 14-6).

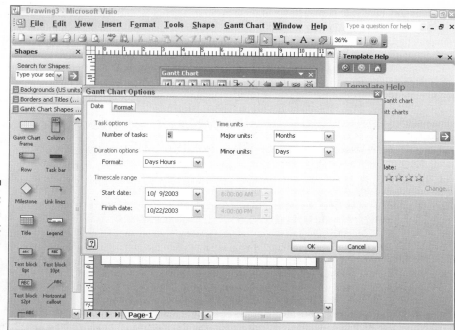

Figure 14-5:
Choose Gantt chart settings for units, duration format, dates, and so on.

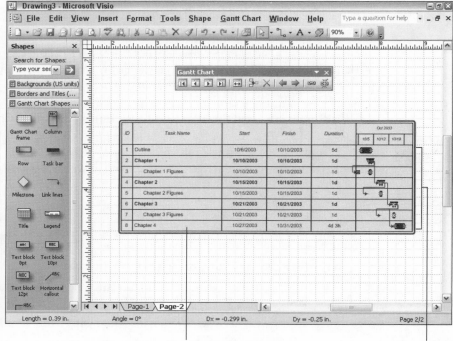

Figure 14-6:
This Gantt
chart was
generated
from data in
a text file.

Gantt chart shape placed by wizard   Your data

If by chance an error exists in your file, you get an error message like the one
shown in Figure 14-7. The error message tells you exactly which line in your
text file the wizard didn't understand. Go back to your text file and check for
errors on the suggested line.

Figure 14-7:
The error
message
directs you
to the line in
the text file
where the
error exists.

Importing data from Microsoft Excel

Maybe your project data is stored in a Microsoft Excel spreadsheet rather
than in a text file. In that case, each task appears on a separate spreadsheet
row, but each piece of information, or *field*, appears in a separate column

(instead of being separated by commas). The Excel data shown in Figure 14-8 is identical to the text data shown in Figure 14-4.

The same rules apply for Excel that apply to text files! Check that the content and format of your data meet the requirements discussed in the "Creating a Gantt chart by importing data" section, and then follow these steps:

1. **Choose File⇨New⇨Project Schedule⇨Gantt Chart.**

   Visio creates a Gantt Chart drawing and displays the Gantt Chart Options dialog box. The Gantt chart toolbar is displayed and the menu bar now contains a Gantt Chart menu.

2. **Select the options you want (that is, the number of tasks, the units, the duration format, and the start and finish dates), and then click OK.**

3. **Choose Tools⇨Import.**

   Visio displays the first screen of the Gantt Chart Wizard.

4. **Choose the Information That's Already Stored in a File option, and then click Next.**

5. **Choose Microsoft Excel File, and then click Next.**

Field names   Individual tasks

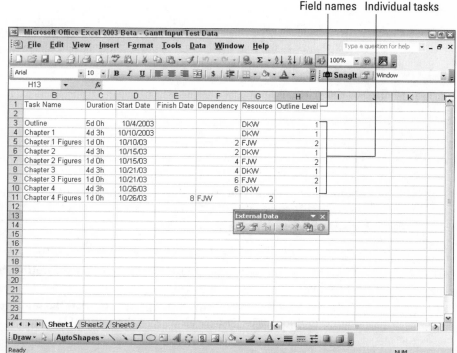

Figure 14-8: This Excel database file contains all the data needed to generate a Gantt chart in Visio.

6. **Continue following the steps throughout the wizard. When you get to the last screen, click Finish.**

   Visio creates the Gantt chart based on the data in your Excel spreadsheet. If you get unexpected results, go back to your Excel file and check all data and formats.

Importing data from Microsoft Project

You can also import data from a Microsoft Project file to create a Gantt chart in Visio.

Wait a minute! Is there something wrong with this picture? Why would you want to create a Gantt chart in Visio using data you import from Microsoft Project when Project itself creates Gantt charts?

The answer is simple. A colleague might send you (or you might have access to) a Microsoft Project file, but you might not have the program to view the file. In this case, use the same steps outlined previously for importing data from a text or Excel file, but specify your Project file as the source file.

Creating data rather than importing

If your data doesn't exist yet and you don't have access to other project management software, you can enter the raw data right into the Gantt Chart Wizard. The wizard creates a text (.txt) file or Excel (.xls) file template for you, opens it, and includes sample data for all the required fields. A sample of an Excel template created by the wizard is shown in Figure 14-9. Just replace the sample data with your data.

Follow these steps:

1. **Choose File➪New➪Project Schedule➪Gantt Chart.**

   Visio creates a Gantt Chart drawing and displays the Gantt Chart Options dialog box. The Gantt chart toolbar is displayed and the menu bar now contains a Gantt Chart menu.

2. **Select the options you want (that is, the number of tasks, the units, the duration format, and the start and finish dates), and then click OK.**

3. **Choose Tools➪Import.**

   Visio displays the first screen of the Gantt Chart Wizard.

4. **Click the Information that I Enter Using the Wizard option, and then click Next.**

5. **Enter the tasks options, duration options, time units, and timescale range that apply to your project, and then click OK.**

Individual project tasks   Column headings

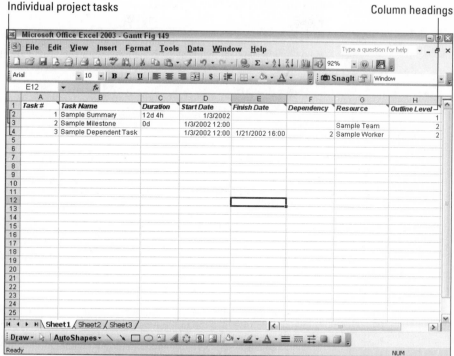

6. **Continue through the rest of the wizard screens. When you get to the last screen, click Finish.**

   Visio places a Gantt Chart shape in your drawing, inserting your data.

Creating a calendar by importing Outlook appointments

Since you can print a calendar from Microsoft Outlook directly, why would you want to import Outlook data to a Visio calendar? Here are a few reasons:

✔ In Visio, you can reformat the calendar, changing its size, shape, coloring, and special effects such as highlights, shadows, and imported clip art. (You can't do all this in Outlook.)

✔ You can print and distribute the reformatted calendar

✔ You can publish the calendar on the Web

To import an Outlook calendar into Visio, use these steps:

1. **Choose File⇨New⇨Project Schedule⇨Calendar.**

   Visio creates a new Calendar drawing and add a Calendar menu to the standard menu bar.

2. **Choose Calendar⇨Import Outlook Data Wizard.**

   The first screen of the Calendar Wizard appears.

3. **Choose New Visio Calendar.**

   The second page of the wizard appears, where you choose calendar dates and times to include.

4. **Continue providing information on the wizard screens, clicking the Next button after completing each screen.**

5. **At the last wizard screen, click Finish.**

   Visio creates a calendar shape that spans the dates you specified. It includes all appointments scheduled for those dates. A sample file reformatted in Visio is shown in Figure 14-10.

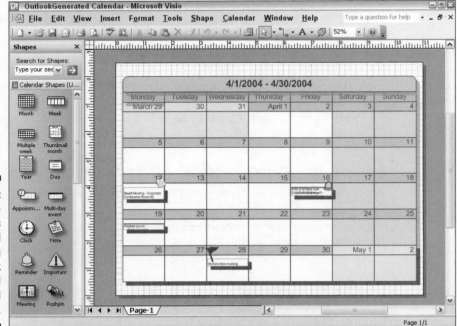

Figure 14-10:
This calendar was generated using Outlook data and reformatted in Visio.

Incorporating Visio Shapes and Drawings in Non-Visio Documents

The *object linking and embedding* (OLE) feature of Microsoft Windows makes it possible to share many types of data and graphic images between Windows-compatible applications. A Visio drawing or selected Visio shapes can be linked to a document or embedded in a document, as long as the program that produces the document supports OLE. (Most Windows programs support OLE.) Linking and embedding produce the same results visually, but they're different behind the scenes, as you find out in this section.

When a program doesn't support OLE, you can *export* Visio drawings or shapes to non-Visio documents. This section describes these three methods for sharing data and images between programs. Table 14-1 summarizes the differences between the linking, embedding, and exporting methods.

Linking shapes and drawings

Linking creates a special connection between two files: the *source file* (where the data is created and displayed) and the *destination file* (where the data is displayed only). When you link data to a destination file, the original data stays in the source file where you created it. When you open the destination file, you see a *representation of the data*, like a snapshot, but it isn't really part of the file.

Scratching your head? Think of it like this: Suppose you link a Visio drawing (the source file) to an Excel spreadsheet (the destination file). When you open your Excel spreadsheet, you see the Visio drawing displayed right before your eyes — like magic! But like the magician's sawed-in-half assistant, it isn't really there. It's as if Excel opens up a door in the spreadsheet and moves your drawing right into the doorway. You see the drawing, but it isn't part of your Excel file. You still have only one drawing, and it's located in Visio.

Sending drawings to Outlook

Microsoft Outlook uses the Microsoft Exchange Server format for storing files. If you want to store a drawing in an Outlook folder, you can. Open the Visio drawing and choose File➪Send To➪Exchange Folder. Choose the folder that you want and then click OK. Your drawing is stored as an embedded object in the Outlook folder you chose (such as Drafts). You can open the drawing in Outlook, and then send it to someone using File➪Send To.

Table 14-1	Link, Embed, or Export?		
	Link	**Embed**	**Export**
Description	Establishes a connection between a Visio drawing or shape and the non-Visio file or document to which the shape is linked.	Places the Visio drawing or shape in a non-Visio file without making a connection between the two.	Converts the Visio drawing to a different file format that a non-Visio program can accept.
Result	A representation of the Visio drawing or shape appears in the non-Visio document. When you update the drawing or shape in Visio, it's updated automatically in the non-Visio document as well.	A Visio drawing or shape that becomes part of the non-Visio document as an embedded object.	A converted Visio drawing or shape. The conversion changes the Visio drawing or shape to a graphics file (such as .gif, .tif, or .bmp), which can be inserted or pasted into a non-Visio file.
Use It When...	Changes to the original Visio drawing or shape should be reflected in the non-Visio document. You want to keep a drawing up-to-date in several different non-Visio files. You have access to the original Visio drawing on your computer or network. You want to keep the non-Visio file size.	Updating a drawing in the non-Visio document isn't important. File size isn't a concern. The Visio drawing isn't stored on your computer.	The non-Visio program is not compatible with Microsoft OLE (that is, linking and embedding won't work).

Why would you care about the behind-the-scenes workings of linking? The fact that the Visio drawing isn't part of your non-Visio file keeps the file size down. One more thing — and this is a biggie: If you update the drawing in Visio, the drawing is automatically updated in the non-Visio document too. The next time you open your non-Visio file, the Visio drawing or shapes are automatically updated as soon as you open the file. You don't have to worry about keeping track of which version is where or which version is most current.

You might not care whether the original Visio drawing is identical to the Visio object in the non-Visio file. But you can still edit the drawing in the non-Visio file if you need to using in-place editing. With this slick feature, you double-click the drawing in the non-Visio program. Visio opens a mini-Visio window and displays Visio menus and toolbars so you can edit the drawing or shape right where you are. When you finish updating the drawing, save it and then click anywhere outside the image. The non-Visio application's toolbars and menus are redisplayed and you can keep working without ever having to start Visio. (Remember that the original drawing is untouched.)

All of these reasons make linking a good option to choose when you want to use a drawing in several different non-Visio files and keep it updated in all its locations. To link data from a Visio drawing to another file, follow these steps:

1. **In Visio, open the drawing that you want to link to another file.**

   Note that the file must be saved before it can be linked.

2. **Choose Edit⇨Copy Drawing.**

3. **Open the document in the non-Visio program where you want to link the Visio drawing.**

4. **Choose Edit⇨Paste Special.**

   Some programs may use a different command for linking files. If this command is not on your menu, check the online help or user documentation for the program that you're using.

5. **In the Paste Special dialog box, select Microsoft Visio Drawing Object from the list box (see Figure 14-11).**

6. **On the left side of the box, click the Paste Link button, and then click OK.**

   The drawing or shapes that you linked are now displayed in the non-Visio program's document.

Figure 14-11:
This Paste
Special
dialog
box from
Microsoft
Word lists
several file
formats,
including
Microsoft
Visio
Drawing
Object.

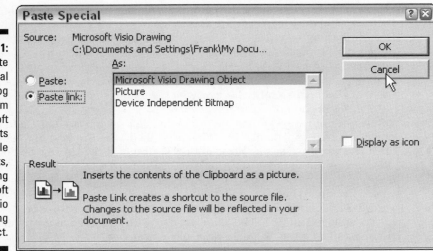

Embedding shapes in drawings

You've probably been embedding objects for years without even knowing it — every time you cut and paste (or copy and paste) from one program to another, you're embedding objects.

Embedding is different from linking because the data you embed becomes part of the destination file (which automatically increases the size of the destination file). Once embedded, if you change, or update, the data in the destination file, the data in the source file is *not* automatically updated. Likewise, if you change the data in the source file, the data in the destination file remains unchanged. Embedding keeps the two files separate.

Just like with linking, when you embed a Visio drawing or shape into a non-Visio file, you have in-place editing capability. Double-click the Visio object in the non-Visio file. The Visio object appears inside a mini Visio window, and the Visio menus and toolbars are displayed. Edit the object, and then click anywhere outside the object to return to your non-Visio file. The original Visio file remains unchanged. To save the embedded Visio object, save the non-Visio file.

Embedding is a good option when you want the data to be part of your destination file, when you're pretty sure the data won't be updated (or, if it is, you don't care whether the original is updated), when there's a possibility that you won't be storing the source file on your computer, and when increased file size is not an issue.

To embed a Visio shape or an entire drawing in a non-Visio file, use these steps:

1. **Open the document in the program where you want to link the Visio shape or drawing.**

2. **Open the Visio drawing that you want to use.**

3. **In your Visio drawing, select the shape or shapes that you want to paste in the non-Visio document.**

   To use the entire drawing, choose Edit⇨Select All.

4. **To copy the shape(s) from Visio, choose Edit⇨Copy or click the Copy button on the Standard toolbar.**

5. **Switch to the other program and click in the document where you want to paste the shape or shapes.**

6. **Choose Edit⇨Paste, or click the Paste button on the Standard toolbar.**

   The shape or shapes are pasted into the non-Visio document.

As mentioned, this method makes no connection between the two files. These steps are similar to dropping a clip art image into a document. No association or connection between the two files or the data in each file is formed. If you need a connection between the two, use linking, described in the preceding section.

Exporting and importing shapes and drawings

Some computer programs are not OLE compatible; in other words, they don't support Edit⇨Copy and Edit⇨Paste or Edit⇨Paste Special. When you want to use a Visio shape or drawing in a program that doesn't support OLE, you can export the file. *Exporting* converts the data in a Visio file to a non-Visio file format — one that you choose. In the non-Visio program, you then *import* the file as a picture.

Table 14-2 lists all the file types that you can use to export a Visio drawing. The file type that you choose for exporting depends on two things: the program that you want to use the drawing in and how you're going to use the drawing. For example, if you just want to insert the drawing in another file as a picture, use a common graphics format, such as *.bmp, .tif, or .gif. If you want to use the drawing in an AutoCAD file, choose the AutoCAD drawing or AutoCAD Interchange format.

Table 14-2	File Formats for Exporting Visio Drawings
Drawing (Visio 2003 drawing)	AutoCAD Drawing
Stencil (Visio 2003 stencil)	AutoCAD Interchange
Template (Visio 2003 template)	Web Page
XML Drawing	Compressed Enhanced Metafile
XML Stencil	Enhanced Metafile
XML Template	Graphics Interchange Format (.gif)
Visio 2002 Drawing	JPEG File Interchange Format (.jpg)
Visio 2002 Stencil	Portable Network Graphics
Visio 2002 Template	Tag Image File Format (.tif)
Scalable Vector Graphics	Windows Bitmap (.bmp)
Scalable Vector Graphics — Compressed	Windows Metafile (.wmf)

To export a Visio drawing (or selected shapes from a drawing), follow these steps:

1. **Start Visio and open the drawing that you want to export.**

   If you want to export a few shapes rather than the entire drawing, hold down the Shift key as you click the shapes that you want to export.

2. **Choose File⇨Save As to display the Save As dialog box.**

3. **In the Save In drop-down menu, select the folder where you want to save the drawing.**

4. **In the File Name box, type a name for the file.**

5. **In the Save As Type drop-down menu, choose a file format.**

   Refer to Table 14-2 and Figure 14-12.

6. **Click the Save button.**

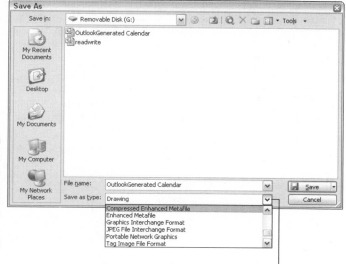

Figure 14-12:
The Save
As Type box
lists all
available file
formats.

Click to display the list of file formats

In the non-Visio program, use the program's Import command to bring the Visio drawing into the document.

Sending drawings through e-mail

If you use electronic mail and want to e-mail drawings to other Visio users, you can do so as long as your e-mail program supports the *Messaging Application Program Interface* (MAPI) protocol. (Check with your network administrator to see whether your program supports the MAPI protocol.) To view the Visio drawing, the message recipient must have Visio or the Visio Viewer running on his or her computer, as mentioned later in this chapter.

To e-mail a drawing to another Visio user, use these steps:

1. **Start Visio and open the drawing that you want to send through e-mail.**

2. **Choose File⇨Send To⇨Mail Recipient (as Attachment).**

   Visio displays an e-mail message window for you. The file name is inserted in the Subject line and appears in the Attach box.

3. **Enter the recipient's e-mail address in the To box.**

4. **If you want to include a message, type it in the message area.**

5. **Click the Send button.**

If you're running Microsoft Office 2000 or later, you can use the Office features that let you route an e-mail message to more than one user (for instance, so that all users in your group can review a Visio drawing). To add a routing slip to an e-mail message, follow these steps:

1. **Open Visio and the drawing that you want to send.**

2. **Choose File⇨Send To⇨Routing Recipient.**

   The Routing Slip dialog box appears, as shown in Figure 14-13.

3. **Click the Address button.**

   The Address Book dialog box appears.

4. **Select the recipients in the Address Book, and then click OK.**

   Visio returns to the Routing Recipient dialog box.

5. **To route the drawing in a specific order, click a name in the list and then click the Move arrow (either up or down) to reorder the names.**

   Do this for all names until they are in the order that you want.

6. **If you reordered the routing (in Step 5), click the One After Another option in the Route to Recipients box. Otherwise, click the All at Once option.**

7. **Choose Return When Done to have the drawing sent back to you after everyone views it, or choose Track Status to receive an update after each person on the list views the drawing.**

8. **To add a message to the e-mail, type the text in the Message Text box.**

9. **Click OK.**

10. **Choose File⇨Send To⇨Next Routing Recipient to send the message.**

Figure 14-13:
Enter the
addresses
of all
recipients.

Using Visio Viewer to Share Visio Drawings

Even if some of your colleagues don't have Visio, you can still send them a Visio drawing. To view the drawing, they must download and install Visio Viewer from the Microsoft Download Center:

```
http://office.microsoft.com/downloads
```

When you open a drawing using Visio Viewer, the drawing is displayed in a Microsoft Internet Explorer (Version 5.0 or later) window. Note that you can view a drawing created in Visio 2003 only with Visio Viewer 2003. However, you can view drawings created in earlier versions of Visio (Version 5.0, 2000, and 2002) using Visio Viewer 2002, also downloadable from Microsoft's download center.

At the time of this writing, Visio Viewer 2003 isn't yet available. Please continue to check the Microsoft Web site periodically for updates.

Saving Visio Drawings for the Web

The Internet contains so much information — and graphics are a huge part of that. Gone are the days of waiting ten minutes for a picture to download. High-speed access makes your Visio drawings download almost as fast as a puny text file!

Many software companies are making it easier than ever to save files specifically for publishing to the Web, and Microsoft is no exception. The File menu in Visio now contains a Save As Web Page command, which automatically saves your drawing in .html (Hypertext Markup Language) format. You can save new Visio drawings directly to this format, or save existing Visio drawings in Visio format as well as .html. Your drawings will look as cool on your Web page as they do in Visio.

Use these steps to save a drawing as a Web page:

1. **Start Visio and create or open the file that you want to save.**
2. **Choose File➪Save As Web Page.**

   You might need to click the down arrow at the bottom of the file menu to display this command. The Save As dialog box appears, as shown in Figure 14-14.

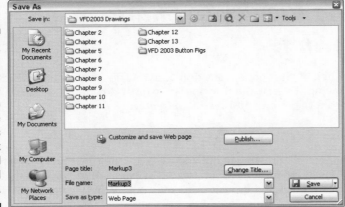

Figure 14-14:
When you
choose
File⇨Save
As Web
Page, the
Save As
dialog box
has special
Web-related
options.

3. **In the Save In box, choose the folder in which you want to save the file.**

4. **In the File Name box, type a name for the file.**

5. **If you want to change the name that appears in the title bar in the Web browser when the page is displayed:**

   a. **Click the Change Title button.**

   b. **Type a name in the Set Page Title dialog box.**

   c. **Click OK.**

   Visio returns to the Save As dialog box.

6. **In the Save As Type box, choose Web Page, if it's not already chosen for you.**

7. **Click the Save button. (To save the file as Read Only, click the down arrow next to the Save button and select Read Only.)**

   Visio saves the file and displays it in a Microsoft Internet Explorer window.

8. **To close the file, click the X in the upper-right corner, or choose File⇨Close.**

The file is now ready to be published to a Web site. Use whatever procedures you normally do to upload the file.

Part V
The Part of Tens

The 5th Wave   By Rich Tennant

"YES, I THINK IT'S AN ERROR MESSAGE."

In this part . . .

Ah, the "Part of Tens" — a mysterious title that hints that you're going to discover at least ten things about *something*. It's a curious yet helpful part of all *For Dummies* books. *Curious* because there really isn't any standard thing you'll find here. *Helpful* because you find some helpful hints, tips, tricks, and trivia that you won't find anywhere else in the book!

This book's "Part of Tens" contains answers to ten frequently asked questions. (No, really, they *are* frequently asked!) You also get some quick, to-the-point steps that answer your "How do I . . ." questions, as well as some downright practical tips for working with Visio. Finally, I point you to some online Visio resources where you can find sample drawings, third-party stencils, advice from pros (maybe even a chat room!), and Microsoft Visio resources.

Chapter 15

Answers to Ten Frequently Asked Questions about Visio

In This Chapter

▶ Can I work with other file types in Visio?

▶ Can I save a Visio drawing in a non-Visio file format?

▶ Can I copy a shape from one stencil to another?

▶ How do I change the number of recently opened files listed on the File menu?

▶ How do I get a summary of all the shapes, pages, and layers in a drawing?

▶ Can I customize my drawing environment?

▶ How do I print gridlines in a drawing?

▶ Can I use Undo more than once?

▶ How can I find out how many shapes are on a layer?

▶ How do I not print a layer?

*I*t doesn't matter how long you've used a program, questions always pop up about doing some of the most common or practical tasks. Often our questions may seem trivial, but the answers might save you a great deal of time and make you more productive. I hope this chapter answers some of *your* questions about Visio.

Can I work with other file types in Visio?

Yes, you can work with other file types in Visio. You can *paste*, *insert*, or *open* files, shapes, charts, text, spreadsheets, data, pictures, images, or other objects from a few dozen file types and programs. In general, the objects become shapes in Visio. The extent to which you can alter them varies depending on the type of object. Refer to Chapter 14 for more information.

Can I save a Visio drawing in a non-Visio file format?

Yes, you can save a Visio drawing in a non-Visio file format. Choose File⇨ Save As to display the Save As dialog box. In the Save As Type box, you'll find nearly two dozen file formats. Refer to Chapter 14 for a list of file types and specific steps for saving Visio drawings in different formats.

Can I copy a shape from one stencil to another?

Yes, you can copy a shape from one stencil to another, as long as the stencil you're copying to is a custom stencil, that is, one that you create. Custom stencils that you create are editable. They are the *only* stencils to which you can add (or delete) shapes. (You can't edit Visio master stencils.)

Want another bonus? You can change Visio shapes and save your changes on a custom stencil. Refer to Chapter 11 for specific steps on creating and editing custom stencils.

How do I change the number of recently opened files listed on the File menu?

To change the number of recently opened files listed on the File menu, choose Tools⇨Options. Click the General tab on the Options dialog box. In the General Options area, click the arrow for the Recently Used Files List. (The default setting is 4.) Note that changing this number also changes the number of files listed in the Open area of the task pane.

How do I get a summary of all the shapes, pages, and layers in a drawing?

To get a summary of all the shapes, pages, and layers in a drawing, choose View⇨Drawing Explorer Window. Visio displays all elements of the current drawing — pages, shapes, layers, styles, masters, fill and line patterns — in a hierarchical tree structure. The drawing name appears at the top. If a folder shape is preceded by a plus symbol (+), the folder contains more information. Just click the + to display that information.

Can I customize my drawing environment?

Yes, you can customize many aspects of your drawing environment. For example, you can hide rulers and grid lines by removing the check mark from these options on the View menu. You can set the page size, orientation, and drawing scale by choosing File⇨Page Setup. You can maximize the drawing space by closing the task pane on the right side of the screen (just click the X in the upper-right corner). And you can change the display style for stencils to conserve screen space by right-clicking the stencil title bar and choosing View.

How do I print gridlines in a drawing?

To print gridlines in a drawing, choose File⇨Page Setup, then go to the Print Setup tab. In the Print area, check the Gridlines box, and then click OK. This setting applies to the current drawing only but remains in effect until you change it. To prevent gridlines from printing, go back to File⇨Page Setup and remove the check mark from the Gridlines box on the Print Setup tab.

Can I use Undo more than once?

Yes, you can use Undo more than once. The default Undo Level is set to 20, so you can undo up to the last twenty actions you took. To set the Undo Level to a number other than 20, choose Tools⇨Options and go to the General tab. Change the number in the Undo Levels box and then click OK. (Hey, you can go wild here; set up to 99 if you want!)

To undo multiple past actions at once, click the down arrow next to the Undo button on the Standard toolbar and then scroll to the last action you want to undo. Visio reverses the action you select *and all other actions* taken since. You can't undo past actions *selectively*.

How do I find out how many shapes are on a layer?

To find out how many shapes are on a layer, first make sure that the drawing is open. Then click the Layer Properties button on the View toolbar, or choose View⇨Layer Properties. In the Layer Properties dialog box, click the # column heading. Visio displays the number of shapes on each layer. (Note that this doesn't provide an accurate count of the entire number of shapes in a drawing because some shapes may be assigned to multiple layers.)

If your drawing doesn't use layers and you still want a shape count, choose View⇨Drawing Explorer Window. Click the folder for the page you want, and then click the Shapes folder. Drawing Explorer lists all the shapes on the current page. (Here's a little bonus: If you click a shape name in the list, Visio selects the shape in the drawing window.)

How do I not print a layer?

To not print a particular layer, first make sure that the drawing is open. Then click the Layer Properties button on the View toolbar, or choose View⇨Layer Properties. In the Layer Properties dialog box, find the layer you don't want to print, and click to clear the check mark in the Print column. The next time you print the drawing, this layer is not printed. To restore printing of this layer, click to add the check mark back to the Print column.

Chapter 16

Ten Common Tasks in Visio

*L*et's face it, as you work with any software program, you need to perform plenty of mundane tasks that just don't seem to fit easily in the table of contents or index of the user's manual or don't pop up automatically in online help files when you search. You know that the answer has to be there somewhere — if you could just find it! This chapter covers ten of those tasks that you might find yourself wondering about as you work with Visio.

Rotating shapes to a specific angle

Sometimes you want to rotate a shape to a specific angle, such as 45 degrees. The quickest way to do this is to select the shape, grab the shape's rotation handle, and start rotating the shape right or left. Watch the status bar, which displays the exact angle as you rotate the shape. Rotating counterclockwise produces a positive number; rotating clockwise produces a negative number.

If you prefer to type a specific angle, you can choose View⇨Size & Position Window. Select the object you want to rotate. In the Angle box of the Size and Position window, enter the angle. To rotate the shape in a counterclockwise direction, use a positive number. To rotate the shape clockwise, enter a negative number.

Centering a drawing before printing

Centering a drawing before you print it is a simple option that you might miss if you don't happen to be looking at the Shape menu. Whether shapes in the drawing are selected or not, choose Shapes⇨Center Drawing. Visio repositions all the shapes on the page so that they are centered in relation to the page borders.

However, this doesn't necessarily mean that all the shapes are on the page. If your drawing is too large for the page, you can rearrange or resize shapes, change your page size or orientation (choose File⇨Page Setup and then click the Page Setup tab), or scale the drawing (choose File⇨Page Setup and then click the Drawing Scale tab). For information about working with page size, orientation, and scale, refer to Chapter 3.

Resizing a page to fit the content of a drawing

If you can't or don't want to move, adjust, rearrange, or resize shapes in a drawing to fit on standard-size paper, you can always adjust the page size to fit the content of the drawing. (You can print an odd-sized drawing on multiple pages or by using a large-scale printer or plotter. See the next section.) With the drawing displayed, choose File⇨Page Setup. On the Page Size tab, click the Size to Fit Drawing Contents button, and then click OK. Visio automatically resizes your drawing page.

If you prefer to adjust the drawing page manually, just point your mouse to any edge of the paper near a corner, and then press and hold the Ctrl key. The mouse pointer changes to a double-headed diagonal arrow, which you can drag to resize. (Don't point directly at the corner. If you do, you get a rotation handle, which lets you rotate rather than resize the page.) Release the Ctrl key and mouse button when the page is the size you want it.

Creating a drawing that spans several pages

This tip and the preceding one are related. If you want to create a large drawing to print on oversized paper or tiled across several pages, you can set up the drawing in two ways. If you know the paper size, define it up front: choose File⇨Page Setup, select the Print Setup tab, and set the paper size.

If you're not sure how large the drawing will be, just start creating the drawing and let it evolve. When you think you have the drawing the way you want it, use one of the methods in the preceding tip to size the page to fit the drawing contents. Then choose File⇨Page Setup and click the Print Setup tab. Check the preview; it shows you how your drawing size compares to your paper size. Adjust the paper size as necessary

Saving a company logo as a stencil shape

To save a company logo as a stencil shape, bring your company logo into the current Visio drawing. To do so, you can choose Insert⇨Picture⇨From File, or you can choose File⇨Open, or you can copy the logo in a different program and then choose Edit⇨Paste in Visio.

Create a stencil by choosing File⇨Shapes⇨New Stencil, or open an existing custom stencil. Drag the logo that you placed in the drawing onto the stencil. Right-click the shape in the stencil, choose Rename Master, and then type a new name. To make the logo available in any drawing, open the custom stencil whenever you open or create a new drawing. For more information on creating custom stencils, refer to Chapter 11.

Creating and adding a background design to a drawing

You can create a custom background from clipart, photos, or other types of drawings. Paste or insert the object, size it to fit the page, drag it onto a custom stencil to save it, and then give it a name that indicates it is a background shape. (See Chapter 11 for help creating custom stencils.) Backgrounds are usually set to be semitransparent so that they don't overpower your drawing. See the next tip to find out how to adjust transparency.

Adding a Visio-created background to a drawing is a simple matter of dragging a shape into the drawing. Choose File⇨Shapes⇨Visio Extras⇨Backgrounds to open the Backgrounds stencil. Drag a shape onto the drawing. Don't worry about the shape fitting the page; Visio fits the background shape to the page size automatically.

Look at the page tabs at the bottom of the drawing window, and you'll see that the background shape is automatically placed on a new background page. If your drawing had only one page, Visio automatically assigns the background to the only foreground page. Check out Chapter 9 to find out more about using background pages.

Adjusting the transparency of shapes and text in a drawing

The absolute quickest way to adjust transparency is to select the shape or text, and then click the Transparency button on the Format Shape toolbar. Select a percentage setting from the drop-down list, or click More Transparency Levels to display a dialog box where you can use a slider to select a specific percentage.

An alternative to this method is to right-click the shape or text and choose Format⇨Fill or Format⇨Text to display a dialog box where you can adjust transparency.

Adding the same shape or image to all pages in a drawing

When you want to add a shape or an image to all the pages in a drawing, please don't try pasting the shape onto every page! Add the shape to a background page instead. Then choose File⇨Page Setup, click the Page Properties tab, and assign the background to each foreground page individually.

Note: If you're creating a drawing, create your background page first and complete it, and then start inserting foreground pages. In the Page Setup/Page Properties dialog box, the name for the background page pops up automatically as the suggested background, saving you the step of having to assign the background individually to each foreground page. Refer to Chapter 9 for more information about working with pages and backgrounds.

Unlocking a shape

A shape that displays gray handles when you select it is locked. Some Visio grouped shapes are made up of many components and are purposely locked so that you don't tamper with them! The entire group or just a component of the group might be locked.

To unlock a shape or a component of a grouped shape, right-click it and choose Format➪Protection. The Protection dialog box that appears indicates by a check mark all aspects of the shape that are locked. You can unlock aspects individually (such as Width or Rotation) by clicking them to remove the check mark. To unlock all aspects (that is, to protect no aspects), click the None button.

Note that some shapes that appear to be locked (because their selection handles are gray) are not locked in every aspect. For instance, you might be able to add text but not be able to rotate the shape. Only the Protection dialog box tells you for sure which aspects are locked.

Copying formatting from one shape to another

If you missed the description of how to copy formatting from one shape to another in Chapter 8, pay close attention now, because this is a terrific time-saving tool! Select the shape or text whose formatting you want to copy, and then click the Format Painter button on the Standard toolbar. Your mouse pointer changes to a paint brush. Point to the shape you want to apply the format to and click. Visio copies the format to the shape instantly.

Format Painter works for shape formatting (such as color, shadow, and transparency) as well as text formatting (font, size, style, text color, and so on.) But be aware that it works only once for each shape you apply it to. (It's not like the Paste button, which you can use to paste something again and again and again.) If you want to "paint" formatting to another shape, you have to click the Format Painter button again to pick up the formatting, and then click the shape you're applying it to.

Chapter 17

Ten Tips for Working Successfully with Visio

*I*t's always nice to have a few tips for working successfully with a program. Some of the tips in this chapter come from Visio's top trainers. Others are just practical ideas that make you more productive once you make them a habit.

Use keyboard shortcuts

You can significantly speed up your work if you take the time to memorize some of the Visio keyboard shortcuts for menu commands. If a command has a shortcut, it's listed to the right of the command name in the menu. Other keyboard shortcuts aren't listed anywhere; you just pick them up as you go. See the Cheat Sheet at the front of the book for a list of valuable keyboard shortcuts.

Work from existing drawings when you can

You can usually save yourself a lot of work by working from an existing drawing rather than starting a new one from scratch. If the drawing you need to create is similar to another one, load the similar drawing, and then choose File⇨ Save As to save a copy of the existing drawing under a different file name. Now you can edit the new copy, changing shapes and text where necessary. Think of the time you'll save, now that you don't have to fool around with templates, opening additional stencils, reformatting, and more.

Fool around with snap and glue

Snap and glue are two of Visio's most powerful features. They make creating drawings a lot easier, but they can be confusing at first because you have so many choices. Dynamic or static? Snap and glue to *what*? Connection points? Handles? Grid? Guides? All or none? Set snap and glue *strength*? Enough, already!

The best way to figure out snap and glue is to play with them. Create a drawing you don't care anything about and go wild! Try every combination of snap and glue options that you can think of. Drag in some shapes. Move them around. Reset the snap and glue strength. Turn off some of the snap and glue options. Move the shapes around again. Turn off all the options. Now move the shapes around again. Play around with snap and glue to see what happens. The more you experiment, the more comfortable you'll feel.

Group your shapes

The more adept you become at creating shapes, the more you realize that a good shape is often a combination of many shapes. When you spend a lot of time creating various components, you don't want to lose any of the pieces when you start dragging and copying them. The best way to avoid losing pieces is to group them.

Remember that you can group groups, too. Suppose you're drawing a personal computer. You might want to group the keyboard shapes, the system unit shapes, and the monitor shapes separately, but then select all three and group them together as the final shape. That way, you can select one component, such as the keyboard, and move it without ungrouping the entire shape. Refer to Chapter 8 for details on grouping shapes.

Use guides to position and move shapes

A guide is sort of like a Visio clothesline — or maybe *shapeline* is more appropriate! Use a guide when you want to hang shapes from the same line — horizontal, vertical, or diagonal. In addition to positioning and aligning shapes, you can use a guide to move shapes. Just drag the guide, and all the attached shapes move along with it. To review guide use, see Chapter 7.

Work with drawing layers

Drawing layers are one of the most useful features in Visio because they help you organize your work, particularly complex, detailed drawings. For certain drawing types, Visio gives you a head start here by placing shapes on layers automatically.

You have many options when working with layers. You can place a shape on more than one layer (often a shape might apply to more than one category of shapes). You can display and print layers selectively. And you can lock entire layers to protect shapes from change. See Chapter 10 for details on creating and using layers.

Quickly edit the text in a drawing

When you work with a text document, you probably run spell-check automatically before you print or distribute the document. When you work with a drawing, it's just as important to do the same! Choose Edit➪Select All to select all shapes on the current page, and then press F7 or choose Tools➪Spelling to quickly run the spell checker. This checks the spelling of all the text on the page, including stand-alone text (such as titles) and text used to label shapes. Choose Edit➪Find to find text on the current page. To search for and replace text on the page, choose Edit➪Replace. Note that you need to check each page of a drawing separately.

Use your pasteboard

"Pasteboard? What's that?" you ask. You may not have noticed the blue area surrounding a drawing page. (In fact, you don't see the pasteboard if you zoom in on the drawing page.) When the pasteboard is visible, you can drag shapes onto it and use it as a holding area for shapes that you're not ready for yet.

The pasteboard is a great place to store shapes when you're opening a lot of stencils. You can drag the shapes onto the pasteboard and then close the stencils that you're not using anymore. The shapes are stored with the drawing, but they aren't printed. When you're ready to use the shapes, just drag them into the drawing area. If you think you'll use a shape more than once, hold the Ctrl key as you drag to copy rather than move the shape into the drawing.

Find your drawings quickly in Windows Explorer

If you have a lot of Visio drawings, you might not recall exactly what's in them by looking at the file name. To identify — and open — a drawing quickly, use the visual method in Windows Explorer.

In Windows Explorer, go to the directory where your Visio file is located. Click the Views icon on the Windows Explorer toolbar and choose the Thumbnails option. Visio displays a thumbnail-sized picture of your file so you can visually review the contents. To open the file, double-click it. This quick method doesn't even require that Visio be running first; Windows Explorer will start it for you!

Print a drawing without opening it

You can use Windows Explorer also to print a file quickly. In the Windows Explorer window, find the file you want to open. On the Start menu, click Printers and Faxes to open the Printers and Faxes window, which displays all printers available to your computer. Arrange these two windows so you can see the printer icon you want to use and the Visio file you want to print. Now, back in the Windows Explorer window, drag the Visio file icon onto the printer icon in the Printers and Faxes window. Windows Explorer opens your file and Visio and prints it automatically.

Chapter 18

Ten Places to Look Online for Visio Resources

As you might expect, this chapter starts out with a great big fat disclaimer! Web sites change, as do people, companies, places, and products. I can make no guarantees as to the reliability, authenticity, integrity, or any other *ity* of non-Microsoft sources. At the time of this writing, however, all resources listed in this chapter were reliable.

Help from Microsoft

Microsoft provides a wealth of useful online information — almost too much! The potential problem with all this information is that it's often difficult to find what you want. Use the sites in this section as a launchpad to further information on Visio.

Microsoft Office's Online home page is a great place to start. Click the Visio link to find tips, articles, updates, downloads, and more:

```
http://office.microsoft.com/home/
```

Go to the following for Visio updates (click the Visio links):

```
http://office.microsoft.com/officeupdate/default.aspx
```

For online training and tutorials in Visio, go to the following address. Most of what's provided is helpful but the topics are limited:

```
http://office.microsoft.com/training/default.aspx
```

At Microsoft's Assistance Center page for Visio, you can find a variety of information on working with Visio. Much of this information is duplicated in the Visio Help files:

```
http://office.microsoft.com/assistance/topcategory.aspx
```

Following is another launchpad site for finding newsgroups, community Web sites, technical chats, and user's groups. Look for resources here that suit your Visio needs and level of expertise:

```
www.microsoft.com/communities/default.mspx
```

MVPs.org

For a great general information site maintained by Visio experts who have been heavily involved with Visio since it was introduced in 1992 by Shapeware (the creator of Visio), visit the following:

```
www.mvps.org/visio/
```

Another site maintained by this group contains a huge variety of downloadable files — some older than others:

```
http://www.mvps.org/visio/CompuServe.htm
```

Google

Google is well-known as a search engine extraordinaire. In addition to helping you find almost any information you're looking for, Google also sponsors user groups, where people can share information. As luck would have it, you can choose from several Visio groups!

First go to Google's home page:

```
www.google.com
```

Then, for a list of Visio user's groups, click the Groups button at the top of the page, and type **microsoft.public.visio** in the search box on the next page. At the time of this writing, 17 user groups were listed, providing general information to technical help for developers. This is a great way to ask questions and share information user-to-user.

Yahoo!

If you're a software developer or network designer, you might want to join this Yahoo group (members only):

```
http://groups.yahoo.com/group/Microsoft_Visio/
```

Third-Party Suppliers of Visio Shapes and Stencils

Many companies and independent organizations create and supply Visio shapes. Some shapes are even free. This section lists several great resources for Visio shapes and stencils.

MVPs.org

MVPS, which was listed previously in the chapter, is maintained by Visio experts, some of whom are Microsoft employees. You can find a list of third-party suppliers of shapes, stencils, and templates for Visio at the following:

```
www.mvps.org/visio/3rdparty.htm
```

ShapeDev.com

The ShapeDev site contains Visio shape development tutorials and Visio stencils available for free download:

```
http://www.shapedev.com/
```

SoftApproach Corporation

SoftApproach is a third-party supplier of Visio stencils and templates primarily for business and technology:

```
www.amazingvisio.com/visio_Index.htm
```

Siemon Company

The Siemon Company supplies Visio shapes for networking diagrams:

```
www.siemon.com/visio/
```

Altima Technologies

Altima Technologies, a subscription-based download service, specializes in stencils for networking diagrams. Literally thousands of shapes are listed, categorized by high-tech manufacturers such as 3Com, Hewlett-Packard, and Sony Electronics, to name a few (without showing any favoritism or partiality!). Go to the following:

```
www.netzoomstencils.com/home/index.asp
```

Visimation

Visimation supplies Visio add-ons for users and developers at the following address:

```
www.visimation.com/visio-shapes.asp
```

They also offer one of the widest varieties of Visio shapes I've ever seen, including biology, border art, police and fire, and restaurant shapes.

Index

• *G* •

Notes

Notes

Notes

Notes

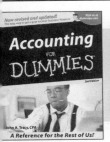

FOR DUMMIES®

A world of resources to help you grow

HOME, GARDEN & HOBBIES

Feng Shui FOR DUMMIES
0-7645-5295-3

Gardening FOR DUMMIES
0-7645-5130-2

Guitar FOR DUMMIES
0-7645-5106-X

Also available:

Auto Repair For Dummies
(0-7645-5089-6)

Chess For Dummies
(0-7645-5003-9)

Home Maintenance For Dummies
(0-7645-5215-5)

Organizing For Dummies
(0-7645-5300-3)

Piano For Dummies
(0-7645-5105-1)

Poker For Dummies
(0-7645-5232-5)

Quilting For Dummies
(0-7645-5118-3)

Rock Guitar For Dummies
(0-7645-5356-9)

Roses For Dummies
(0-7645-5202-3)

Sewing For Dummies
(0-7645-5137-X)

FOOD & WINE

Cooking FOR DUMMIES
0-7645-5250-3

Cookies FOR DUMMIES
0-7645-5390-9

Wine FOR DUMMIES
0-7645-5114-0

Also available:

Bartending For Dummies
(0-7645-5051-9)

Chinese Cooking For Dummies
(0-7645-5247-3)

Christmas Cooking For Dummies
(0-7645-5407-7)

Diabetes Cookbook For Dummies
(0-7645-5230-9)

Grilling For Dummies
(0-7645-5076-4)

Low-Fat Cooking For Dummies
(0-7645-5035-7)

Slow Cookers For Dummies
(0-7645-5240-6)

TRAVEL

Italy FOR DUMMIES
0-7645-5453-0

Hawaii FOR DUMMIES
0-7645-5438-7

Las Vegas FOR DUMMIES
0-7645-5448-4

Also available:

America's National Parks For Dummies
(0-7645-6204-5)

Caribbean For Dummies
(0-7645-5445-X)

Cruise Vacations For Dummies 2003
(0-7645-5459-X)

Europe For Dummies
(0-7645-5456-5)

Ireland For Dummies
(0-7645-6199-5)

France For Dummies
(0-7645-6292-4)

London For Dummies
(0-7645-5416-6)

Mexico's Beach Resorts For Dummies
(0-7645-6262-2)

Paris For Dummies
(0-7645-5494-8)

RV Vacations For Dummies
(0-7645-5443-3)

Walt Disney World & Orlando For Dummies
(0-7645-5444-1)

Available wherever books are sold. Go to www.dummies.com or call 1-877-762-2974 to order direct.

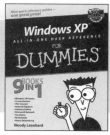

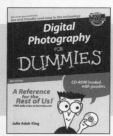

FOR DUMMIES®

The advice and explanations you need to succeed